Illustrated
Turbo Pascal® 6.0

Paul L. Schlieve

Wordware Publishing, Inc.

Library of Congress Cataloging-in-Publication Data

Schlieve, Paul L.
    Illustrated turbo pascal 6.0 / Paul L. Schlieve.
         p.   cm.
    Includes index.
    ISBN 1-55622-202-5
    1. Pascal (Computer program language)   2. Turbo Pascal (Computer
program).   I. Title.
QA76.73.P2S3295   1991
005.265—dc20   91-30230
                                                                  CIP

Copyright © 1992, Wordware Publishing, Inc.

1506 Capital Avenue
Plano, Texas 75074

Printed in the United States of America

ISBN 1-55622-202-5

10 9 8 7 6 5 4 3 2 1

9112

IBM and PC-DOS are trademarks of International Business Machines Corporation.
MS DOS is a registered trademark of Microsoft Corporation.
Turbo Pascal is a registered trademark of Borland International, Inc.
WordStar is a registered trademark of MicroPro International Corporation.
SideKick is a registered trademark of Borland International, Inc.

All inquiries for volume purchases of this book should be addressed to Wordware Publishing, Inc.,
at the above address. Telephone inquiries may be made by calling:

(214) 423-0090

Contents

Contents (continued)

Contents (continued)

Recommended Learning Sequence

Recommended Learning Sequence (cont.)

Recommended Learning Sequence (cont.)

Preface

This book is written both as a reference and as a learning tool. As a reference, its alphabetic arrangement makes locating information about specific commands quick and easy. As a learning tool, the recommended learning sequence and module exercises provide both instruction and self-evaluation.

The book is designed for those using Turbo Pascal 6.0 on the IBM PC and compatible computers. Although Turbo Pascal is available for other computers, concentrating on the needs of the MS-DOS user avoids the confusion of having to read through information about multiple operating systems and language variants to find the information relevant to your system. Concentrating on version 6.0 eliminates the confusion caused by trying to address multiple releases of the program in a single book.

Each command is illustrated through the use of short sample programs. Each sample program is constructed to highlight the operation of one language feature or a small family of related procedures. Every effort has been made to make the sample programs as short and simple as possible to prevent hiding the language feature under a myriad of details.

Module 1
ABOUT THIS BOOK

INTRODUCTION

This book describes the computer programming language Turbo Pascal. This software system, a product of Borland International, is the most popular version of Pascal. Specifically, the book provides a detailed treatment of version 6.0 of Turbo Pascal for the IBM PC and compatibles.

Borland provides four manuals with Turbo Pascal 6.0. Since the quantity of information can be overwhelming, *Illustrated Turbo Pascal 6.0* arranges the information in a logical order and presents the information with examples. Each command and technique is illustrated with examples. For a broad range of users, it is designed for first-time Pascal programmers needing a sequential introduction to the system, and for users familiar with Pascal programming who need a reference manual with numerous examples to extract the full benefits of this complex software system.

Since Turbo Pascal 6.0 contains hundreds of different commands, this book explains only the most common commands. Once you have mastered these, you will be ready to tackle the more advanced commands in the Turbo Pascal manuals.

This book assumes you have a basic familiarity with your computer system. It is assumed that your computer is assembled, that you can load the disk operating system, format and copy a disk, and display a disk directory. No familiarity is assumed for more advanced topics, for example, 8088 family Assembly Language programming, inline machine code, I/O redirection, and DOS interrupts. Where advanced topics are discussed, an introduction to the topic is provided, in addition to examples showing its exploitation through the use of Turbo Pascal.

WHAT IS PASCAL?

The natural language of computers consists entirely of 0s and 1s. Whatever you want a computer to do, the command must first be converted into a long string of 0s and 1s. While this is natural for computers, it is awkward for humans. As a result, people have created a number of programming languages designed to serve as a middle step in communicating with computers. You translate your instructions into a programming language, then the computer translates that into 0s and 1s.

There have been many attempts to design a perfect computer language that would allow more effective programming of computers. In this development process, some language features were discovered that make it easier to write structured, changeable computer programs.

In 1968 Nicklaus Wirth designed the Pascal computer language to teach good programming practices. The design of Pascal makes it easy to express computer programming solutions to problems, but it makes it difficult to make some of the more hard-to-correct errors that are common to earlier languages.

WHY TURBO PASCAL?

Turbo Pascal is a particular version of Pascal that has several significant features that make it an ideal tool for both learning Pascal and doing serious software development.

- Turbo Pascal is extremely fast, both in the time required to *compile* (translate the Pascal statements into machine language) a program and the time required to run a program. Compilation times are so fast for short programs that they are insignificant.

- Although the Turbo Pascal Compiler can use text files created by many file editors, the Turbo Pascal Editor is directly linked with the error handling routines in the Compiler. When the Compiler detects an error, control is automatically transferred to the Editor, and the cursor points to the place in the program where the error is detected.

- Turbo Pascal allows you to relax some of the rules of rigid matching of data types in standard Pascal, where such relaxation makes sense.

- Turbo Pascal allows you to take full advantage of the special hardware features of your IBM personal computer or compatible. You can manipulate graphics and sound. Advanced programmers can incorporate Assembly Language routines and directly communicate with the Input/Output ports and Disk Operating System functions of the computer.

- The Turbo Pascal integrated environment includes a source-level debugger that allows you to step through your program one line at a time.

- Turbo Pascal provides support for object-oriented programming, the latest advance in programming style. Turbo Pascal's objects combine the best aspects of Object Pascal for the Macintosh and the C++ language in the creation of an excellent blend of flexibility and performance.

- The TurboVision program library, included with Turbo Pascal 6.0, allows you to quickly create programs that use the same user interface as Turbo Pascal itself.

- The inclusion of both the integrated environment compiler and command-line compilers in the package allows both interactive development of programs of reasonable size, and for compilation of larger program modules. An extended memory version of the command-line compiler allows the creation of programs with many thousands of lines of source statements.

THE WRITING STYLE

Understanding several practices followed in the writing of this book can make the reading easier for you.

- Turbo Pascal reserved words and predeclared identifiers are set in italic type.
- Discussion of Turbo Pascal features and procedures is in paragraph form.
- Steps that you perform in the Typical Operations are numbered.
- Keys you type or press are indicated by bold type.
- Two-key combinations are indicated by a statement such as "Press Ctrl-C to cancel the operation." The word "press" is your clue that you must use a function key or key combination. The notation Ctrl-C means that you press and hold the key marked "Ctrl," then press and release the letter "c," and finally release the key marked "Ctrl."

ORGANIZATION

This book is not designed to be read in page-number order. A logical learning sequence is provided to guide you through the text. If you are learning Turbo Pascal, follow the Recommended Learning Sequence found in the front of the book. Once you know Turbo Pascal, you can use the book as an alphabetic reference.

The book is divided into modules. Each module contains information on one command or feature of Turbo Pascal. Each module has three sections. The first section is a description of the command or feature. It serves as a formal definition and is useful as a reference guide. The second section contains applications. That information describes ways you use the command to solve problems. The third section contains a typical operation, a sample session you work through to illustrate the use of a particular command or feature.

Continue the learning sequence with Module 2, Sample Session.

Module 2
SAMPLE SESSION

DESCRIPTION

In this module you use the Turbo Pascal Editor to create a short program. You save the program on disk and run the program. You see how the Editor and Compiler are integrated into a total Pascal programming system.

APPLICATIONS

It is most convenient to develop Pascal programs using the integrated environment. The integrated environment maintains the Editor, your program statements, and the compiled program resident in memory. Frequently saving your work file on disk is the best insurance against power failure and catastrophic editing mistakes. When the program is fully debugged, you then use the compile-to-disk option to produce an executable file on your disk. In that way, you do not have to recompile programs each time they are used.

Compiling and testing in the integrated environment mode is fastest and speeds development time. When developing programs thousands of lines in length, which exceed the size of the editor workspace, it is best to develop the program in small pieces, testing each piece fully in the memory-resident mode before using the advanced features of the system to link the pieces together in a large programming system.

TYPICAL OPERATION

This session introduces you to the Turbo Pascal Editor and demonstrates the creation of a simple Turbo Pascal program. The Editor is used to create and modify the Pascal programs you write. If you are familiar with the WordStar® word processing program, you will notice that the Turbo Pascal Editor is very similar to WordStar.

STARTING TURBO PASCAL The instructions given in the following steps are applicable to both floppy-disk based and hard disk equipped computers.

1. Start the computer with the Disk Operating System (DOS) disk and enter the date and time.

2. Place your working copy of the Turbo Pascal program disk in the disk drive, or change to your Turbo Pascal subdirectory (this directory is named "TP" if you accept the TurboPascal installation defaults) if you have a hard-disk based system.

3. Type **TURBO** from the DOS prompt and press **Enter**. Notice the following display.

The top line of the screen shows the Turbo Pascal drop-down menu system. There are several ways to activate a drop-down menu. You can press Alt-letter, where letter is the lighlighted letter, F, E, S, R, etc. corresponding to the File, Edit, Search, and Run menus. You can press F10 to highlight the menu bar, then press the Left Arrow and Right Arrow keys to highlight a menu, and finally press Enter to display the menu on the screen.

Below the menu bar is an Editor window. When you start Turbo Pascal, a single editing window is displayed that occupies the full screen. Centered at the top of the screen is the default filename NONAME00.PAS, which will be used to save your program text unless you specify a different name when you select the Save option.

The bottom line of the screen displays function key labels corresponding to frequently used functions in the integrated environment. These functions duplicate items available on the drop-down menu system but are also placed at the bottom of the screen because they are so frequently used.

A computer program is a set of statements that the computer can follow to carry out a task. DOS (Disk Operating System) is a computer program that allows the computer to communicate with the disk drive, keyboard, monitor, and printer. The Editor is a program that creates and changes text and stores it on the disk. The Compiler is a program that translates Pascal programs into machine language.

The language you speak, English, is too complex and variable in meaning to be understood by a computer. The binary language of zeros and ones of machine language is not easily understood by humans. Computer programming languages, such as Pascal, have been developed to bridge this gap between man's language and a machine language. The Pascal programming language contains English-like words and mathematical symbols arranged according to rigid rules of structure and syntax that are understandable to machines.

THE EDITOR You create a Turbo Pascal program with the Editor. When you start Turbo Pascal, you are automatically placed in the Editor, ready to begin your work. Notice that the cursor appears in the upper left corner of the Edit window.

The first statement in a Pascal program is the program statement. The program statement gives the program a name. Turbo Pascal does not require the use of the program statement, but using it to identify the program name helps make the program more readable.

NOTE

If you make a mistake, press Backspace to erase your error, then retype the line. The semicolon is important. The Pascal Compiler uses the semicolon to separate Pascal program statements.

4. Type **program simple;** and press **Enter**.

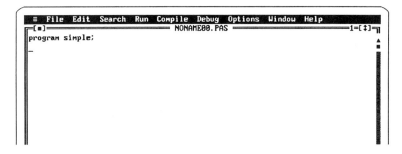

The main body of the program starts with the reserved word, *begin*. Reserved words are the words having predefined meaning to Turbo Pascal, and their meaning cannot be changed. The word *begin* tells the computer where to start working.

5. Type **begin** and press **Enter**.

```
 ≡  File  Edit  Search  Run  Compile  Debug  Options  Window  Help
┌─[■]════════════════════ NONAME00.PAS ═══════════════════1=[↕]═┐
│program simple;                                                ▲
│begin                                                          ▪
│_                                                              ▪
│                                                               
│                                                               
│                                                               
│                                                               
│                                                               
│                                                               
│                                                               
│                                                               
│                                                               
│                                                               
│                                                               ▼
```

One technique to make computer programs more readable is the use of indention. Pascal ignores all spacing and indention between statements in your programs.

6. Press the **Spacebar** four times to indent the next line of text four spaces.

```
  ≡  File  Edit  Search  Run  Compile  Debug  Options  Window  Help
╒[■]══════════════════════ NONAME00.PAS ══════════════════1=[↕]╕
│program simple;                                                  ▲
│begin                                                            ▪
│                                                                 ▪
│    ─
```

CEATING LITERAL OUTPUT For a program to be useful, it must perform a function. One of the most basic functions is the production of text on the screen. The Pascal statements *write* and *writeln* are used to produce program output.

NOTE

Remember that the text that you type is shown as boldface print. Look carefully at the instructions to determine exactly what you must type. Pay special attention to punctuation marks, such as the semicolon. If you have any doubts, look ahead to the next screen display to see how your screen should look.

7. Type **writeln('This is as simple as it gets!');** and press **Enter**.

```
  ≡  File  Edit  Search  Run  Compile  Debug  Options  Window  Help
╒[■]══════════════════════ NONAME00.PAS ══════════════════1=[↕]╕
│program simple;                                                  ▲
│begin                                                            ▪
│    writeln('This is as simple as it gets!');                    ▪
│    ─
```

The cursor returns to the position immediately below the "w" in *writeln*.

When you run a Pascal program from within the integrated environment, the program returns to the Editor immediately upon completion. In the case of this short program, the computer returns to the Editor so rapidly that you would not see the program output. Therefore, add a *readln* statement as the last executable statement in the program. A *readln* statement with no operators causes the program to pause until you press Enter.

8. Type **readln;** and press **Enter**.

```
  ≡  File  Edit  Search  Run  Compile  Debug  Options  Window  Help
╒[■]══════════════════════ NONAME00.PAS ══════════════════1=[↕]╕
│program simple;                                                  ▲
│begin                                                            ▪
│    writeln('This is as simple as it gets!');                    ▪
│    readln;
│
│    ─
```

The last statement in a Pascal program is *end*. Unlike other Pascal statements, which are separated by semicolons, the last *end* in the program is followed by a period. The *end* statement closing the program matches the *begin* statement at the start of the program and should be aligned with the *begin* statement.

9. Press the **Backspace** key once, then type **end.** (You must type the period.)

Check your text carefully against the preceding screen display. Have you forgotten a semicolon? Did you type a period after the *end* statement? If necessary, backspace to correct your error now, before you save and compile.

SAVING YOUR WORK Before going on, save your work to protect yourself against power failures and other hazards.

NOTE

Remember that hyphenated key sequences, such as Alt-F, are activated by first pressing and holding the Alt key, then typing and releasing the second key (in this case "F"), and finally, releasing the Alt key.

10. Press **Alt-F** to drop down the File menu.

11. Type **S** to save the file. (Pressing the Down Arrow, highlighting Save, and pressing Enter has the same effect.)

Because you have not yet specified a name for the file, Turbo Pascal displays the "Save File As" dialog box, requiring you to specify a filename for the program text.

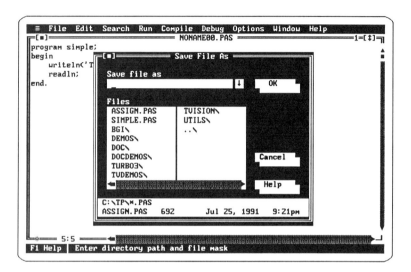

12. Type **SIMPLE** as the filename and press **Enter**. It is not necessary to type the .PAS extension; Turbo Pascal adds it automatically. Your file is saved and you are returned to the editor screen.

RUNNING A PROGRAM   One of the drop-down menus is "Run," which in turn contains the Run command. The Run command starts the Compiler to translate the program in memory into machine language, then transfers control to your program.

13. Press **Alt-R** to activate the Run menu, then press **Enter** to execute the Run command.

14. Press **Enter** to return to the Turbo Pascal Editor.

15. Press **Alt-F** then type **Q** to quit Turbo Pascal and return to DOS.

16. Turn to Module 31, Help Menu, to continue the learning sequence.

Module 3
ABSOLUTE

DESCRIPTION

```
var varname : vartype  absolute address;
```

Absolute is a specification added to a *var* statement to allow variables to be located at a specific location in memory.

varname The name of the variable.

vartype The type of the variable.

address The location in memory where the first byte of *varname* is located. The location may be specified either by two integer constants representing a segment and an offset in the address space, or by the name of another variable. If the name of another variable is used, *varname* is placed "on top" of the variable, and the two variables refer to the same location in memory. The predefined Turbo Pascal constants *CSeg* and *Dseg* may be used to place absolute variables at specific locations relative to the code and data segments respectively.

For example,

```
var X    : real;
    Xlook: array[1..6] of char absolute X;
```

declares X as a *real* number and declares Xlook as a 6-byte array of characters occupying the same location in memory as X. This technique allows you to ignore completely the type checking of Pascal and freely transfer values from one variable type to another. Because the technique defeats the data protection mechanism provided by Pascal's strong typing, it should be used with extreme caution. This particular example, however, could be useful as a debugging aid to examine the contents of the real variable X using Turbo Pascal's 6-byte *real* numbers.

The statement

```
var Value : byte absolute $0050:$0004;
```

declares *Value* as a byte variable at absolute address 0050:0004, which happens to be memory used by DOS. (This byte is used with single-drive systems. A value of 0 means that the diskette for drive A was last used. A value of 1 means that the diskette for drive B was last used.) Note that this part of memory is a dangerous place in memory to be. When you use absolute variables, Turbo Pascal does nothing to protect you from yourself. You can overwrite your Pascal program, your data, the Turbo Pascal system, or the Disk Operating System. You can create errors that require you to turn off the power to reset your system. More dangerously, you can cause errors that allow you to continue but cause the system to behave in an unpredictable manner. Extreme caution is essential when working with absolute variables.

APPLICATIONS

One of the most productive applications of the *absolute* statement is the manipulation of the screen using memory-mapped video. You can create an array or other data structure and cause it to overlap the video memory. Any modification of the memory is instantly reflected on the screen. You can use this technique to examine screen images for printing, to save screen images for restoration of screen contents after closing a window, and for writing a disk file containing a screen image. The multitude of graphics systems available for the IBM PC each have their own locations in the computer memory system for storing graphics information. However, the display of text information is relatively constant across different systems. When displaying text information, the IBM Personal Computer and compatibles use two bytes to store each character of the display. The first byte is used to store the ASCII code for the character. The second is used to store an attribute code containing color information. Therefore, an 80 x 25 screen requires 80 x 25 x 2, or 4000 bytes of memory.

The address of the first byte of the IBM Monochrome Display Adapter memory is located at the hexadecimal address $B000:0000. The Hercules graphics adapter, which emulates the IBM Monochrome Display Adapter in text mode uses the same base address. The address of the first byte of character text displayed on the IBM graphics displays, including the Color Graphics Adapter (CGA), Enhanced Graphics Adapter (EGA), Multi-Color Graphics Adapter (MCGA), and Video Graphics Array (VGA) is located at $B800:0000. The address $B800:0000 is also used by the PCjr, even though it is phantom memory. The declaration

```
type image=array[1..4000] of byte;
var Screen: image absolute $B800:0000;
    ScreenSave:image;
```

declares a variable named Screen as a 4000-byte array. (Remember that the $ informs Turbo Pascal that the number is expressed in hexadecimal format.) The first byte of the array corresponds to the address of the first byte of the Color Graphics Adapter. (The address also applies to the Enhanced Color Graphics Adapter and Video Graphics Array.) If you have a monochrome display attached to an IBM Display and Printer Adapter or a Hercules Graphics Card, you can overlay the text screen with this declaration:

```
type image=array[1..4000] of byte;
var Screen: image absolute $B000:0000;
    Screensave: image;
```

TYPICAL OPERATION

In this session you examine the ROM BIOS date and machine ID in your computer. Any program making use of absolute locations in the computer's memory must make assumptions about the hardware. The best way to make your programs run on the fewest number of machines is to make use of absolute memory references. However, in the real world, you sometimes cannot ignore the machine you are using. For example, IBM PCs with ROM BIOS dates prior to 10/27/82 cannot make use of many of the latest hardware options for the PC, including such accessories as the Enhanced Graphics Adapter, without upgrading the ROM BIOS. IBM places the date of each ROM BIOS in segment $F000 at offset $FFF5. Another example is the machine ID. IBM identifies each class of personal computers by a 1-byte identification code located at the next-to-the-last byte of the computer's memory, segment $F000 and offset $FFFE. The original PC with a 64K system board has a machine ID of $FF (255 decimal); the PC-XT, the portable PC, and the revised PC with a 256K system board have a machine ID of $FD (254 decimal); the PCjr has a machine ID of $FD (253 decimal); and the PC-AT has a machine ID of $FC (252 decimal). To determine the date and machine type, you must examine those memory locations. An absolute variable is a natural choice.

NOTE
If your computer is not manufactured by IBM, there is no guarantee that a date is located in this spot in memory; non-IBM machines are not predictable in their use of the machine ID. At least one XT-compatible identifies itself as a PCjr. The addresses, however, are located in ROM, and your compatible has *something* located there. You may want to vary the value of the offset and the length of the array to do some ROM snooping. You cannot damage anything by reading the ROM BIOS.

1. If you are continuing your work session, clear the Editor workspace. Otherwise, start Turbo Pascal.

2. Enter the Editor and type the following program.

```
program RomDate;
uses Crt;
var i : integer;
    notice : array[1..8] of char absolute $F000:$FFF5;
    ID     : byte absolute $F0000:$FFFE;
begin
    ClrScr;
    write('The ROM BIOS date is: ');
```

```
    for i:=1 to 8 do write(notice[i]);
    writeln;
    writeln('The machine ID is: ',ID);
    readln;
end.
```

3. Run the program.

```
The ROM BIOS date is: 03/30/87
The machine ID is: 248
```

The date displayed on your screen reflects the revision date of your ROM BIOS. The machine ID is expressed in decimal notation and reflects the type of machine you use. The sample screen is from an IBM PS/2 Model 80. You probably have a different date and ID on your system.

4. Press **Enter** to return to the integrated environment.

5. Turn to Module 38, Move, to continue the learning sequence.

Module 4
ARITHMETIC

DESCRIPTION

The symbols for integer arithmetic operations are as follows:

Not operator:

not	Bitwise negation

Multiplying operators:

*	Multiplication
shl	Shift Left
and	Arithmetic And
div	Division
shr	Shift Right
mod	Remainder

Adding operators:

+	Addition
–	Subtraction
or	Arithmetic Or
xor	Arithmetic Exclusive Or

The symbols for real arithmetic operations are:

*	Multiplication
/	Division
+	Addition
–	Subtraction

The order of precedence for operators is:

1. Unary minus (minus with one operand only)
2. *not*
3. Multiplying operators: *, /, *div, mod, and, shl, shr*
4. Adding operators: +, –, *or, xor*
5. Relational operators: =, <>, <, >, <=, >=, *in*

Within a single level of precedence, expressions are generally evaluated from left to right. However, the compiler may change the order to optimize the expression. If the order of operations within a single level of precedence must be computed in a particular order, use parentheses to specify the required order of operations.

APPLICATIONS

Integer data types and real data types have different operations that are performed on them. Because different types of data are stored differently in memory, the computer uses separate operations for each. Even though the only visible difference in the symbols is in the division and shift operators, from the computer's point of view, a difference exists between integer arithmetic and real arithmetic for all operations.

INTEGER ARITHMETIC Although the arithmetic operations are familiar, Pascal uses different notation for some operations to prevent confusion between symbols. You can see several differences between the list of integer operators and the list of operators used in mathematics. Multiplication is designated by * instead of x or X to prevent the multiplication operation from becoming confused with a variable named "X." Integer multiplication is only performed if both operands are integers. If one of the operators is real, the integer data is converted to real data, the numbers are multiplied together with real multiplication, and the result is real data. You can use the *shl* operator to perform a binary shift on an integer. This is useful for the special case of multiplying by a power of 2. The second operator in the *shl* operation specifies the number of binary digits to shift left.

The *not* operator performs bitwise negation of an integer. For example, the number 0 is represented as 0000000000000000. Reversing all the bits produces 1111111111111111, the 2s-complement form of −1. The expression not 64 is −65. First, look at the binary representation for 64:

Decimal   Binary

  64   0000000001000000

Reversing all the digits, the result is

1111111110111111

which is the 2s complement form of −65. The 2s complement of a number is determined by reversing all the bits and adding 1. First, reverse the bits,

0000000001000000

then add 1,

0000000001000001

The magnitude of the number is 65, but because of the 1 in the sign bit, the computer interprets the number as –65.

The three operations associated with integer division are the *div* operation, the *mod* operation, and the *shr* operation. The *div* operation computes the quotient of two integers, ignoring the remainder. The *mod* operation computes the remainder of the division operation, ignoring the quotient. The *shr* operation is a binary right shift, corresponding to division by 2. The *shr* and *shl* operations are inverses of each other.

An integer arithmetic expression may include either real or integer data. If you use real data with integer operators (*div, mod, shr, shl, and, or, xor*), the Compiler automatically generates code to convert the real data to integer data before performing the operation. If you use both integer data and real data with operators that can be either integer or real (*, +, –), integer data is converted to real data, and real number arithmetic is used.

The *or* operator performs a bitwise *or* operation on the two integer operands. For each bit position:

> 1 or 1 produce 1
> 1 or 0 produce 1
> 0 or 1 produce 1
> 0 or 0 produce 0

For example, 3742 or 1842 is 4031. An examination of the binary representation illustrates the process:

Decimal	16-bit Binary Representation
3742	0000111010001101
1842	0000011100110010
4031	0000111110111111

The xor operator performs a bitwise exclusive or operation on the two integer operands. For each bit position:

> 1 and 1 produce 0
> 1 and 0 produce 0
> 0 and 1 produce 0
> 0 and 0 produce 1

For example, 3724 xor 1842 is –4032. An examination of the binary representation illustrates the process:

Decimal	16-bit Binary Representation
3742	0000111010001101
1842	0000011100110010
–4032	1111000001000000

The result is not 61504. The first bit is interpreted as a sign bit, and the remaining bits are interpreted as the 2s complement of the value.

The system does not check for overflow conditions when performing integer arithmetic. You must be careful that the intermediate results of an arithmetic expression do not exceed the minimum or maximum values for the integer type that you use. For example, using the basic integer type, the expression (10000 * 5) – 20000 generates an overflow condition when 10000 is multiplied by 5. As a consequence, your result is not what you expect, although no error message is produced.

REAL ARITHMETIC   A real arithmetic expression may contain real data, integer data, and real operators. The computer converts the integer data to real data as it performs an operation.

ARITHMETIC PRECEDENCE   The meaning of arithmetic expression could be confusing if Pascal did not have rules for determining the order in which operations are performed.

In Pascal, multiplication and division are performed before addition and subtraction. The order of operations within a level of precedence is usually performed from left to right. The expression

$$45 + 23 * 4 - 10 \text{ div } 2$$

is evaluated as follows: "23 * 4" is evaluated first, giving 92; the multiplication takes precedence over the addition and precedes the division from left to right. The expression "10 div 2" is evaluated next, because division takes precedence over both addition and subtraction. This leaves 45 + 92 – 5. Addition and subtraction have the same precedence, so the order of operations proceeds from left to right, and 45 + 92 – 5 yields 132.

Following the rules of precedence is important! If these operations are performed from left to right, ignoring the rules of precedence, the result is 131.

Although all popular implementations maintain the same order of operator precedence, in Turbo Pascal 6.0 and many other Pascal compilers, the order of evaluation of operations of equal precedence is undefined and does not necessarily proceed from left to right. Turbo Pascal performs optimization to speed the calculation of arithmetic expressions. This inconsistency can lead to exotic and difficult-to-detect errors. The safest course of action is to use parentheses to specify the exact order of operations when the order of operation is important and in doubt.

ALTERING PRECEDENCE   Sometimes you may find it difficult to express a formula using the natural precedence provided by Pascal. Other times, the natural precedence may not be immediately apparent when you look at a formula. Parentheses are used to change the order of operations and to make formulas more readable. The previous example

$$45 + 23 * 4 - 10 \text{ div } 2$$

could be rewritten

$$45 + (23 * 4) - (10 \text{ div } 2)$$

This use of parentheses does not change the order of operations in any way, but it does make the formula more readable. To force all the operations in this formula to take place from left to right, write the statement as

$$(((45 + 23) * 4) - 10) \text{ div } 2$$

The operation in the innermost parentheses is performed first $(45 + 23 = 68)$. The second level of parentheses directs the next operation $(68 * 4 = 272)$. The outer level of parentheses dictates the next operation $(272 - 10 = 262)$. This result is divided by 2, giving 131.

Even when the natural order of precedence provides the correct order of operations, it is good programming practice to clarify the operation with the use of parentheses.

TYPICAL OPERATION

In this session you use the *writeln* statement to display the result of several arithmetic operations.

1. If you are continuing your work from a prior session, press **Alt-F** and type **N** begin a new Edit window; otherwise type **TURBO** from the DOS prompt to start the Turbo Pascal system.

2. Type the following program.

```
program Math;
uses Crt;
begin
    ClrScr;
    writeln(not 64);
    writeln(not 0);
    writeln(8*3);
    writeln(3 shl 2);
    writeln(1 shl 16);
    writeln(7 div 2);
    writeln(7 mod 2);
    writeln(7 shr 2);
    writeln(7 shr 16);
    writeln(7+3);
    writeln(7.0+3.0);
    writeln(7-2);
    writeln(7.0-2.0);
    writeln(6E10-100);
    writeln(3742 xor 1842);
```

```
      writeln(3742 and 1842);
      writeln(3742 or 1842);
      writeln((((45 + 23) * 4) - 10) div 2);
      writeln(45 + (23 * 4) - (10 div 2));
      writeln(45 + 23 * 4 - 10 div 2);
      readln;
end.
```

3. Press **Alt-F** and type **S** to save the program. Type **MATH** as the program name and press **Enter**.

4. Press **Alt-R** and **Enter** to run the program.

Verify that the results shown follow the rules for arithmetic expressions as discussed.

5. Press **Enter** to return to the Turbo Pascal integrated environment.

6. Turn to Module 60, String, to continue the learning sequence.

Module 5
ARRAY

DESCRIPTION

An *array* is one kind of list. Each element in the array is always the same type. An *array* is a list of numbers, a list of names, or a list of times for the hundred-yard dash.

To declare a single-dimensional array:

```
var VariableList: array of [Lower..Upper] of DataType
```

To declare a two-dimensional array:

```
var VariableList: array of [Lower1..Upper1,Lower2..Upper2] of DataType
```

VariableList   is either a single variable name or a list of variable names separated by commas.

Lower (*Lower1, Lower2, Lower3, . . .*)   is the lowest value index for the array and must be an ordinal constant or literal. *Lower* may be positive, negative, or zero.

Upper (*Upper1, Upper2, Upper3, . . .*)   is the highest value index for the array and must be an ordinal constant or literal.

MULTIPLE-DIMENSIONAL ARRAYS   Arrays are not limited to containing only integer, real, and other simple data types. Arrays can consist of any type of data. One of the useful complex data types is an array of type array.

An array of arrays is often referred to as a two-dimensional array. You can think of a two-dimensional array as a collection of rows and columns of data.

A two-dimensional array requires two subscripts to reference an element in the array. The type of the indexes depends on the definition of the array. The subscripts can be of the same or different types, it just depends on how you define the array.

APPLICATIONS

The variable type string is a list of characters of dynamically changing length. In fact, the string type in Turbo Pascal is interchangable with an array of *char* of the declared length of the string. Using this fact allows you to refer to the characters in a string with subscript notation. For example, If Name:='Thomas Jefferson,' Name[0] refers to the length of the string, Name[1] contains the "T" from "Thomas," and Name[8] contains the "J" from "Jefferson." When manipulating strings on a character-by-character basis, subscript notation is frequently easier to write than repeated use of the *Copy* string function.

The array provides a similar type of structure for all data types. Sometimes, situations arise in which data must be processed as a group. For example, the problem of producing an alphabetized roster of a football team requires retaining the names of all the football players in memory to alphabetize them. The techniques used so far have enabled doing this only by providing a different variable name for each player. You could do this by using variable names, such as QUARTERBACK, FULLBACK, RIGHTHALFBACK, LEFTHALF-BACK, LEFTGUARD, RIGHTGUARD, etc. This is a solution, but keeping track of the variable names is difficult.

Another solution is to name the variables systematically, such as PLAYER1, PLAYER2, PLAYER3, PLAYER4, PLAYER5, etc. This designation allows the variables to be referenced in a more systematic fashion. This still requires program code that considers each player's data individually. To print the names of the 40 members of a football team, you could write:

```
procedure printteam;
begin
    writeln(Player1);
    writeln(Player2);
    writeln(Player3);
    writeln(Player4);
    writeln(Player5);
    writeln(Player6);

 {additional statements go here}

    writeln(Player38);
    Writeln(Player39);
    Writeln(Player40);
end;
```

Pascal provides a data type called an array that implements this idea in a more elegant fashion. The array takes the idea of PLAYER1, PLAYER2, PLAYER3, PLAYER4, etc. and allows you to reference any arbitrary element in the list by referring to the number of the element. Using array notation, the players would be referenced by the notation PLAYER[1], PLAYER[2], PLAYER[3], PLAYER[4], etc.

The advantage of this technique is that you can now write the procedure for printing the football team roster in far fewer programming steps. The same procedure, using array notation, could be written:

```
procedure printteam;
var I:integer;
```

```
begin
    for I:=1 to 40 do writeln(Player[I]);
end;
```

The advantages are apparent for a 40-member football roster. The same code that prints 40 names also prints 4000, assuming, of course, you have enough memory to store that many names. An array that holds the names of 40 football players is declared with this statement:

```
var Player : array [1..40] of string[30];
```

An array to hold uniform numbers could be declared with the following statement:

```
var Jersey : array [1..40] of integer;
```

An array to hold times in the hundred yard dash could be declared with this statement:

```
var Dash : array [1..40] of real;
```

One application appropriate for an array of multiple dimension is a seating chart for an airplane. Depending on the size of the airplane, the number of rows of seats and the number of seats in each row may vary, but all major airlines use computer programs to keep track of the seating in their airplanes.

An airline seat assignment program needs to keep track of which passenger is assigned to which seat. As a result, the base type of the array must be capable of storing a name. A string type is appropriate for this application. The rows of seats in an airplane are numbered starting with row 1 at the front of the plane. The seats in each row are usually assigned letters. An airplane with 20 rows of seats with four seats in each row could be represented with a data structure like this:

```
var Seat[1..20,'A'..'D'] of string;
```

As a programmer working for a major airline, the method of assigning seats for an airplane is the same for a large number of planes, only the exact size of the plane changes. One way to make your procedure or program easy to modify is to make the size of the plane a constant. You could use the statements:

```
const Maxrow=20;
        Maxseat='D';
var Seat[1..Maxrow, 'A'..Maxseat] of string;
```

These three statements have exactly the same meaning as the previous declaration. If all references to the size of the array are made in terms of MAXROW and MAXSEAT, then to change the program to handle an airplane of a different size, change only the values of two constants. This is much simpler than going through the program changing all the 20s and 6s to other numbers. It also prevents you from missing one or more numbers or changing others incorrectly.

Still another way to declare this same array is

```
const Maxrow=20;
type Row=array['A'..'D'] of string;

var Seat[1..Maxrow] of Row;
```

There are several ways to define this and many other data structures. When you have a choice, always choose the method that gives the most clarity to your program and provides the greatest ability to incorporate changes later.

TYPICAL OPERATION

A football coach wants to produce an alphabetized list of the team's starting offensive lineup to distribute to the sports writers.

The functions of the program are broken into three distinct actions:

- Read the names of the players.
- Sort the names of the players.
- Print the list of the players.

It is often necessary to arrange information in alphabetic or numeric order. The techniques used to sort information are the same. One of the simplest methods for sorting a list of data is the bubble sort.

THE BUBBLE SORT   The bubble sort works on the following principle:

- Look at the first item in the list.
- Compare this item, individually, with every other item in the list.
- If the comparison shows that the first item should precede the item being examined, go on to the next item.
- If the comparison shows that the first item should come after the item being examined, swap the positions of the two items.
- Look at the second item in the list.
- Perform the compare-and-swap procedure between the second item and every item below it in the list.
- Look at the third item in the list.
- Perform the compare-and-swap procedure between the third item and every item below it in the list.
- Continue the procedure until you reach the end of the list.

Use this technique to implement the Sort procedure in the Football program.

Module 5

This technique calls for two *for* loops, one inside the other. The index of the outer for loop points to the current top of the list. The index of the inner for loop starts just below the current top of the list and goes to the bottom of the list.

1. Start the Editor and type the following program:

```
program Football;
uses Crt;
const NumberOfPlayers = 11;
type PlayerList = array[1..NumberOfPlayers] of string[30];
var Player : PlayerList;

procedure Readlist(var List:PlayerList;  HowMany:Integer);
var i : integer;
begin
    for i:=1 to HowMany do
    begin
        write('Enter the name of player ',i,':');
        readln(List[i]);
    end;
end;

procedure Sortlist(var List:PlayerList;
HowMany:Integer);
var Hold:string[30];
    Top,Current:integer;
begin
    for Top:=1 to HowMany-1 do
    begin
        for Current:=Top+1 to HowMany do
        begin
            if List[Top] < List[Current] then
            begin
                Hold:=List[Top];
                List[Top]:=List[Current];
                List[Current]:=Hold;
            end;
        end;
    end;
end;

procedure
PrintList(List:PlayerList;HowMany:Integer);
var i:integer;
begin
    for i:=1 to HowMany do writeln(List[i]);
end;

begin
    ClrScr;
    ReadList(Player,NumberOfPlayers);
    ClrScr;
    writeln('The original list is: ');
    PrintList(Player,NumberOfPlayers);
```

```
        write('Press Enter to continue.');
        readln;
        ClrScr;
        SortList(Player,NumberOfPlayers);
        writeln('The sorted list is: ');
        PrintList(Player,NumberOfPlayers);
        readln;
    end.
```

There are several ways to accomplish most programming tasks. This program demonstrates several elements of good programming style. The declaration section,

```
program Football;
const NumberOfPlayers = 11;
type PlayerList = array[1..NumberOfPlayers] of string[30];
var Player : PlayerList;
```

could be written more simply as:

```
program Football;
var Player : array[1..11] of string[30];
```

This approach, however, hides the meaning of the number 11. The statements used in the program clearly indicate the meaning of the number 11. When football season is over and the program must be modified for the basketball coach, it is easy to identify exactly what changes must be made to sort a five-member basketball starting lineup. The single required change is to the const statement, where it is clear that NumberOfPlayers should be 5. Of course, changing the name of the program to Basketball would add to the program's readability.

The Readlist and Sortlist procedures each use both a var parameter and a value parameter. Both procedures modify the contents of the player list. Therefore, the array with player names must be a var parameter. The number of players is not modified, therefore, it is specified as a value parameter.

The PrintList procedure is called twice. The first time it is called, it prints the list in the same order as the names are entered. The second time it is called, it prints the list in the sorted order. Because the PrintList procedure does not change the values of any data, there is no reason to provide it with var parameters. Using value parameters exclusively helps guard against unwanted side effects.

   2. Save the program with the name FOOTBALL.PAS.

3. Run the program. Use the names: Jackson, Smith, Green, Taylor, Brooks, Newhouse, Martinez, Walters, Brown, Jones, and Kent.

```
The original list is:
Jackson
Smith
Green
Taylor
Brooks
Newhouse
Martinez
Walters
Brown
Jones
Kent
Press Enter to continue.
```

4. Press **Enter**.

```
The sorted list is:
Brooks
Brown
Green
Jackson
Jones
Kent
Martinez
Newhouse
Smith
Taylor
Walters
Press Enter to end the program.
```

PROGRAMMING MATRIX ADDITION Matrices are used for the representation and manipulation of data in many applications in mathematics, engineering, and economics. Matrix addition is one of the operations commonly performed when manipulating matrices.

To be added together, two matrices must have the same number of rows and columns. The sum of two matrices is a matrix. The sum is computed by adding each element in the first matrix with the corresponding element in the second matrix, giving the element in the same position in the final matrix. For example

$$
\begin{bmatrix} 3 & 5 & 2 \\ 1 & 9 & 2 \end{bmatrix} + \begin{bmatrix} 1 & 4 & 5 \\ 6 & 0 & 1 \end{bmatrix} = \begin{bmatrix} 3+1 & 5+4 & 2+5 \\ 1+6 & 9+0 & 2+2 \end{bmatrix} = \begin{bmatrix} 4 & 9 & 7 \\ 7 & 9 & 3 \end{bmatrix}
$$

Your first inclination in writing a general-purpose computer routine that adds matrices is to use a function. A function is ideally suited to the task, but remember that a function is limited to returning simple data types (CHAR, INTEGER, REAL, user-defined ordinal types). The only way to return a result that is a complex data type, such as an array, is to use a procedure.

If the two matrices to be added are named MATA and MATB and the result is named MATSUM, the procedure could be written as:

```
procedure MatAdd (Mata,Matb:Matrix;var Matsum:Matrix);
var Row,Col:integer;
begin
    for Row:=1 to 2 do
        for Col:=1 to 3 do
            MatSum[Row,Col]:=Mata[Row,Col]+Matb[Row,Col];
end;
```

This assumes, of course, that MATRIX is defined as array[1 . . 2, 1 . . 3] of integer. This procedure is not a good, general-purpose routine. It is limited since it can add only 2 x 3 matrices. It is impractical to have a separate procedure to add every size matrix. The procedure is much more generally applicable if it can add matrices of any size. Of course, there is a limitation that the maximum size of the matrices must be specified at the time the program is written. However, it is a fairly straightforward matter to make a general-purpose routine that can add any size matrix up to and including some maximum size.

The limitation of the maximum size restriction on the matrices can be reduced by specifying the size of the matrices as global constants at the beginning of the program.

```
program Matrices;
{MAXROW and MAXCOL specify the maximum dimension of the matrices in this program.}
const Maxrow=10;
      Maxcol=10;
type Matrix = array[1..Maxrow,1..Maxcol] of integer;
```

Specifying the maximum number of rows and columns in the main program declaration assures that all matrices have the same maximum sizes. If it later becomes necessary to modify the program to work with matrices of a different size, these modifications are accomplished by changing only two constant declarations. The comment, while not required by the Compiler, is essential in this case to document the meaning of these constants properly. Later modifications can be made in the array bounds eliminating a search through the program code to discover (or remember) how you planned to accommodate future modifications to the program.

Just because the maximum size of each matrix is specified as 10 x 10 (or any other size) does not mean that every matrix must be that size. The actual size of each matrix can be maintained in separate variable locations.

The definition of the general matrix addition procedure is almost identical to the definition used for the 2 x 3 specific case. The first difference is the addition of two more parameters to specify the actual number of rows and columns in the matrices.

```
procedure Matadd (Mata,Matb:Matrix;Nrow,Ncol:integer;var Matsum:Matrix);
```

The variables NROW and NCOL are used to specify the actual number of rows and columns in the matrix.

```
procedure Matadd (Mata,Matb:Matrix;Nrow,Ncol:integer;var Matsum:Matrix);
var Row,Col:integer;
begin
    for Row:=1 to Maxrow do
        for Col:=1 to Maxcol do
            Matsum[Row,Col]:=Mata[Row,Col]+Matb[Row,Col];
end;
```

The small extra effort involved in writing a general-purpose procedure pays for itself quickly the next time you write a similar program that can use procedures you have already written.

1. Begin a new Editor window and type the following program:

```
program Matrices;
uses Crt;
const Maxrow=10;
      Maxcol=10;
type Matrix = array[1..Maxrow,1..Maxcol] of integer;
var MatA, MatB, Sum : Matrix;
    Row,Col:Integer;

procedure Getsize(var Row,Column:integer);
begin
    ClrScr;
    Gotoxy(10,10);
    write('How many rows? ');
    readln(Row);
    Gotoxy(10,10);
    write('How many columns? ');
    readln(Column);
    ClrScr;
end;

procedure GetMat(var Mat:Matrix;Numrow,Numcol:integer);
var Row, Col : integer;
begin
    ClrScr;
    for Row:=1 to Numrow do
```

```
            for Col:=1 to Numcol do
            begin
                write('Enter row ',Row,', column',Col,':');
                read(Mat[Row,Col]);
            end;
    end;

    procedure MatAdd(Mata,Matb:Matrix;Nrow,Ncol:integer;var Matsum:Matrix);

    var Row, Col : integer;
    begin
        for Row:=1 to Maxrow do
            for Col:=1 to Maxcol do
                Matsum[Row,Col]:=Mata[Row,Col] + Matb[Row,Col];
    end;

    procedure Outmat(var Mat:Matrix;Numrow,Numcol:integer);

    var Row,Col:integer;
    begin
        writeln;
        for Row:=1 to Numrow do
        begin
            for Col:=1 to Numcol do write (Mat[Row,Col]:6);
            writeln;
            writeln
        end;
        gotoxy(28,24);
        write('Press Enter to continue.');
        readln;
        ClrScr;
    end;

    begin
        Getsize(Row,Col);
        Getmat(Mata,Row,Col);
        Getmat(Matb,Row,Col);
        Matadd(Mata,Matb,Row,Col,Sum);
        ClrScr;
        writeln('The first matrix is:');
        outmat(Mata,Row,Col);
        writeln('The second matrix is:');
        outmat(Matb,Row,Col);
        writeln('The sum of the matrices is:');
        outmat(Sum,Row,Col);
        readln;
    end.
```

2. Save the program.

3. Run the program. Specify 2 rows and 3 columns.

Use $\begin{bmatrix} 3 & 5 & 2 \\ 1 & 9 & 2 \end{bmatrix}$ as the first matrix.

Use $\begin{bmatrix} 1 & 4 & 5 \\ 6 & 0 & 1 \end{bmatrix}$ as the second matrix.

```
The first matrix is:
     3    5    2
     1    9    2
                    Press any key to continue.
```

```
The second matrix is:
     1    4    5
     6    0    1
                    Press any key to continue.
```

```
The sum of the matrices is:
     4    9    7
     7    9    3
                    Press Enter to continue.
```

4. Experiment with matrices of other sizes and with different values.

5. Turn to Module 3, Absolute, to continue the learning sequence.

Module 6
ASSIGN

DESCRIPTION

The *assign* statement makes the connection between the program filename and the DOS filename. All file operations in Turbo Pascal work with the program filename. The only place the DOS filename (or device name) appears is in the *assign* statement. The format of the statement is

```
Assign (filevar, DOS-filename);
```

filevar
The *filevar* is formed according to the Turbo Pascal rules for naming.

DOS-filename
The *DOS-filename* is either the name of a DOS-defined device, such as LPT2, or a valid DOS filename, which may include a drive specifier and a path.

APPLICATIONS

Unless you are working with a Turbo Pascal predefined file, such as *Input*, *Output*, or *Lst* (from the Printer unit) which are, in effect, preassigned, you must use the *assign* statement to make the connection between the program filename and the DOS filename. The *assign* statement is the only statement that uses a DOS filename. All other Turbo Pascal file operations are performed on the program filename. If your program contains a file definition such as

```
var Outdata : File of integer;
```

and the DOS filename for the disk file containing the information is PROG.DAT, you use the statement

```
assign(Outdata,'PROG.DAT');
```

to connect "Outdata" with "PROG.DAT." All further references in the program are made in terms of Outdata, but because of the association of the *assign* statement, the operations are carried out on the disk file PROG.DAT.

TYPICAL OPERATION

In this session you add the *assign* statement to the TEXTIO program and the INTIO program. Use the filename INFO.TXT as the filename for the text file and INFO.DAT as the filename for the file of integers.

1. Use the Open command on the File menu to load the program TEXTOUT into an Editor window. Add the *assign* statement as shown in the following program listing.

```
program TextIO;
uses Crt;
var         S:string;
    Diskfile : text;
begin
    ClrScr;
    assign(Diskfile,'INFO.T'T');
    writeln(Diskfile,'This information is placed on the disk.');
    readln(Diskfile,S);
    writeln(S);
end.
```

2. Save the program as INTEGER.

3. Load the program INTIO into the Editor.

4. Add the *assign* statement as shown in the following listing.

```
program IntegerInOut;
uses Crt;
var     i,j: integer;
    Diskfile: File of Integer;
begin
    ClrScr;
    assign(Diskfile,'INFO.DAT');
    for i:= 1 to 10 do write(Diskfile,i);
    for i:= 1 to 10 do
    begin
        read(Diskfile,j);
        writeln(j);
    end;
readln;
end.
```

5. Save the program.

6. Turn to Module 53, Rewrite, to continue the learning sequence.

Module 7
CASE

DESCRIPTION

The *case* statement is similar to multiple *if* statements. If the case-selector variable matches one of the constant lists, the statement or compound statement associated with the list is executed. If no match is found, the *case* statement does nothing, and execution continues with the next statement in the program.

```
case case-selector of
     constant-list : statement {;
     constant-list : statement}
end;
```

case-selector   The *case-selector* is a scalar variable. It can be an integer, real, character, or user-defined scalar. It cannot be a real variable or a string.

constant-list   The *constant-list* can be a single value, several single values separated by commas, or a subrange of values designated by separating the minimum value and the maximum value by two periods.

APPLICATIONS

The *if* statement is ideally suited for selecting one of two possible actions. Frequently, programs must handle decisions involving more than two classifications. An educational management program might perform different actions based on the classifications of freshman, sophomore, junior, senior, and special. A military program might distinguish between general, colonel, major, captain, lieutenant, and private.

The File menu of the Turbo Pascal system provides an excellent example of an appropriate application for a *case* statement. When at the File menu you have nine options: Load, Pick, New, Save, Write to, Directory, Change dir, OS shell, and Quit. If each of these were procedures and the user input was a *char* variable, then the following program code segment could be used to make the decision about which procedure to execute:

```
Choice := Readkey;
Choice:=Upcase(Choice);
if Choice = 'O' then Load
else
    if Choice='N' then NewWindow
    else
```

```
        if Choice='S' then SaveWindow
        else
            if Choice='A' then SaveWindowAs
            else
                if Choice='L' then SaveAll
                else
                    if Choice='C' then ChangeDirectory
                    else
                        if Choice='P' then PrintWindow
                        else
                            if Choice='G' then GetInfo
                            else
                                if Choice='D' then DosShell
                                else
                                    if Choice='X' then Quit;
```

Even with careful indention to improve readability, the structure above is difficult to follow. It is easy to make errors in program coding. Using this technique for a longer menu would greatly compound the potential for confusion and error.

CASE STATEMENT WITH PROCEDURES   Pascal provides the *case* statement to control multiple-option decisions. Expressing this same program segment with a *case* structure follows:

```
Choice:=Readkey;
Choice:=Upcase(Choice);
case Choice of
    'O' : Load;
    'N' : NewWindow;
    'S' : SaveWindow;
    'A' : SaveWindowAs;
    'L' : SaveAll;
    'C' : ChangeDirectory;
    'P' : PrintWindow;
    'G' : GetInfo;
    'D' : DosShell;
    'X' : Quit;
end;
```

The *case* statement is much easier to code and infinitely more readable than the nested *if* construction. The action of the statement is obvious at a glance. You do not have to study your way through multiple levels of *if* statements to understand what it does.

A *case* statement can be used to identify whether a character is a vowel. The case statement in the program could be written as:

```
Character:=Upcase(Character);
case Character of
    'A',.'E','I','O','U' : write ('It''s a vowel.');
    'B'..'D'             : write ('It''s a consonant.');
    'F'..'H','J'..'N'    : write ('It''s a consonant.');
    'P'..'T'             : write ('It''s a consonant.');
```

```
      'V'..'X','Z'            : write ('It''s a consonant.');
      'Y'                     : write ('It could be either.');
   end;
```

TYPICAL OPERATION

In this session you create a program to select one of five messages to place on the screen, based on user input.

1. Start Turbo Pascal or begin a new Editor window. Type the following program.

2. Start the Editor and type the following program.

```
program Message;
uses Crt;
var Choice: char;

begin
    ClrScr;
    write ('Press the letter of your choice, (A-E): ');
    Choice:=Readkey;
    writeln(Choice);
    case Choice of
        'A','a'  : writeln('A stitch in time saves nine.');
        'B','b'  : writeln('Don''t cry over spilt milk.');
        'C','c'  : writeln('Blood is thicker than water.');
        'D','d'  : writeln('The squeaky wheel gets the grease.');
        'E','e'  : writeln('A watched pot never boils.')
    end;
    readln;
end.
```

Pay special attention to the double apostrophe in the word "Don't." Because the apostrophe is used as a quotation mark, to print the apostrophe you must place two of them together.

3. Run the program.

4. Type **C**.

```
Press the letter of your choice, (A-E): C
Blood is thicker than water.
```

5. Run the program. Type **b**.

```
Press the letter of your choice, (A-E): b
Don't cry over spilt milk.
```

Notice the single apostrophe in the word "Don't."

6. Run the program. Type **K**.

The program does not print a message. If a match is not found for one of the conditions specified in the *case* statement, it does not produce an error. None of the options are performed, and control passes to the statement immediately following the *case* statement. In this program, it was the end of the program.

7. Turn to Module 26, For, to continue the learning sequence.

Module 8
CHARACTER FUNCTIONS

DESCRIPTION

Turbo Pascal provides several functions for working with character and other scalar data. The *ord* and *chr* functions are mutual inverses. The *upCase* function converts a lowercase character to its uppercase equivalent.

Ord(*C*)	*C* is a *char* or other scalar value. If C is a character, the function returns an integer value that corresponds to the position of C in the ASCII character set. If C is a scalar, such as a user-defined enumerated type, the ordinal value (position) of the scalar is returned.
Chr(*I*)	*I* is an *integer* value. The function returns a *char* value equal to the position of C within the character set.
UpCase(*Source*)	*Source* is a character. The function returns a character in which each character of *source* that is a lowercase character is converted to the corresponding uppercase character, and all other characters are unaffected.

Remember that a character and a string are different data types. This includes both strings defined as having a length of one and longer strings containing exactly one character. If you need to use a character function to operate on individual characters contained in a string, use subscript notation to refer to the individual characters. For example, if S is a string, the statement

```
S[1]:=Upcase(S[1]);
```

converts the first character of the string S to an uppercase character. (Remember to guarantee that S[1] actually contains valid data before applying the Upcase function.)

APPLICATIONS

The computer has no way of directly storing letters and symbols in memory. The computer is limited to storing numbers. To store letters and symbols, systems of number codes have been developed. Then, instead of storing a letter, the computer stores the corresponding code for the letter. These numbers are assigned in alphabetical order. Most personal computers use an extended ASCII character set. ASCII is an acronym standing for

American Standard Code for Information Interchange. "A" is assigned code number 65, which is one less than "B"; and the "a," code 97, is one less than "b." As you can see, the uppercase and lowercase letters have different number codes. The code for "A" is always different than the code for "a."

Two functions are available to convert characters into integers and integers into characters. Be careful in converting integers to characters as there are more integers than characters.

These two functions are inverses of each other.

```
Ord(Chr(I)) = I                    Chr(Ord(C)) = C
```

For example, Ord('A') returns the value 65, and Chr(65) returns the character value "A."

When you need a character in your program that is not readily typed from the keyboard, use the Chr function to create the character from an integer. For example, the top-of-form or line-feed character for most printers has the ASCII value of 10. You can send this value to the printer (using the *Printer* unit) with the statement

```
write(Lst, Chr(10));
```

To guard against forgetting what Chr(10) stands for, assign the value to a variable, and use the variable when a form-feed is needed. The key steps are:

```
var FormFeed:Char;

begin
    FormFeed := Chr(10);

    Write(Lst,FormFeed,'This message is printed at the top of the paper.');

end.
```

The *upCase* function is excellent when accepting input from users. For example, the Turbo Pascal Main Menu allows you to type either "S" or "s" to save a program. While it is possible to check for both cases, a simpler technique is to use the statement sequence

```
var choice:char;

    read(choice);
    choice:=UpCase(choice);
```

to guarantee that the value of *choice* is always an uppercase character. Note that Turbo Pascal does not allow you to freely interchange characters with strings of length one; *upCase* cannot be used with *string* data without first converting it to *char* data.

TYPICAL OPERATION

In this session you use the *Chr* function to display characters on the screen.

1. Start Turbo Pascal or create a new Editor window. Type the following program.

```
program Charfunc;
uses Crt;
var I:integer;

begin
    ClrScr;
    writeln('Enter an integer: ');
    readln(I);
    writeln('The character representation is: ',chr(I));
    readln;
end.
```

2. Run the program. You are prompted "Enter an integer:"

3. Type **69** and press **Enter**.

```
Enter an integer:
69
The character representation is: E
```

4. Run the program again. Type **227** and press **Enter**.

```
Enter an integer:
227
The character representation is: π
```

The character representing *Pi* is displayed on the screen. To print the character on your printer you need a printer capable of printing the IBM extended character ASCII character set.

Appendix A contains the complete character set and corresponding ASCII codes.

5. Turn to Module 61, String Functions, to continue the learning sequence.

Module 9
CLOSE

DESCRIPTION

When a Turbo Pascal program ends, all open files are automatically closed. It is also possible to explicitly close a disk file with the *close* statement.

close(*filevar*)   *filevar* is the name of the file variable defined in the *var* statement. It is not the DOS filename.

If the file is used for output, the *close* statement forces a physical write for the last record in the file and updates the disk directory to show the status of the file.

APPLICATIONS

It is good practice to explicitly close every file as soon as you are finished using it. Even if the program only opens files for input, the system can quickly exceede the maximum number of files allowed by DOS. Closing them immediately minimizes the number of file buffers that must be maintained in memory and helps prevent exceeding the maximum number of DOS file handles. For output files, closing guarantees that the last record is physically written to the disk, and not just maintained in a partially filled buffer waiting to be written. Closing output files promptly is added protection against data loss from a power failure.

TYPICAL OPERATION

In this session you add the close statement to the TEXTIO and INTIO programs that you modified most recently in the *Reset* module.

1. Load the program TEXTIO into the Editor. Add the *close* statement as shown in the following listing.

```
program TextIO;
uses Crt;
var        S:string;
    Diskfile : text;
begin
    ClrScr;
    assign(Diskfile,'INFO.TXT');
    rewrite(Diskfile);
    writeln(Diskfile,'This information is placed on the disk.');
    reset(Diskfile);
    readln(Diskfile,S);
    close(Diskfile);
    writeln(S);
end.
```

2. Save and run the program.

```
This information is placed on the disk.
C:\TP>
```

The output is unchanged, but your code is now of higher quality. It is always best to explicitly close files when you are finished with them.

3. Load the program INTIO into the Editor. Add the *close* statement as shown in the following listing.

```
program IntegerInOut;
uses Crt;
var     i,j: integer;
    Diskfile: File of Integer;
begin
    ClrScr;
    assign(Diskfile,'INFO.DAT');
    rewrite(Diskfile);
    for i:= 1 to 10 do write(Diskfile,i);
    reset(Diskfile);
    for i:= 1 to 10 do
    begin
        read(Diskfile,j);
        writeln(j);
    end;
    close(Diskfile);
end.
```

4. Save and run the program.

```
1
2
3
4
5
6
7
8
9
10

C:\TP>
```

Again, the program is unchanged. It is, however, always a good idea to close files when you complete your work with them.

5. Turn to Module 15, CRT Unit, to continue the learning sequence.

Module 10
CLRSCR

DESCRIPTION

The *ClrScr* procedure, part of the *Crt* unit, clears text from the screen and places the cursor in the upper left corner of the screen in preparation for output. To use *ClrScr* your program must also contain the statement *uses Crt*.

The *Crt* unit provides routines to manage the computer screen. One of these routines is the *ClrScr* instruction to clear the screen. To access the *Crt* unit routines, you must place the statement *uses Crt;* at the beginning of the program.

If you use the *Window* statement to define an active text window smaller than the full screen, the *ClrScr* command clears text only from the active window; it leaves the remainder of the screen unchanged.

APPLICATIONS

When a Turbo Pascal program starts to run, it does not automatically erase the contents of the text screen. To eliminate the clutter from the screen when the program starts, use the *ClrScr* statement as the first statement in your program.

A program that allows text to scroll off the top of the screen is less professional than one that presents information a full screen at a time. Anytime you need to erase text from the screen, use the *ClrScr* command.

The *ClrScr* command does not erase graphics from the screen, including text that is created in a graphics mode. To erase graphics from the screen use either the *SetGraphMode*, *ClearDevice*, or *ClearViewPort* procedures from the *Graph* unit. These procedures are discussed in the Graphics Unit module.

TYPICAL OPERATION

In this session you clear the screen before writing on the screen.

1. Start Turbo Pascal by typing **TURBO** at the DOS prompt.

2. Press **Alt-E** to start the Turbo Pascal Editor; then type the following program:

```
program ClearText;
uses Crt;
begin
    ClrScr;
    writeln('The ClrScr statement clears text from the screen.');
    writeln('Further output starts in the upper left corner.');
    readln;
end.
```

The *uses Crt* statement references the unit containing *ClrScr* and makes it available to the program. The *ClrScr* statement actually performs the work of clearing the screen.

3. Press **Alt-F** to drop down the File menu.

4. Type **S** to save the program. Type **CLEARTXT** as the program name and press **Enter**.

5. Press **Alt-R** and **Enter** to run the program.

```
The ClrScr statement clears text from the screen.
Further output starts in the upper left corner.
```

6. Press **Enter** to return to the integrated environment.

7. Turn to Module 12, Compile Menu, to continue the learning sequence.

Module 11
COMMENTS AND COMPILER DIRECTIVES

DESCRIPTION

Comments are English text that are placed in the program source statements to describe the operation of the program and the meaning of program variables. Turbo Pascal ignores any text placed between the braces, { and }, or between the metasymbols (* and *).

Compiler directives are a set of instructions to the Turbo Pascal Compiler specifying how your program is compiled. The compiler directive does not perform any function itself, rather it determines the way other statements are interpreted.

Compiler directives are indicated by starting the directive with the characters {$, followed by a list of directives separated by commas. The set of compiler directives is ended with a brace, }. There cannot be a space between the opening brace { and the dollar sign $. Alternately, you may begin a compiler directive with (*$ and close it with *). You may place multiple directives between a single pair of braces or (* and *) metasymbols. These multiple directives must be separated by commas, and the string of directives must not contain any spaces.

The actions performed by compiler directives are also available in the Compiler Options portion of the Turbo Pascal environment. However, placing the directives in the source file has the advantage of permanently associating the directive with the program.

The compiler switch directives available in Turbo Pascal are as follows:

A   Align Data   Default A–
     This directive fine-tunes the placement of data in the computer's memory. When alignment is turned on, all data types occupying more than a single byte of memory are aligned on an even-numbered address. This allows faster program execution on computers using the 8086, 80286, and 80386 processors because the computer can use 16-bit data transfers instead of multiple 8-bit memory transfers to access the information stored there. The negative side of alignment is that it can leave byte-size gaps of unused memory. You must decide whether conservation of memory or maximum speed is the most important for each application. Each var and const declaration section is automatically aligned on a word (even-byte) boundary regardless of the setting of the Alignment directive. When developing software for 8088-based computers, remember that all memory access in an 8088 computer occurs

one byte at a time. Therefore the A+ directive holds no advantage for 8088-based computers.

B   Boolean Evaluation   Default B–

When evaluating a Boolean expression with an *and* or an *or* operator, it is not always necessary to evaluate the complete expression. For example, if X=0, the evaluation of the expression (X=0) or (I<SIN(3*Y)) can be stopped immediately after the system determines that X=0. It is not necessary to evaluate the SIN function. This short-circuit Boolean evaluation normally produces the fastest, cleanest, and easiest to debug programs. However, if you make use of a function that modifies global variables or produces output as part of a Boolean expression, you may want to guarantee that the complete Boolean expression is always evaluated. In this case, you may use the {$B+} directive to force the evaluation of the complete Boolean expression. The preferred practice, however, is to write functions without side effects and allow short-circuit evaluation of Boolean functions.

D   Debug Information   Default D+

When active, the Turbo Pascal Compiler generates a line number table that is usable by the Turbo Pascal System to locate run-time (execution) errors. Although the debug information requires extra memory (or disk for disk-based compilation), it does not affect the speed of program execution. If you want to use the stand-alone Turbo Debugger to debug your program, set the compiler destination to disk and stand-alone debugging to On.

E   Emulation   Default E+

Enables or disables the use of a run-time 8087 emulation library in generating program code. When emulation is enabled, by default or through the E+ compiler directive, the Compiler produces a larger .EXE file, but the resulting code can be executed on any computer, regardless of whether a math co-processor is present. Compiling a program with the E– directive produces a smaller .EXE file but requires the presence of a math co-processor in each machine that runs the program if any 8087 data types are used in the program.

F   Force Far Calls   Default F–

This option controls the machine language linkage between Turbo Pascal procedures and functions. In the default state, F–, Turbo Pascal determines whether the calls should be near calls or far calls. In the active state, all calls are generated as far calls.

I   I/O Error Handling   Default I+

The I directive selects the method of I/O error handling. In the active, default state, {$I+}, all I/O operations are checked for errors. Errors cause the abnormal termination of the program and the display of a runtime error message. In the passive state, {$I–}, it is your responsibility to check for I/O errors with the predeclared function IoResult.

L   Local Debug Information   Default L–
      Generates local debug information. With this option active, Turbo Pascal maintains a
      list of local identifiers in each procedure and function so that the debugger can
      reference them during a debugging session.

N   Numeric Processing   Default N–
      The default is using Turbo Pascal software libraries to evaluate all real-number
      expressions. However, when active, N+, the compiler takes advantage of the math
      co-processor to generate the real number math operations. You must have a math
      co-processor to use the N+ directive, unless you also use the E+ directive to provide
      for software emulation of the 8087 when it is not physically present.

O   Overlay Code Generation   Default O–
      If you want separately compiled units to be overlayed in memory, it is necessary to
      instruct Turbo Pascal to add additional error-checking code through the use of the O+
      directive. Just because a unit is compiled in the O+ state does not require it to be
      overlaid, it only enables overlaying the code. Note that overlaid code must also use
      Far calls; in practice the O+ directive is almost always used with the F+ directive,
      {$O+,F+}.

R   Index Range Check   Default R–
      The R directive controls the use of run-time checks of array indices. In the default
      passive state, {$R–}, no checks are made to assure that array indices do not exceed
      the array bounds. As a result, an out-of-control array access may modify a region of
      memory that only later produces an obscure error. When active, {$R+}, checks are
      made on the value of the index for every array access. Out-of-range errors are
      identified immediately. The range checking does, however, slow down program
      execution. As a general rule, always enable range checking when developing and
      debugging a program. When you can guarantee that there are no errors in the array
      access, disable range checking to improve program performance.

S   Stack Checking   Default S+
      The S compiler directive controls the generation of stack-checking code. In the default
      active state, {$S+}, the system checks for available space for local variables on the
      stack before each call to a subprogram. In the passive state, {$S–}, no checks are
      made. In general, it is advisable to leave this directive in its default state, especially in
      programs that perform deeply nested recursive operations.

V   Var-String Type Checking   Default V+
      The V compiler directive selects type checking on strings passed as *var* parameters.
      In the default active state, {$V+}, strict type checking is performed. All strings passed
      as actual parameters must match the length of the formal parameters. In the passive
      state, {$V–}, the lengths of strings passed as actual parameters do not have to match
      the lengths of strings specified as formal parameters.

The compiler parameter directives available in Turbo Pascal include:

I   Include Files   {$I *filename*}
     The I directive followed by a filename instructs the compiler to import the specified
     file at that point and include its contents in the compilation. The format is {$I
     filename} where *filename* is a valid DOS filename. The filename may contain an
     optional drive specification and a path.

L   Link Object File   {$L *filename*}
     This directive causes the Compiler to link the named file with the program or unit
     being compiled. The code is written in assembly language for procedures and
     functions declared to be external. The file must be an Intel relocatable object file (.OBJ
     file).

M   Memory Allocation Sizes   {$M *stacksize, heapmin, heapmax*}
     This directive allows you to specify the program's memory allocation parameters.
     (The directive has no effect when compiling units.) All values are integers. *Stacksize*
     must be in the range 1024 to 65520 and specifies the size of the stack segment. The
     default value is 16384. The heap is the area of memory used to store dynamic
     variables—variables created with the procedures *new* and *GetMem*. *Heapmin* must be
     in the range of 0 to 655360 and specifies the minimum size heap required for program
     execution. *Heapmax* may be no smaller than the value specified for *heapmin*, nor
     larger than 655360.

O   Overlay Unit Name   {$O *filename*}
     The O directive is used in a program to specify that a particular unit whould be treated
     as an overlay. The O directive has no effect if placed in a unit. The directive must be
     placed after the *uses* clause for the particular unit. When you use the O directive in
     your program, the code for the specified unit is placed in a file with the extension
     .OVR instead of in the program's .EXE file. Remember to compile units that will be
     used as overlays with the compiler directives {$O+,F+} to generate the required code
     in the overlay itself.

APPLICATIONS

Comments are used to explain the strategies used in constructing a program to document an
algorithm, or to explain the use of constants and variables in a program. Comments should
not be used to belabor the obvious. For example, the following comment adds nothing to its
associated statement and is therefore worthless:

```
{Assign the number 12 to factor.}
Factor :+ 12;
```

The following comment, used with the same programming statement, is a valuable addition
to its associated program code:

```
{Factor represents the number of inches per feet and is used in performing
unit conversions.}
Factor :=12;
```

The first example tells us nothing we can't tell from the Pascal text. The second example explains why the number 12 is assigned to the variable Factor. The value assignment is obvious from the Pascal statements. The reason for the assignment is a valid use for comment text.

Compiler directives are used to modify the interpretation of other Turbo Pascal statements. Further discussion of the action of compiler directives is found with the affected statements in other modules in the book.

Turn to Module 78, Write and Writeln, to continue the learning sequence.

Module 12
COMPILE MENU

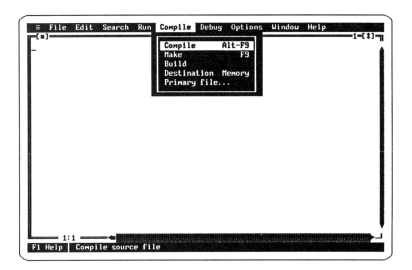

DESCRIPTION

Press Alt-C to drop down the Compile menu.

Compile Compiles the file currently loaded either into RAM or onto the disk, depending on the setting of "Destination."

Make When you create programs that use your own separately compiled units, the Make command compiles the current file in the Editor (or the specified Primary file) and any separately compiled units that have changed since the last time they were compiled.

Build When you create programs that use your own separately compiled units, the Build command compiles the current file in the Editor (or the specified Primary file) and all separately compiled units that the primary file uses. Build is similar to Make, but it is unconditional in its recompilation.

Destination Specifies where the compiled version of the program should be placed. For program development, the fastest and most convenient place is memory. However, when the development process is complete, compiling to disk creates an .EXE file that is run from the DOS prompt without having Turbo Pascal in memory. For very large programs or computers with limited memory, compiling to disk may be the only viable option.

Find Error Turbo Pascal identifies two kinds of errors. Errors in Pascal syntax are identified when you compile the program, and you are automatically returned to the Editor to correct the program syntax. For this command to work, you must also enable Debug information in the Options/Compiler menu.

Primary file This option allows you to specify which file the compiler uses to control the action of a Make or Build.

Get info Displays a window of information about the current Turbo Pascal program.

APPLICATIONS

Compiling the program is the required step to translate it from Pascal into machine language. All programs must be compiled before they are executed. (The Run command on the Run menu automatically compiles the program if you have not already done so.) Programs are compiled either into an EXE file on the disk or into a memory image that can be run within Turbo Pascal. Separately compiled units are compiled into a proprietary unit format with a file extension .TPU.

Make and Build are provided for use with separately compiled units. Make uses the DOS date and time on your units to determine if recompilation is necessary. Build recompiles all supporting units. If your file dates and times are incorrect, possibly from forgetting to set the system date and time, Make does not sense all the required dependencies. It is good practice to periodically use a Build command to force recompilation of all supporting units to force them into synchronization.

The Primary file option allows you to specify the file controlling the Make or Build operation. If you do not specify a primary file, the system assumes that the program currently in the Editor is the primary file.

When you distribute your programs, you normally want to distribute only an EXE file that the user can run from the DOS prompt. Change the destination to Disk to create an EXE file. Unlike some other compilers, Turbo Pascal does not require a separate link operation to create an EXE file. The linker is an integral part of the compiler.

When a Turbo Pascal program encounters an invalid condition, such as division by zero, the program terminates abnormally. When this happens, use the Find error command to instruct Turbo Pascal to identify the location in the program where the error occurred.

TYPICAL OPERATION

In this session you compile a program into a disk file, then execute the program from the DOS prompt.

1. From the DOS prompt, type **TURBO** and press **Enter** to start the Turbo Pascal system.

2. Press **Alt-F** to drop down the File menu. Notice that the Open option is highlighted. Press **Enter** to select Open.

The selection window displays all the files in the current directory with an extension of .PAS. Your display is probably different and may include sample programs that come with the Turbo Pascal system.

3. Type **SIMPLE** and press **Enter**, or use the mouse to double click on SIMPLE.PAS.

4. Press **Alt-C** to drop down the Compile menu.

5. Press **Down Arrow** to highlight "Destination Memory."

6. Press **Enter** to change "Destination" to "Disk." (Note that the menu disappears so that you don't actually see the change made.)

7. Press **Alt-C** and type **c** to start the compiler.

The compiler window shows that the file SIMPLE.PAS was compiled onto the disk.

8. Press **Enter** (or another key) to close the compiler window.

9. Press **Alt-F** and type **D** for DOS shell.

10. Type **DIR   *.EXE** and press **Enter** to display the directory of executable files on your disk directory.

11. Type **DIR   *.EXE** and press **Enter** to display the directory of Pascal files on your disk directory.

Note that your display will vary from the one shown, but that the file SIMPLE.EXE is included in the list.

```
C:\TP>exit
Type EXIT to return to Turbo Pascal...

IBM DOS Version 4.00
          (C)Copyright International Business Machines Corp 1981, 1988
          (C)Copyright Microsoft Corp 1981-1986

C:\TP>dir *.exe

 Volume in drive C is SCHLIEVE
 Volume Serial Number is 3D2D-1ED6
 Directory of  C:\TP

UNZIP     EXE      23044 10-23-90   6:00a
TURBO     EXE     325397 10-23-90   6:00a
TPC       EXE      69214 10-23-90   6:00a
TPTOUR    EXE      79065 10-23-90   6:00a
SIMPLE    EXE       1968 08-18-91   7:24p
          5 File(s)   256679936 bytes free

C:\TP>_
```

12. Type **SIMPLE** and press **Enter** to execute the program from the disk. The program SIMPLE.EXE executes and places its output on the screen.

13. Turn to Module 58, Simple Data Types, to continue the learning sequence.

Module 13
CONST

DESCRIPTION

```
const name = value
     {name = value};
```

A constant is similar to a variable: both allow you to give a name to a value used in a program. The difference between a constant and a variable is that a constant is provided a value when the program is written.

Constants are declared and given a value in a *const* statement. The *const* statement (which is short for constant) is usually placed immediately after the *program* statement and before the *var* statement, although this rule is not enforced by the Turbo Pascal Compiler. Turbo Pascal also allows you to have more than one *const* statement in a program block.

APPLICATIONS

Constants are useful for values that do not change in a program. Using constants provides a self-documenting alternative to repetitive use of numeric literals. A statement such as *TextColor(Red)* is self-explanatory, where the equivalent statement, *TextColor(4)*, requires an accompanying comment to make the meaning clear.

USER-DEFINED CONSTANTS In a program for performing measurement conversions, the measurement conversion factors are ideal applications for constants. Some declarations might include the following:

```
program Measure;
Const InchesPerFoot = 12;
     FeetPerYard = 3;
     FeetPerRod = 17.5;
     RodsPerChain = 4;
   {Other program statements}
begin
   {Other program statements}
end.
```

The constant declaration is different from a variable assignment. Notice that the equals sign (=) is used instead of the assignment symbol. This difference between assignment and declaration is because you are making a statement of equality, not assigning a value to a variable.

PREDEFINED CONSTANTS The values True and False are predefined as Boolean values and their meanings are self-evident. Other constants, such as those defining color names as numbers, are keyed to the numbers used for color text on the IBM Personal Computer and compatibles. The use of these constants is discussed more fully in the TextColor and other modules.

TYPICAL OPERATION

In this session you use a user-defined constant in computing the area of a circle. The function *Pi* is predefined in Turbo Pascal's *Sys* unit, which is used implicitly in every Turbo Pascal program. The precision of *Pi* depends on whether or not you have a math co-processor. Although technically *Pi* is a function, you can use it as a constant.

1. Start Turbo Pascal and type the following program in an Editor window.

```
program Area;
uses Crt;

const FeetPerYard = 3;

var CircleArea, RadiusInFeet, RadiusInYards : Real;

begin
    ClrScr;
    RadiusInYards:=10.0;
    RadiusInFeet:= RadiusInYards * FeetPerYard;
    CircleArea:=Pi * RadiusInFeet * RadiusInFeet;
    writeln ('The area in square feet is: ',CircleArea);
    readln;
end.
```

2. Save the program with the name AREA, then run the program.

```
The area in square feet is:   2.8274333882E+03
```

3. Press **Enter** to return to the Turbo Pascal environment.

The program uses the user-defined constant FeetPerYard to compute the value of the variable RadiusInFeet. The computation for Area uses the predeclared function *Pi* in performing the calculations. The answer is displayed in exponential notation and corresponds to approximately 2827.4 square feet.

4. Turn to Module 11, Comments and Compiler Directives, to continue the learning sequence.

Module 14
CONSTRUCTOR

DESCRIPTION

You must initialize each individual use, or instance, of an object with a constructor. A constructor is a special type of procedure that contains the initialization code for an object.

APPLICATIONS

Every object containing virtual methods must have a constructor procedure. When you create a new instance of an object, you must call the constructor procedure before you call any virtual procedures for the object. Failure to do so will lock up your computer.

TYPICAL OPERATION

In this session you modify the initializitation methods of the ScrnObj unit to designate them as constructors.

1. Load SCRNOBJ.PAS (Most recently used in Module 73, Virtual) into the Turbo Pascal Editor.

2. Replace the word *procedure* with constructor in the Initialize method of both Point and Ball.

```
Unit ScrnObj;

interface
type Point = object
        X, Y : word;
        constructor Initialize(XPos,YPos : word);
        procedure ChangeLocation(XDisplacement,YDisplacement :
            integer); virtual;
        function XLocation : word;
        function YLocation : word;
     end;

     Ball = object(Point)
        Radius : word;
        constructor Initialize(XPos,YPos,Size: word);
        procedure ChangeLocation(XDisplacement,YDisplacement :
            integer); virtual;
      end;
```

3. Save the unit.

4. Select New from the File menu. Then type the following program in the Editor.

```
program VirtualDemo;
uses Crt,Graph,ScrnObj;
var i,GraphDriver,GraphMode : integer;
    APoint : point;
    ABall  : ball;
    X,Y : array[1..4] of word;

begin
    GraphDriver:=Detect;
    InitGraph(GraphDriver,GraphMode,'');
    {Set up some points to move to.}
    X[1]:=GetMaxX div 2 - GetMaxX div 4;
    X[2]:=X[1] + GetMaxX div 2;
    X[3]:=X[2];
    X[4]:=X[1];
    Y[1]:=GetMaxY div 2 - GetMaxX div 4;
    Y[2]:=Y[1];
    Y[3]:=Y[1] + GetMaxY div 2;
    Y[4]:=Y[3];
    {Make a point and move it around.}
    APoint.Initialize(GetMaxX div 2,GetMaxY div 2);
    readln;
    For i:=1 to 4 do
    begin
        Apoint.MoveTo(X[i],Y[i]);
        readln;
    end;
    {Make a ball and move it around.}
    ABall.Initialize(GetMaxX div 2, GetMaxY div 2, GetMaxY div 20);
    readln;
    For i:= 1 to 4 do
    begin
        ABall.MoveTo(X[i],Y[i]);
        readln;
    end;
    readln;
end.
```

5. Save the program as VIRTUAL.PAS.

6. Select Make from the File menu.

7. Run the program. Press **Enter** to move the point, then the ball, from location to location.

8. Turn to Module 18, Destructor, to continue the learning sequence.

Module 15
CRT UNIT

DESCRIPTION

The *Crt* unit contains a number of useful items that are helpful in writing Pascal programs. These constants and procedures are all oriented toward improved control over both the screen and the keyboard. The *Crt* unit includes the constants

```
BW40      = 0;        { 40x25 B/W on Color Adapter }
CO40      = 1;        { 40x25 Color on Color Adapter }
BW80      = 2;        { 80x25 B/W on Color Adapter }
CO80      = 3;        { 80x25 Color on Color Adapter }
Mono      = 7;        { 80x25 on Monochrome Adapter }
Font8x8   = 256;      { Add-in for ROM font }
```

that are used with the Textmode procedure. They include the color constants:

```
Black          = 0;
Blue           = 1;
Green          = 2;
Cyan           = 3;
Red            = 4;
Magenta        = 5;
Brown          = 6;
LightGray      = 7;
DarkGray       = 8;
LightBlue      = 9;
LightGreen     = 10;
LightCyan      = 11;
LightRed       = 12;
LightMagenta   = 13;
Yellow         = 14;
White          = 15;
Blink          = 128;
```

and a number of miscellaneous variables for providing better control over the Turbo Pascal screen and keyboard environment.

```
CheckBreak: Boolean;        { Enable Ctrl-Break }
CheckEOF: Boolean;          { Enable Ctrl-Z }
DirectVideo: Boolean;       { Enable direct video addressing }
CheckSnow: Boolean;         { Enable snow filtering }
LastMode: Word;             { Current text mode }
TextAttr: Byte;             { Current text attribute }
WindMin: Word;              { Window upper left coordinates }
WindMax: Word;              { Window lower right coordinates }
```

The *Crt* unit also contains a number of useful procedures and functions.

procedure AssignCrt(var F: Text);

> Allows the use of fast Crt output routines that require absolute IBM compatibility at the video hardware level. This speeds up output operations at the expense of compatibility with some MS-DOS compatible, but not IBM-compatible computers. You declare a text file, assign the Crt to it with *AssignCrt*, and then direct your screen output to the text file.

function KeyPressed: Boolean;

> A Boolean function that becomes True when the user presses a key on the keyboard. A full explanation is provided in Module 37, Keypressed.

function ReadKey: Char;

> A keyboard input routine that does not echo keystrokes to the screen. A full explanation is provided in Module 49, Readkey.

procedure TextMode(Mode: Integer);

> A procedure to control the screen mode. A full explanation is provided in Module 67, Textmode.

procedure Window(X1,Y1,X2,Y2: Byte);

> A procedure to control text windows on the screen. A full explanation is provided in Module 75, Window.

procedure GotoXY(X,Y: Byte);

> A procedure to locate the text cursor anywhere on the screen. A full explanation is provided in Module 29, Gotoxy.

function WhereX: Byte;

> A function that returns the X-coordinate of the current location of the screen cursor.

function WhereY: Byte;

> A function that returns the Y-coordinate of the current location of the screen cursor.

procedure ClrScr;

> A procedure to clear the text screen, or a window within the physical screen if the *window* procedure was used to create a window.

procedure ClrEol;

> A procedure to clear the remainder of one line on the screen, starting at the current location of the screen cursor and going to the right edge of the window or physical screen.

procedure InsLine;

> A procedure to insert a blank line on the screen at the location of the current text cursor. Lines below the current line scroll downward. The line previously at the bottom of the screen (or window) is lost. The background is either black, or as previously set with *TextBackground*.

procedure DelLine;

> A procedure to delete the line on the screen at the location of the current text cursor. All lines below the current line scroll up one position. A new, blank line is placed at the bottom of the screen.

procedure TextColor(Color: Byte);

> A procedure to set the text foreground color. This procedure is more fully explained in Module 66, TextColor.

procedure TextBackground(Color: Byte);

> A procedure to set the text background color. This procedure is more fully explained in Module 65, TextBackground.

procedure LowVideo;

> A procedure to set the intensity of text colors to 0 . . 8. This procedure maps the screen colors 7 . . 15 to their low-intensity equivalents.

procedure HighVideo;

> A procedure to set the intensity of text colors to 7 . . 15. This procedure maps the screen colors 0 . . 8 to their high-intensity equivalents.

procedure NormVideo;

> A procedure to set the intensity of the screen colors to whatever the intensity was when the program started. Use this *NormVideo* prior to exiting a program to restore the user's original choice of video intensity.

procedure Delay(MS: Word);

> A procedure to pause for a specified number of milliseconds. This procedure is explained more completely in Module 17, Delay.

procedure Sound(Hz: Word);

> This procedure creates sound using the PC's speaker. It is explained more fully in Module 59, Sound and NoSound.

procedure NoSound;

> Turns off the sound that was started with procedure *Sound*. This procedure is explained more fully in Module 59, Sound and NoSound.

APPLICATIONS

The facilities in the Crt unit are the building blocks for developing a quality user interface for your programs. The routines are fast and bug-free, providing quality access to the interface features of the IBM PC and compatibles. Although many of these features can be accessed through direct memory access, DOS functions, and BIOS calls, using the facilities of Crt provides faster development and good quality final code.

TYPICAL OPERATION

In this session you use the fast output routines accessed through *AssignCrt*.

1. Start Turbo Pascal, or continue your work session by clearing the Editor workspace. Type the following program.

```
program FastIO;
uses Crt;
var Screen: text;
begin
    ClrScr;
    AssignCrt(Screen);
    Rewrite(Screen);
    Writeln(Screen,'This output is written faster than normal.');
    Close(Screen);
    Readln;
end.
```

2. Save the program as FASTIO then run the program.

```
This output is written faster than normal.
```

It is difficult to see the speed increase on a single line, but when painting screenfuls of text, the speed increase is noticeable, especially on slower machines.

3. Press **Enter** to return to the integrated environment.

4. Turn to Module 74, While, to continue the learning sequence.

Module 16
DEBUG MENU

DESCRIPTION

The commands on the Debug menu allow you to specify the values you want to examine when using the integrated source-level debugger. A "watch" is a Pascal expression consisting of variables, constants, and literals. You may add watch expressions, delete watch expressions, change a watch variable, or remove all watch variables.

The watch option allows you to Add, Delete, and Edit watches. You may also remove all watches with a single command.

A breakpoint is a place where your program stops automatically during debugging. While editing your program, place the cursor on a line containing an executable program statement, press Alt-B, and type T for "Toggle breakpoint" to set a breakpoint on that line. (Pressing Ctrl-F8 has the same effect.) The Breakpoints dialog box allows you to edit, delete, view, or clear all breakpoints. You may have a maximum of 21 breakpoints active in a program at any one time.

You may access the Debug menu commands both when editing the program and when tracing the program in the debugger.

APPLICATIONS

Turbo Pascal's ability to monitor the changing values of expressions while stepping through program execution represents a major advance in computer programming over previous programming systems. For most programmers, the debugger is the most useful tool there is for finding logic errors in a program. Most logic errors have, as one of their effects, incorrect values stored in one or more variable locations. As a result, the use of watch expressions and breakpoints in the Turbo Pascal debugger becomes a universal tool for finding errors in program logic.

TYPICAL OPERATION

In this session you set up the ASSIGN program, created previously, for examination with the debugger.

1. From the Turbo Pascal menu screen, press **Alt-F** to select the File menu, then type **O** for the Open command.

2. Type **Assign** as the filename and press **Enter**. (The Turbo Pascal system automatically assumes that you want files with the extension .PAS unless you explicitly type another file extension.) The program is recalled to the screen.

3. Press **Alt-D** and type **WA** to add a watch expression. Type **j** as the watch expression and press **Enter**. A Watch window appears at the bottom of the screen.

```
≡  File  Edit  Search  Run  Compile  Debug  Options  Window  Help
───────────────────────── ASSIGN.PAS ─────────────────────────1─
program Assign;
uses Crt;
var x, y, z: real;
    i, j, k: integer;
    s, t, r: string[255];
    b      : boolean;

begin
    ClrScr;
    i := 2 + 3;
    j := 27350 - 21845;
    k := i * 2 + 1;
    x := 2 / 3;
    y := 3.14159 * 5 * 5;
    z := x + y;
┌[■]─────────────────────── Watches ───────────────────2=[↑]┐
  j: Unknown identifier
└                                                           ┘
 F1 Help  F7 Trace  F8 Step  ↵ Edit  Ins Add  Del Delete  F10 Menu
```

NOTE

The value of "j" is undefined until the program is run and the assignment statement executes.

4. Press **Ctrl-F7**, type **k** in the Add Watch dialog box, and press **Enter**.

5. Press **Ctrl-F7**, type **z** in the Add Watch dialog box, and press **Enter**.

6. Press **F6** to switch to the window containing the ASSIGN.PAS source statements. Don't worry that the Watch window disappears. It is merely "under" the source window on the desktop. Place the cursor under the "r" in the statement "r:= s + t;" and press **Ctrl-F7**. Notice that "R" appears in the Add watch dialog box. Press **Enter** to add "R" to the list of watch expressions. (The Watches window remains hidden behind the program statements.)

```
  ≡  File  Edit  Search  Run  Compile  Debug  Options  Window  Help
─────────────────────────── ASSIGN.PAS ──────────────────────1──
program Assign;
uses Crt;

var X, Y, Z: real;
    i, j, k: integer;
    S, T, R: string[255];
    B      : Boolean;

begin
    ClrScr;
    i:=2+3;
    j:=27350 - 21845;
    k:=I * 2 + 1;
    X:=2/3;
    Y:=3.14159 * 5 * 5;
─[■]═════════════════════════ Watches ═══════════════════════2=[↑]═
    j: Unknown identifier
    k: Unknown identifier
    z: Unknown identifier
    R: Unknown identifier
─────────────────────────────────────────────────────────────────
F1 Help  F7 Trace  F8 Step  ↵ Edit  Ins Add  Del Delete  F10 Menu
```

7. With the cursor on the line "r:= s + t;" press **Alt-D** to drop down the Debug menu, then type **T** to make this line a breakpoint. The Editor highlights the line to show that it is marked as a breakpoint.

8. Press **F6** to bring the Watches window to the front. Notice that "R" appears in the Watches window.

9. Do not stop. Continue this activity directly with Module 54, Run Menu.

Module 17
DELAY

DESCRIPTION

```
Delay(milliseconds)
```

The *Delay* instruction, part of the *Crt* unit, pauses for *milliseconds* before allowing program execution to continue.

APPLICATIONS

The *Delay* procedure is useful anytime you need to force a program delay. One application is to display a copyright notice on the screen for a specific period of time. Another application is varying the length of notes in conjunction with the *sound* and *nosound* procedures.

TYPICAL OPERATION

In this session you modify the music program from the *Sound* module to increase the length of the notes.

1. Start Turbo Pascal and load MUSIC.PAS.

2. Enter the Editor and add the *Delay* statement as shown in the following:

```
program Music;
uses Crt;
var Pitch:real;
        i:integer;
begin
    Pitch:=220;
    for i:=1 to 12 do
    begin
        {Compute the 12th root of 2.}
        Pitch:=Pitch*exp(ln(2)/12);
        Sound(Trunc(Pitch));
        Delay(500);
    end;
    Nosound;
end.
```

3. Save the program, then run it.

The scale plays at a controlled rate.

4. Turn to Module 35, Intr, to continue the learning sequence.

Module 18
DESTRUCTOR

DESCRIPTION

A *destructor* is an object method that performs the tasks associated with abandoning a dynamically created object. It is possible to define more than one *destructor* method for an object type to allow for variations in the steps required for destroying the object. For example, different *destructor* methods might be used to destroy a "visible" versus an "invisible" graphics screen object. The destructor methods are defined in the same way as constructor and other object methods. In general, all *destructor* methods should be defined as *virtual*. For example,

```
type Point = object
        X, Y : word;
        constructor Initialize(XPos,YPos : word);
        destructor Cleanup; virtual;
        procedure ChangeLocation(XDisplacement,YDisplacement :
            integer); virtual;
        function XLocation : word;
        function YLocation : word;
        procedure MoveTo(XPos,YPos : word); virtual;
    end;
```

A *destructor* method is used in combination with an extended form of syntax for the *dispose* statement. If APoint is a dynamically created object and Cleanup is its destructor, the syntax of the extended form of the *dispose* statement is as follows.

```
dispose(APoint,Cleanup);
```

When this statement executes, the Cleanup method first executes as an ordinary method. The final activity, however, is for the destructor to determine the number of bytes of memory that are allocated on the heap for this instance of the object and for *dispose* to deallocate the memory. If no special cleanup activities are required, only the deallocation of memory, the destructor can be an empty method, as shown in the following statements.

```
destructor Point.Cleanup;
begin
end;
```

There are three parts to using dynamically allocated objects. First, you create the object with a call to the standard procedure *new*, followed immediately by a call to the objects constructor method. For example,

```
type PointPtr = ^Point;
var APoint : PointPtr;
    |         |
    New(APoint);
    Apoint^.Initialize(100,100);
```

You may alternately use an extended syntax of *new* to both dynamically allocate the object and call its constructor in a single statement. The following statement is equivalent to the previous initialization sequence.

```
New(APoint,Initialize(100,100));
```

Notice that the call to the constructor method is not written as Apoint^. Initialize(100,100). The compiler determines the correct object method from the type of the object.

The second part of using objects is to actually refer to their methods. This is done as a natural extension to Pascal's traditional handling of the fields in a dynamically allocated record. For example, to use the MoveTo method for Apoint, refer to the method as

```
Apoint^.MoveTo(150,100);
```

The final consideration in using dynamically allocated objects is their deallocation with the extended form of the *dispose* statement, as shown in the following.

```
dispose(APoint,Cleanup);
```

APPLICATIONS

The *destructor* method, combined with the extended syntax for *new* and *dispose* allow objects to be dynamically allocated and deallocated on the heap at run time, instead of occupying valuable memory space in the data segment or on the stack for the duration of the program.

The use of dynamically allocated objects frees you, as a programmer, from needing to know in advance how many objects of what types are required when the program runs.

In writing a windowing system, where the "windows" are defined as objects, you do not have to place artificial limits on the number of windows that the program may use. In writing an object-oriented drawing program, you do not have to decide in advance the number and mix of various graphics elements such as points, circles, lines, and arcs that are required.

TYPICAL OPERATION

In this session you modify the ScreenObj unit to provide objects that may be allocated dynamically. You then modify the Virtual calling program to use those objects.

1. Load SCRNOBJ.PAS, most recently used in Module 14, Constructor, into the Turbo Pascal Editor. Modify the interface portion of the unit by adding the destructor declarations as shown.

```
Unit ScrnObj;
interface
type Point = object
          X, Y : word;
          constructor Initialize(XPos,YPos : word);
          destructor Cleanup; virtual;
          procedure ChangeLocation(XDisplacement,YDisplacement :
              integer); virtual;
          function XLocation : word;
          function YLocation : word;
          procedure MoveTo(XPos,YPos : word); virtual;
     end;

     Ball = object(Point)
         Radius : word;
         constructor Initialize(XPos,YPos,Size: word);
         destructor Cleanup; virtual;
         procedure ChangeLocation(XDisplacement,YDisplacement :
             integer); virtual;
       end;
```

2. Add the definition of the Point.Cleanup method to the implementation section as shown.

```
constructor Point.Initialize;
begin
    X:=XPos;
    Y:=YPos;
    PutPixel(X,Y,White);
end;

destructor Point.Cleanup;
begin
    PutPixel(X,Y,Black); {Remove the point visually from the screen.}
end;

procedure Point.ChangeLocation;
begin
    PutPixel(X,Y,Black);
    X:=X+XDisplacement;
    Y:=Y+YDisplacement;
    PutPixel(X,Y,White);
end;
```

3. Add the definition of the Ball.Cleanup method to the implementation section as shown.

```
constructor Ball.Initialize;
begin
```

```
    Point.Initialize(XPos,YPos);
    Radius:=Size;
    SetColor(White);
    X:=XPos;
    Y:=YPos;
    Circle(X,Y,Radius);
end;

destructor Ball.Cleanup;
begin
    SetColor(Black);
    Circle(X,Y,Radius);
end;

procedure Ball.ChangeLocation;
begin
    SetColor(Black);
    Circle(X,Y,Radius);
    X:=X+XDisplacement;
    Y:=Y+YDisplacement;
    SetColor(White);
    Circle(X,Y,Radius);
end;
```

4. Save the unit.

5. Load VIRTUAL.PAS, created in Module 14, Constructor, into the Editor. Add the *type* statement and modify the *var* statement as shown.

```
program VirtualDemo;
uses Crt,Graph,ScrnObj;
type PointPointer = ^Point;
     BallPointer  = ^Ball;
var i,GraphDriver,GraphMode : integer;
    APoint : PointPointer;
    ABall  : BallPointer;
    X,Y : array[1..4] of word;
```

6. Modify the main program as shown.

```
begin
    GraphDriver:=Detect;
    InitGraph(GraphDriver,GraphMode,ïï);
    {Set up some points to move to.}
    X[1]:=GetMaxX div 2 - GetMaxX div 4;
    X[2]:=X[1] + GetMaxX div 2;
    X[3]:=X[2];
    X[4]:=X[1];
    Y[1]:=GetMaxY div 2 - GetMaxX div 4;
    Y[2]:=Y[1];
    Y[3]:=Y[1] + GetMaxY div 2;
    Y[4]:=Y[3];
    {Make a point and move it around.}
    new(APoint,Initialize(GetMaxX div 2,GetMaxY div 2));
```

```
      readln;
      For i:=1 to 4 do
      begin
          Apoint^.MoveTo(X[i],Y[i]);
          readln;
      end;
      {Make a ball and move it around.}
      new(ABall,Initialize(GetMaxX div 2, GetMaxY div 2, GetMaxY div 20));
      readln;
      For i:= 1 to 4 do

      begin
          ABall^.MoveTo(X[i],Y[i]);
          readln;
      end;
      readln;
      dispose(APoint,Cleanup);
      dispose(ABall,Cleanup);
end.
```

7. Save the program, then select Make from the Compile menu and Run from the Run menu. Notice that the program runs as before.

8. Turn to Module 68, Turbo Vision, to continue the learning sequence.

Module 19
DIRECTORY FUNCTIONS

DESCRIPTION

It is often useful to perform basic disk management activities from within a program. The following procedures provide access to commonly used DOS directory functions.

erase(*FileVar*)	Removes the directory entry for the disk file associated with *FileVar*. Although an open file can be erased, you should make a practice of closing files before erasing them.
rename(*FileVar,NewName*)	Renames the file associated with *FileVar* as *NewName*. *FileVar* is the program filename specified in the *var* statement. *NewName* is a literal string, or a string variable containing the new DOS filename. *NewName* must follow the rules of naming for DOS. After using *rename*, continue to refer to the file within your program as *FileVar*, understanding that the operations are actually taking place on the disk file *NewName*. Never *rename* an open file.
ChDir(*path*)	Changes the current DOS directory to the path specified by *path*. *Path* is a string literal or variable following the rules for forming DOS path specifications.
MkDir(*path*)	Creates a new subdirectory as specified by *path*. *Path* is a string literal or variable following the rules for forming DOS path specifications.
RmDir(*path*)	Removes the subdirectory specified by *path*. DOS does not allow the removal of a subdirectory that contains files. You must first erase all files from the subdirectory before removing the subdirectory.
GetDir(*Drive,path*)	Specify Drive as an integer where 0=DOS default drive, 1=A, 2=B, etc. The procedure returns the current path for the drive in the string variable path.

APPLICATIONS

It is frequently useful to manipulate files and directories from within a program. You may need to create temporary files in your program to store large data structures for which there is no room in memory. When the temporary files are no longer needed, use the *Erase* procedure to prevent them from unnecessarily robbing the user of disk space.

Frequently, software installation procedures are performed by DOS batch files. However, the DOS batch facility provides nowhere near the flexibility of Turbo Pascal for excellent screen design, interactivity, and error trapping. The Turbo Pascal directory functions offer excellent flexibility for writing all, or portions, of a software installation program in Turbo Pascal instead of a DOS batch file.

TYPICAL OPERATION

In the first activity of this session you create a subdirectory on the default disk drive, assign it as the current subdirectory, create a file in the new subdirectory, then reset the current subdirectory to its status at the beginning of the program.

In the second activity you erase the newly created file and subdirectory.

1. If you are continuing your work session, clear the Editor workspace. Otherwise, start Turbo Pascal.

2. Enter the Editor and type the following program:

```
program Directory;
var NewFile : text;
    path : string[64];
begin
    GetDir(0,Path);
    MkDir('NEWDIR');
    ChDir('NEWDIR');
    Assign(NewFile,'NEWFILE.TXT');
    ReWrite(NewFile);
    Writeln(NewFile,'This is the new file');
    Close(NewFile);
    ChDir(Path);
end.
```

The program first uses *GetDir* to save the current directory information for the default drive in Path. *MkDir* and *ChDir* are used to make a new directory and establish it as the default directory path. The *assign, rewrite, writeln,* and *close* statements create a short text file in the new directory. The *ChDir* procedure resets the current directory to Path, the original default directory path for the drive.

3. Save and run the program.

The disk drive light glows, and the program ends.

4. Quit Turbo Pascal and return to DOS.

5. Type **DIR** and press **Enter** to display the directory of the default drive and directory.

Notice that your default directory is unchanged. A new subdirectory is added to the list of files in the default directory. Your screen shows the new directory, in addition to the other files previously in your default directory. If drive A is the default drive and contains a blank disk, the screen display is as follows.

```
A>dir

 Volume in drive A has no label
 Directory of  A:\

NEWDIR
      6-21-86   9:22a
         1 File(s)    360448 bytes free
```

6. Type **DIR NEWDIR** and press **Enter** to display the contents of the NEWDIR subdirectory.

```
A>DIR NEWDIR

 Volume in drive A has no label
 Directory of  A:\NEWDIR
```

7. Type **TYPE NEWDIR\NEWFILE.TXT** and press **Enter** to display the contents of NEWFILE.TXT on the screen.

```
A>TYPE NEWDIR\NEWFILE.TXT
This is the new file
```

8. Start Turbo Pascal, enter the Editor and type the following program:

```
program RemoveDirectory;
uses DOS;
var NewFile : file;
    path : string[64];
begin
    Assign(NewFile,'NEWDIR\NEWFILE.TXT');
    Erase(NewFile);
    RmDir('NEWDIR');
end.
```

Because the only operation performed on NewFile in the program is erasure, NewFile is defined as an untyped file. You know that it is a text file because you just created it. Therefore, you could again define it as a text file and delete it. However, in general, when erasing or renaming files, an untyped file is the preferred specification.

9. Save the program as REMOVE then run the program.

10. Quit Turbo Pascal and return to DOS.

11. Type **DIR** and press **Enter** to display the default directory of the default drive.

```
A>DIR

Volume in drive A has no label
Directory of  A:\
File not found
```

The subdirectory and its file are both gone.

12. Turn to Module 30, Graphics Unit, to continue the learning sequence.

Module 20
DISPOSE and MARK/RELEASE

DESCRIPTION

```
dispose (varname);

mark (varname);

release (varname);
```

When you are finished with a data structure created with pointers through the use of the *new* statement, you can release the memory for use again in other dynamic data structures. One technique available is the *dispose* statement. To eliminate the example linked list, use the statement

```
dispose(Entry);
```

which destroys the data structure and makes the memory available to build other dynamic data structures in the program.

Turbo Pascal provides a second method of managing dynamic memory through the use of the statements *mark* and *release*. To reclaim the memory in the example linked list, use the statements

```
mark(Entry);
release(Entry);
```

If Entry is the only dynamic data structure used in the program, the effect of the two approaches to memory management is identical. However, if there is more than one dynamic data structure, the effect is very different.

Mark/release and *dispose* use two entirely different approaches to memory management. You should normally choose one or the other for use in a single program. If you use both in a single program, extra caution is required. The address and size of free blocks of memory generated by *dispose* are kept in a free list. When you allocate memory for a dynamic variable, the system checks the free list to ensure that enough memory is available. When you use the *release* procedure, the free list is destroyed, and the heap manager "forgets" about any free memory below the address of the *mark*. This can have undesirable effects on program performance. If you choose to use both *dispose* and *mark/release* in the same program, make sure that there are no free blocks of memory below the address of the *mark/release* operation. If this sounds too complicated, take the easy way out and stick with using only a single strategy in each program.

The difference between *dispose* and *mark/release* is that *dispose* frees only the memory associated with a single data structure. *Mark/release* frees all memory following the data structure in the dynamic memory space.

If you have four other variables declared in dynamic memory, the following diagram shows the contents of dynamic memory after using the instructions *dispose(Entry)* and the contents of dynamic memory after using the instructions *mark(Entry); release(Entry);*.

Dynamic Memory	After Dispose	After Mark/Release
Variable 1	Variable 1	Variable 1
Variable 2	Variable 2	Variable 2
Entry		
Variable 3	Variable 3	
Variable 4	Variable 4	

It is important to make the distinction that *mark/release* does not alter any variables created in *var* statements. It only clears variables created with the *new* statement.

Dynamic memory is automatically released when a program terminates. It is not necessary to release memory in a program if there is no further use for it.

APPLICATIONS

Dynamic memory structures are excellent tools for storing large quantities of data. A spreadsheet could be implemented as a two-dimensional array of records; however, the size of the spreadsheet would be severely restricted by Turbo Pascal's 64K limit on static data structures. Additionally, empty spreadsheet cells would require as much memory as full spreadsheet cells. A more efficient approach to spreadsheet memory management is to use a linked list of linked lists of records of pointers as the fundamental data structure. While a full development of a spreadsheet is beyond the scope of this module, suffice it to say that the data structure created can expand to fill all available memory in the computer. When the spreadsheet user finishes one spreadsheet analysis and desires to begin another, it is necessary to issue a clear command within the spreadsheet program. If the spreadsheet is implemented as an array, this amounts to assigning each cell in the array a predetermined null value. In a spreadsheet implemented as a dynamic data structure, you want to reclaim all the memory for reuse in subsequent spreadsheet models. This is easily accomplished by using the *mark* statement to mark the beginning of dynamic memory, then using the *release* statement to make the memory available again. If the variable containing the spreadsheet is called Sheet, the statements could appear as follows:

```
{Initialize screen display, etc.}
|    |    |
mark(sheet);
|    |    |
{Instructions for manipulating spreadsheet.}
|    |    |
{Clear Instruction.}
release(sheet);
|    |    |
```

The *release* statement releases all dynamic memory from the marked point on in the program.

Releasing all of dynamic memory is not necessarily what is desired in a program. For example, in writing an integrated package containing a spreadsheet, a database, and a word processor, each applications data may be maintained in a data structure located in dynamic memory. If memory is arranged as follows,

Dynamic Memory

Spreadsheet
Database
Wordprocessor
Unused

using the statements

```
mark(Spreadsheet);
release(Spreadsheet);
```

releases not only the memory allocated to the spreadsheet, but also memory allocated to the database and the word processor. In this case, a more appropriate solution is the use of the *dispose* statement. The statement

```
dispose(Spreadsheet);
```

does not deallocate the memory used by the database and the word processor. Instead, it leaves a hole in the dynamic memory space.

```
Dynamic Memory

┌─────────────────────┐
│                     │
│  Unused             │
│                     │
├─────────────────────┤
│                     │
│  Database           │
│                     │
├─────────────────────┤
│                     │
│  Wordprocessor      │
│                     │
├─────────────────────┤
│  Unused             │
│                     │
└─────────────────────┘
```

The Turbo Pascal memory management system is sophisticated enough to reuse the memory formerly occupied by Spreadsheet when the *new* statement is used to allocate space for dynamic memory structures.

TYPICAL OPERATION

In this session you modify the program created in the *New* module to release dynamic memory when it is no longer needed.

1. Open DYNAMIC.PAS, which you created in the *New* module, or continue your work session directly from the previous module.

When this program deletes elements from the linked list, the memory is not made available again to the system. This means that after many insertions and deletions, the program eventually exhausts all available memory in the computer. Much of this memory, however, may be occupied by deleted elements. Removing the link from an element makes it inaccessible to the program, but it does not make the memory available. You use the *release* statement to allow the memory to be reused by the Turbo Pascal memory management system.

2. Modify the Delete procedure by adding a *dispose* statement as shown:

```
procedure Delete(var Top:Point);
var Back,Next:Point;
    Found:boolean;
    Value:integer;

begin
    write?'What value should be deleted from the list? ');
    readln(Value);
    {Check to see if you must delete the first element in the list.}
    if Top^.Information = value then
        Top:=Top^.Link
    else
    begin
        Back:=Top;
        Next:=Top^.Link;
        Found:=false;
        while (Next <> nil) and not Found do
        begin
            if Next^.Information = Value then
            begin
                Found:=true;
                Back^.Link:=Next^.Link;    {Reset the link}
                dispose(Next);
            end
            else
            begin
                Back:=Next;

                Next:=Next^.Link
            end;
        end;
    end;
end;
```

3. Save and run the program.

```
Perform which operation?
I :Insert an element
D :Delete an element
P :Print the list
Q :Quit the program
Press the letter of your choice:_
```

4. Use the Insert option to insert the numbers 10, 20, 30, 40, and 50 into the list.

5. Print the list.

```
10
20
30
40
50
```

6. Use the Delete option to delete 40 from the list.

7. Print the list.

```
10
20
30
50
```

There is no change in the appearance of the program. It works as before. However, unlike the previous version of the program, the memory occupied by the number 40 is again available for use by the system.

8. Type **Q** to quit the program.

9. Turn to Module 56, Seek, to continue the learning sequence.

Module 21
EDIT MENU

DESCRIPTION

When you start Turbo Pascal, the system places the cursor in the first edit window, prepared for you to begin editing your program. In the integrated environment, everything revolves around the Editor.

The Turbo Pascal Editor allows you to use either a modern drop-down menu style of editing, or commands that are modeled closely after the WordStar® word processing system. The best part is that you don't have to choose between the two systems. All options of both systems are available at all times. You may therefore mix and match commands from the "modern" editor with those of the "classical" editor to create your own preferred way of working.

If you have not previously used a WordStar-type editor, do not try to learn all of the commands at one sitting. Many competent programmers use only the cursor control features on the cursor control pad for moving around the Editor window and the Backspace key for deleting text. As you become more comfortable with the Editor, review the advanced features to make your program editing faster and more enjoyable.

BASIC CURSOR CONTROL   The cursor control functions on the cursor control pad and/or numeric keypad work in an intuitive manner.

Up Arrow	Moves the cursor up one line.
Down Arrow	Moves the cursor down one line.
Left Arrow	Moves the cursor left one space.
Right Arrow	Moves the cursor right one space.
Home	Moves the cursor to the beginning of the line.
End	Moves the cursor to the end of the line.
PgUp	Moves the display to the preceding screen of information.
PgDown	Moves the display to the following screen of information.

Control key equivalents for these special keys are also provided. These extended cursor control functions are less obvious, but they do have a rationale behind them. Many beginners are confused to find that the control key patterns used in the Editor do not have a mnemonic basis; in other words, Ctrl-U does not move up a line. Rather, the design is positional and ergonomic. Once learned, the system is highly efficient for text entry. Find the keys S, E, D, and X on the keyboard. Notice that they form a diamond.

```
    E
  S  D
    X
```

If you remember that E is on top, S on the left, D on the right, and X on the bottom of the WordStar editing diamond, the extended cursor control features make more sense.

Ctrl-E	Moves the cursor up on line. Pressing Ctrl-E is the same as pressing the Up Arrow key on the cursor control pad.
Ctrl-X	Moves the cursor down one line. Pressing Ctrl-X is the same as pressing the Down Arrow key on the cursor control pad.
Ctrl-S	Moves the cursor to the left one space. Pressing Ctrl-S is the same as pressing the Left Arrow key on the cursor control pad.
Ctrl-D	Moves the cursor to the right one space. Pressing Ctrl-D is the same as pressing the Right Arrow key on the cursor control pad.

Building on the basic editing diamond, you add the keys W and Z, making the pattern appear as follows:

```
  W  E
   S  D
  Z  X
```

The W and Z provide variations of the E and X keys. Instead of moving the cursor, W and Z leave the cursor where it is and move the entire display.

Ctrl-W	Scrolls the display down one line.
Ctrl-Z	Scrolls the display up one line.

Building further on up-down movement, you add the R and C keys to the pattern. Ctrl-R and Ctrl-C correspond to the actions of the PgUp and PgDn keys.

```
W   E   R
  S   D
Z   X   C
```

Ctrl-R	Displays the previous screen of information.
Ctrl-C	Displays the following screen of information.

The basic editing pattern can also be extended in a left-right direction with the addition of the keys A and F.

```
  W   E   R
A   S   D   F
  Z   X   C
```

Ctrl-A	Moves the cursor to the left a whole word at a time.
Ctrl-F	Moves the cursor to the right a whole word at a time.

ADVANCED CURSOR CONTROL   There are six key combinations that are used to move the cursor longer distances. All six of the combinations begin with the key combination Ctrl-Q. You can think of Ctrl-Q as the quick key. The Quick commands work with the central part of the editing keyboard.

```
  E   R
S   D
  X   C
```

Ctrl-Q-S	Moves the cursor to the left end of the line.
Ctrl-Q-D	Moves the cursor to the right end of the line.
Ctrl-Q-E	Moves the cursor to the top of the screen. This is the same as pressing the Home key on the cursor control pad.
Ctrl-Q-X	Moves the cursor to the bottom of the screen. This is the same as pressing End on the cursor control pad.
Ctrl-Q-R	Moves the cursor to the top of the file.
Ctrl-Q-C	Moves the cursor to the bottom of the file.

INSERTING AND DELETING TEXT   When you start the Turbo Pascal Editor it is in *Insert* mode. This means that anything you type is added to the Editor's workspace. Any characters previously in the workspace are moved over to make room for what you type. You can see that you are in Insert mode by looking at the shape of the cursor. The Insert mode is designated by an underline cursor. The other available mode is *Overwrite*. In Overwrite you can type over text that is already on the screen. The Overwrite mode is designated by a block cursor in the Edit window.

There are two ways to toggle between Insert and Overwrite. It does not make any difference which method you use. If you prefer, you can use both methods.

Ins   Toggles between Insert and Overwrite.

Ctrl-V   Toggles between Insert and Overwrite.

Most insertions are performed by typing text. One possible exception is inserting a line. You can insert a line by pressing Enter at the end of the line before you want the insertion. You can also insert a line by pressing Ctrl-N.

Ctrl-N   Inserts a line break at the cursor position. The cursor does not move.

Information is deleted in portions of several sizes.

Del   Deletes the character at the same position as the cursor and fills the space with characters from the right of the cursor.

Backspace   Deletes the character to the left of the cursor and fills the space with characters from the right of the cursor.

Ctrl-G   Deletes the character under the cursor and fills the space with characters from the right of the cursor.

Ctrl-T   Deletes the word to the right of the cursor. Ctrl-T is also useful for deleting line breaks.

Ctrl-Y   Deletes an entire line.

Ctrl-Q-Y   Deletes everything from the cursor position to the right to the end of the line.

There is an *undelete* function in the Editor, but the cursor must still be on the line for it to work.

Alt-E-R   Restores the contents of a line as long as the cursor is still on the line.

BLOCK COMMANDS   You can manipulate text in blocks by marking the beginning of a "block" of text, the end of the "block" of text, and then performing an operation on the block. A block can be defined as small as a single character or as large as your entire workspace. The first step in working with blocks is to mark the block.

If you have a mouse, you may block text by moving the mouse cursor to the starting position of the block, pressing and holding the left mouse button, dragging the mouse cursor to the end of the block, and releasing the mouse button.

Without a mouse, you must use control key combinations to mark the beginning and ending points of the block.

The block commands all begin with the key combination Ctrl-K.

Ctrl-K-B   Marks the beginning of a block. This function is also assigned to the F7 function key. The block marker itself does not appear on the screen. When you mark the end of the block, the block is highlighted.

Ctrl-K-K   Marks the end of a block. This function is also assigned to the F8 function key.

Ctrl-K-T   Marks a single word as a block.

Once marked, there are a number of operations that can be performed with blocks. The Edit menu provides access to Cut, Copy, and Paste. These options make use of a clipboard, or temporary storage area within the integrated environment Editor. These options also have shortcut keys assigned through the integrated environment.

Shift-Del	Cuts a block of text and places it on the Turbo Pascal clipboard. The text is removed from its original location in the file.
Ctrl-Ins	Copys a block of text and places the copy on the Turbo Pascal clipboard. The text remains where it was originally located in the file; only a copy is placed on the clipboard.
Shift-Ins	Pastes the contents of the clipboard at the location of the cursor.

You can delete a block of text by "cutting" it to the clipboard and never pasting it anywhere. You may also press Ctrl-Del to clear the contents of the clipboard.

In addition to the menu-driven cut/copy and paste system using a clipboard, the Editor implements copy, move, and delete functions as found in WordStar.

Ctrl-K-C	Copies a block of text. The start of the block is placed at the cursor position. If there is not a marked block of text, nothing happens.
Ctrl-K-V	Moves a block of text. The block is deleted at its former location and inserted at the location of the cursor when the command is issued.
Ctrl-K-Y	Delete a block of text. Once the block is deleted there is no way to restore it except by retyping.

At times, the color scheme used to identify a block can be difficult to read. In such cases you may want to hide the marked block of text.

Ctrl-K-H	Hides a block. Pressing Ctrl-K-H again displays the block. You cannot copy, move, delete, or write a block to a file when the block is hidden.

You may write the contents of a marked block to a disk file and read the contents from a disk into the Editor.

Ctrl-K-R	Read a block from the disk. You are prompted for the name of the file to insert. The name can be a simple filename from the current disk drive and active directory, or it may be a full file specification including a disk drive, path, and filename. The file is inserted beginning at the cursor location.
Ctrl-K-W	Write a block to the disk. You are prompted for the name of the file to write the block to. The name can be a simple filename from the current disk drive and active directory, or it may be a full file specification including a disk drive, path, and filename. For your protection, if the file already exists, you are prompted to verify that you want to replace the old file contents with the block.

The dialog box displayed for both the read and write operation differ only in the title and labeling of the field for specifying the filename.

You may type the name of the file in the specification field, select the file from the list of files with the arrow keys and the Enter key, or you may use the mouse to select the file. Clicking once selects the file, clicking twice on the filename completes the operation.

You can quickly jump to either the beginning or ending point of a block with the following cursor control key sequences.

Ctrl-Q-B   Moves the cursor to the beginning of the block.

Ctrl-Q-K   Moves the cursor to the end of the block.

ENTERING CONTROL CHARACTERS   There are two ways to enter control characters into your file with the Editor. Control characters are displayed in alternate video in the text. Prefixing any key with Ctrl-P causes the corresponding control character to be inserted in the file. For example,

Ctrl-P-T   Places Ctrl-T in your file.

Ctrl-P-B   Places Ctrl-B in your file.

You may enter any of the 256 ASCII (American Standard Code for Information Interchange) codes into your file with the Alt key and the numeric keypad. (A complete listing of the ASCII codes is located in Appendix A.) Press and hold Alt, then type the three-digit ASCII code on the numeric keypad, then release Alt. You must pad codes under 100 with leading 0's. Typing the numeric codes on the typewriter numeric keys does not work. The codes must be typed on the keypad.

Alt-277   Inserts the code for PI in the IBM extended character set.

Alt-191   Inserts the code for the upper right corner of a box.

In addition to typing these special characters into the Editor window, you may use the same technique in the Find and Replace dialog boxes to search for control characters in your file.

TABS   The Turbo Pascal Editor does not provide fixed tab settings. Instead, the automatic tab setting sets tabs to the start of each word on the preceding line.

Ctrl-Q-I   Toggles the automatic tab feature on and off.

PAIR MATCHING

The Pascal language frequently uses several characters in matched pairs. These characters include

braces { }
parentheses ( )
brackets [ ]
double quotes "
single quotes '

Finding the other half of a matched pair can be troublesome using conventional techniques. However, the Turbo Pascal Editor has a special pair matching command. Place the cursor on one member of the pair, then type the pair matching command. Type Ctrl-Q[for "forward matching" or Ctrl-Q] for "backward matching." When searching for the match to parentheses, brackets, or braces the direction of the search is implied by the character itself. For example, the match to the character } must be located before the character. The distinction between Ctrl-Q] and Ctrl-Q[is only important for quotation marks.

APPLICATIONS

The Turbo Pascal Editor is convenient for creating and modifying Turbo Pascal programs. It is also useful for creating ASCII data files for use as program input and for viewing ASCII files created by your programs.

TYPICAL OPERATION

In this session you use the block read, block move, block copy, and replace operations to modify the file SIMPLE.PAS.

   1. Start Turbo Pascal.

2. Start by using the block-read procedure to import the file SIMPLE.PAS. Press **Ctrl-K** and type **R** to display the Read Block from File dialog box.

3. Type **SIMPLE.PAS** and press **Enter** to specify the name of the file.

The contents of SIMPLE.PAS are read into the Editor workspace.

Next, use the block-copy procedure to make a second copy of the writeln statement.

4. Use the cursor control keys to move the cursor to the space immediately under the "b" in "begin."

5. Press **Ctrl-K-B** to mark the beginning of the block.

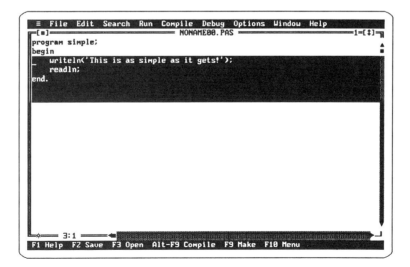

6. Press **Down Arrow** or **Ctrl-X** to move the cursor down one line.

7. Press **Ctrl-K-K** to mark the end of the block.

8. Press **Ctrl-K-C** to copy the block.

9. Turn to Module 55, Search Menu, to continue the learning sequence.

Module 22
FILE

DESCRIPTION

In addition to text files and typed files, Turbo Pascal supports operations on untyped files. Untyped files provide low-level access to any disk file using a record size of 128 bytes. Declare a file variable in a *var* statement of the form

var *FileVar* : *file;*   *Filevar* is the program filename, following the rules for naming identifiers in Pascal. It is not the DOS filename.

APPLICATIONS

Input and output operations on untyped files transfer data directly between the disk file and the file variable. A sector buffer is not used, thus saving the memory required for a sector buffer and a small amount of time associated with moving the data from the sector buffer to the variable location. Untyped files are compatible with all file types. If a file is opened only for an *erase* or *rename* operation, the use of untyped files is preferred.

To use an untyped file, you must first use the *assign* statement to associate the program filename with the DOS filename. To perform input or output operations on the file, it must additionally be opened with either *rewrite* or *reset*. The functions *eof, filepos*, and *seek* work with untyped files; the operations assume a record length of 128 bytes. The *close* command should be used at the end of operations on untyped files.

Turn to Module 19, Directory Functions, to continue the learning sequence.

Module 23
FILE MENU

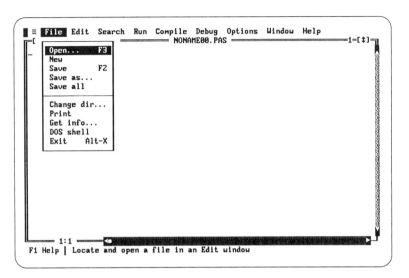

DESCRIPTION

Press Alt-F to drop down the File menu. The File menu provides access to DOS functions from within the Turbo Pascal integrated environment.

Open   Displays a dialog box that allows you to specify the name of the file containing your Pascal program text that should be loaded into the Editor. If you do not specify an extension as part of the filename, Turbo Pascal adds the extension .PAS to the filename. Press F3 as a shortcut to activate the Open file dialog box at any time.

New   Creates a new file in a new Editor window. It is not normally necessary to use this option at the start of a work session, only when a file has been previously loaded into the Editor.

Save   Saves the contents of the Editor workspace into the specified file. The first time you save a new program, the Save command displays the Save as dialog box so that you can specify the filename to use.

Save as   Writes the contents of the current Editor window into a new file. Any subsequent Save operations are also performed with this new filename. This option does not overwrite existing files without your permission.

Save all   Writes the contents of all Editor windows containing changed programs.

Change dir   Displays a dialog box showing the current directory and a visual representation of the directory structure of the current disk drive.

Print   Prints the contents of the active Editor window.

Get info   Displays a dialog box showing the size of the current program in terms of source lines, code size, data size, stack size, and minimum and maximum heap size. The dialog box also shows the memory used by DOS, Turbo Pascal, symbols, the program, and available. A report on Expanded memory is also included, showing the amount used by Turbo Pascal, other programs, and the amount remaining unused.

DOS shell   Allows you to execute a DOS command or run another program without having to reload Turbo Pascal. To return to Turbo Pascal from the DOS prompt type EXIT and press Enter.

Exit   Exits Turbo Pascal and returns you to the DOS prompt in the current directory.

APPLICATIONS

Use the File menu to open existing files, create new files and Editor windows, and save files. Additionally, use the File menu to change the current directory, print the contents of the Editor window, and to exit Turbo Pascal.

The DOS shell command merits special attention. Use the DOS shell command to run the DOS command processor (i.e., get the DOS prompt) from within Turbo Pascal. From this DOS prompt you can use virtually any DOS command or program that will fit into the computer's memory with Turbo Pascal. A common mistake is to forget to return to Turbo Pascal by typing EXIT, and restarting the program by typing TURBO. The effect of this action is to run Turbo Pascal under Turbo Pascal, which works, but allows little memory for your use and frequently results in an "out of memory" error when you attempt to compile a program.

CAUTION
Running the DOS CHKDSK program with the /F parameter can corrupt data files on your disk. Do not run CHKDSK/F from within Turbo Pascal or any other program.

TYPICAL OPERATION

In this session you practice using selected commands in the File menu.

1. Start Turbo Pascal. Press **Alt-F** to activate the File menu.

2. Type **o** to display the Open dialog box.

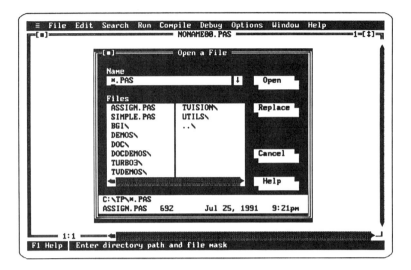

3. Press **Tab**, then use the Up Arrow and Down Arrow keys to highlight the program SIMPLE.PAS, which you created in Module 2. Press **Enter** to select the file, then press **Enter** again to open it. The program appears in an Editor window.

4. Make certain that your printer is connected and turned on. Press **Alt-F** to select the File menu, then type **P** to print SIMPLE.PAS on the printer.

5. Press **Alt-R** and then press **Enter** to run the program. Press **Enter** to return to the integrated environment.

6. Press **Alt-F** to select the File menu, then type **G** to display the Get info dialog box.

7. Press **Enter** to close the Information dialog box.

8. Press **Alt-F** and type **D** to activate the DOS shell.

```
C:\HSG>cd\tp

C:\TP>turbo
Turbo Pascal  Version 6.0  Copyright (c) 1983,90 Borland International
This is as simple as it gets!

Type EXIT to return to Turbo Pascal...

IBM DOS Version 4.00
        (C)Copyright International Business Machines Corp 1981, 1988
        (C)Copyright Microsoft Corp 1981-1986

C:\TP>_
```

Notice that the screen reminds you to type EXIT to return to Turbo Pascal.

9. Type **exit** and press **Enter** to return to the integrated environment.

10. Press **Alt-F** and type **x** to quit Turbo Pascal, returning to the DOS prompt.

11. Turn to Module 71, Uses, to continue the learning sequence.

Module 24
FILE OF

DESCRIPTION

In addition to the *text* predefined file type, Pascal allows the creation of additional file types. Turbo Pascal's typed files are defined in a *type* statement. All file operations are performed with the file variable, defined in a *var* statement.

```
type filetype = file of type-description;

var filevar : filetype;
```

filetype   The *filetype* follows the Pascal rules for naming.

type-description The *type-description* describes a valid Turbo Pascal data type. It can be either a predefined type or a previously defined user-defined type.

filevar   The *filevar* follows the Pascal rules for naming. It does not have to follow the DOS rules for filenames.

A typed file is defined by the reserved words *file of*, followed by the type of the components of the file. A file identifier is declared in a *var* statement by the words *file of*, followed by the identifier of a previously defined file type.

APPLICATIONS

Typed files in Turbo Pascal are organized as records of a particular type—integer, real, byte, char, a structured type, or a user-defined type. With typed files, it makes sense to talk about the "position" within the file because all the elements in the file are the same length. As a result, random access is available with typed files in addition to sequential access methods.

You can declare a file containing integers with this statement:

```
var Numbers : File of integer;
```

You declare a file containing real numbers with this statement:

```
var Numbers : File of real;
```

You can create a file of matrices with the statement

```
type Matrix = Array [1..10,1..10] of real;
var Diskfile: File of Matrix;
```

This declaration defines a file where every record in the file is a 10 x 10 matrix of integers.

Probably the most generally useful file definition is a file based on a record data structure. This is because it allows each component of the file to contain data of different types. A file to contain a mailing list is constructed similar to the following:

```
type Person = record
                    LastName:string[20];
                    FirstName:string[15];
                    MiddleInitial:char;
                    Address:string[35];
                    City:string[15];
                    State:string[2];
                    Zip:string[9];
              end;
var List : File of Person;
```

The only meaningful restriction on the composition of files is that you cannot have a file of files. In other words,

```
var Infile : file of char;
```

is a perfectly legitimate file definition, while

```
var Infile : file of text;
```

is in error, because *text* is a file type, and files cannot contain files.

TYPICAL OPERATION

In this session you begin a program that will write, then read a file of integers.

1. Clear the Editor workspace and type the following program fragment.

```
program IntegerInOut;
uses Crt;
var     i,j: integer;
    Diskfile: File of Integer;
begin
    ClrScr;
    for i:= 1 to 10 do write(Diskfile,i);
    for i:= 1 to 10 do
    begin
```

```
        read(Diskfile,j);
        writeln(j);
    end;
readln;
end.
```

NOTE

Additional statements, including *assign*, *reset*, and *rewrite* are required to make this program fragment into an operational program.

2. Save the program as INTIO.

3. Turn to Module 6, Assign, to continue the learning sequence.

Module 25
FILESIZE

DESCRIPTION

The *filesize* function returns the number of components or records in a file. *Filesize* is a long integer function in the form

```
filesize(FileVar)
```

FileVar   is the name of the file specified in the *var* statement. It is not the DOS filename.

Filesize   is expressed as the number of components in the file, not the number of bytes in the file (except in the special case of a *file of byte*).

APPLICATIONS

Filesize is useful for expanding a random access file. The technique used is to *seek* one element beyond the end of the file, then *write* the new record. Because the first record in every file is record 0, *filesize* corresponds to the record beyond the last record in the file. The statement

```
seek(FilVar, FileSize(FilVar));
```

positions the file pointer properly for adding components to the file with the *write* statement.

TYPICAL OPERATION

In this session you add a component to the inventory file created in the *Seek* module.

1. If you are continuing your work session, clear the Editor workspace. Otherwise, start Turbo Pascal.

The program is similar to the program used to create the datafile. Therefore, save some typing by modifying Create instead of typing the entire program.

2. Use the Editor block read command to import the file CREATE.PAS, developed in the *Seek* module.

3. Change the program name from Create to Extend.

4. Replace the *rewrite* statement with a *reset* statement.

5. Remove the *for* loop from the program.

6. Change the *seek* statement to *seek(Stock,filesize(stock))*.

7. Compute the item number based on *filesize*.

The complete program is as follows:

```
program Extend;
uses Crt;
type Item = record
              Description:string[16];
              Quantity:=integer;
              Price:=real
           end;
var Stock:file of Item;
    Current:item;
    Count:longint;

begin
    assign(Stock,'STOCK.DAT');
    rewrite(Stock);
    seek(Stock,filesize(stock));
    begin
    ClrScr;
    writeln('Item number ',filesize(stock),':');
    write('Enter the DESCRIPTION: ');
    readln(Current.Description);
    write('Enter the QUANTITY: ');
    readln(Current.Quantity);
    write('Enter the PRICE: ');
    readln(Current.Price);
    write(Stock,Current);
    close(Stock);
end.
```

8. Save and run the program. Specify 12 Life Vests at 24.95 as the item.

```
Item number 11:
Enter the DESCRIPTION: Life Vest
Enter the QUANTITY: 12
Enter the PRICE: 24.95
```

9. Load INVENT.PAS (from the *Seek* module) as the current Work file.

The program uses the statement

```
while Choice in [1..10] do
```

to identify the limits of the datafile. This is unacceptable in a production program. A better technique is using the *filesize* function to establish the upper boundary for permissible record magnitude. This is accomplished with a statement such as

```
while (Choice > 0) and (Choice < Filesize(Stock)) do
```

10. Change (as shown) the two bound selectors based on [1 . . 10] to depend on *filesize*.

```
program Inventory;

type Item = record
                Description:string[16];
                Quantity:integer;
                Price:real
            end;

var Stock:file of Item;
    Current:Item;
    Choice:integer;

begin
    ClrScr;
    assign(Stock,'STOCK.DAT');
    reset(Stock);
    Choice:=1;        {Initialize the reference variable}
    while (Choice > 0) and (Choice < Filesize(Stock)) do
    begin
        write('Enter the stock number: ');
        readln(Choice);
        if (Choice > 0) and (Choice < Filesize(Stock)) then
        begin
            seek(Stock,Choice);
            read(Stock,Current);
            with Current do
                writeln(Description:16,Quantity:5,Price:8:2);
        end;
    end;
    readln;
end.
```

11. Save and run the program.

```
Enter the stock number:
```

12. Type **11** and press **Enter**.

```
Enter the stock number: 11
Life Vest          12     24.95
Enter the stock number:
```

The recent addition to the file is displayed on the screen.

13. Type **0** and press **Enter** to end the program.

14. Turn to Module 22, File, to continue the learning sequence.

Module 26
FOR

DESCRIPTION

The *for* statement is used to repeat a single statement or series of statements a specific number of times. An index variable is used to assume a series of values from a starting value to a final value. In the *for/to* form of the loop, the index variable assumes increasing values. In the *for/downto* form of the loop, the index variable assumes decreasing values. The general forms of the statement are:

```
for index := start to final do statement

for index := start to final do
begin
    statement;
    statement;
    statement;
       |    |
    statement
end;

for index := start downto final do statement

for index := start downto final do
begin
    statement;
    statement;
    statement;
       |    |
    statement
end;
```

index   The *index* is an ordinal variable. It can be integer, byte, character, or a user-defined ordinal type. It cannot be a real variable.

start   The starting value for the index variable.

final   The final value for the index variable.

statement Any Pascal statement or compound statement.

Ordinal variables have "order." In other words, it makes sense to talk about the "next" integer or the "next" character. The next integer after 6 is 7. The next character after L is M.

Real variables are not ordinal. It does not make sense to talk about the "next" real number because between any two real numbers there is always another real number.

The action of the *for* statement is as follows:

- Assign *start* to *index*.
- Compare the value of *start* with the value of *final*. If start is greater than or equal to *final*, terminate the loop. (Less than or equal to in the case of the *downto* loop.)
- Perform the statement or statements making up the body of the loop.
- Add one (subtract in the case of a *downto* loop) to the value of *index*.
- Repeat the preceding steps, beginning with the comparison.

It is important to note that if *start* = *final*, a *for/to* loop does nothing. If *start* <= *final*, a *for/downto* loop does nothing.

CAUTION

The value of the loop variable is only defined within the scope of the loop. After the program has exited the loop, the loop variable is undefined. If you use the value of the loop variable after exiting the loop, your program may perform unpredictably.

APPLICATIONS

One of the great strengths of computers is their capability to repeat a function many times. Pascal provides three looping structures: the *while* loop, the *repeat* loop, and the *for* loop. Each of these structures is designed to solve a particular type of repetitive problem. Many looping problems can be solved with any of these loops. By taking advantage of the subtle differences between them, you can make your programs easier to write and read and less prone to contain errors.

Sometimes you know in advance how many times you need to perform a function. An accounting program to generate end-of-year reports might perform a function 12 times—once for each month. Anytime you know the number of times a loop must be performed, the *for* loop is probably the best choice.

It is not necessary to know the exact number when the program is written, only when the program is run. For example, in a program to process string data, you might perform an operation on each character in the string. You do not know how long the string is when you write the program, but the string *length* function allows the program to compute the length when it executes and to use that value to control the *for* loop.

TYPICAL OPERATION

SIMPLE *FOR* STATEMENT   As a first example, print "I like Ike!" on the screen 14 times.

This problem could be solved with 14 *writeln* statements, but that is cumbersome. What if the problem were to print "I like Ike!" 10,000 times? The *for* loop provides a straightforward solution to this problem.

The "I like Ike" problem requires that an action be performed 14 times. Having the action performed once for each letter from "A" to "M" is an option, however, using the numbers 1 to 14 is more easily understood.

1. If you are continuing your work session, clear the Editor workspace. Otherwise, start Turbo Pascal.

2. Start the Editor and type the following program:

```
program Eisenhower;
uses Crt;
var Count : integer;

begin
     ClrScr;
     for Count:=1 to 14 do writeln ('I like Ike!');
readln;
end.
```

The functions of the *for* statement are:

    a. Assign the number one to COUNT.
    b. If COUNT is greater than 14, end the loop; otherwise, continue the loop.
    c. Perform the *writeln* statement.
    d. Set COUNT equal to the next number.
    e. Go to step b.

3. Run the program.

```
I like Ike!
I like Ike!
I like Ike!
I like Ike!
I like Ike!
I like Ike!
I like Ike!
I like Ike!
I like Ike!
I like Ike!
I like Ike!
I like Ike!
I like Ike!
I like Ike!
```

The *writeln* statement is executed once for each value from 1 through 14.

4. Press **Enter** to return to the integrated environment.

There are other ways of repeating this loop 14 times. The value of COUNT could range from 1241 to 1254. The effect is the same. Or, character variables could be used. To illustrate this technique, instead of printing "I like Ike!" for values of COUNT from 1 through 14, print them seven times by letting COUNT vary from A to G.

5. Change the declaration of COUNT to CHAR, then change the *for* statement to go from A to G instead of 1 to 14. Notice the following display.

```
■ ≡ File Edit Search Run Compile Debug Options Window Help
┌─[■]══════════════════════ NONAME00.PAS ═══════════════════════1═[↕]┐
│program Eisenhower;
│uses Crt;
│var Count : char;
│
│begin
│    ClrScr;
│    for Count := 'A' to 'G' do writeln ('I like Ike!');
│readln;
│end.
│
│
│
│
│
│
│
│
│
└────── 7:28 ════◄▮▬▬▬▬▬▬▬▬▬▬▬▬▬▬▬▬▬▬▬▬▬▬▬▬▬▬▬▬▬▬▬▬▬▬▬▬▬▬▬▬▬▬▬▬▬▬▬▶▮
  F1 Help  F2 Save  F3 Open  Alt-F9 Compile  F9 Make  F10 Menu
```

6. Save the file as IKE, then run the program.

```
I like Ike!
I like Ike!
I like Ike!
I like Ike!
I like Ike!
I like Ike!
I like Ike!
```

COMPOUND *FOR* STATEMENT   Instead of repeating just a single statement, you may want to repeat a series of statements. The object of a *for* statement can be a *begin end* group instead of a single statement.

Write a program that displays a list of the first 20 powers of 2 as follows:

• Let RESULT be the variable that the current power of 2 is stored in.

• Assign 1 to RESULT. (This takes care of the first-time-through case.)

- Repeat the following steps 17 times:
    - Multiply RESULT by 2 and place the product back in RESULT.
    - Print RESULT on the screen. (The first time this step is executed, RESULT will equal 2. Therefore, the first number will be 2 to the first power.)
- End of program.

Because the problem requires repeating an action a specific number of times, the *for* loop is an ideal solution.

Repeating the action 20 times can be best expressed using an integer counter. Since this counter corresponds to the current power of 2, use POWER as the counter variable. The powers of 2 get large rapidly. Therefore, a *real* variable is appropriate for holding the result of the calculations. If you have a math co-processor, the *comp* type is ideal for this application.

1. Select New from the File menu. Type the following program:

```
program twos;
uses Crt;
var Power : integer;
    Result: real;

begin
    ClrScr;
    Result:=1;
    for Power:= 1 to 20 do
    begin
        Result:= Result * 2;
        writeln(Power:2,Result:10:0)
    end;
    readln;
end.
```

2. Run the program.

```
 1         2
 2         4
 3         8
 4        16
 5        32
 6        64
 7       128
 8       256
 9       512
10      1024
11      2048
12      4096
13      8192
14     16384
15     32768
16     65536
17    131072
18    262144
19    524288
20   1048576

_
```

You can see that you could not have used an *integer* or *word* variable to keep track of RESULT because the final values are greater than can be accommodated by those data types.

VARIABLE START AND END POINTS   The starting and ending values of the counter variable do not have to be constants; they can also be variables.

Create the following program to print selected letters of the alphabet based on user input.

1. Open a new Editor window and type the following program.

```
program Alpha;
uses Crt;
var Initial, Final, Counter: char;

begin
   ClrScr;
   write('Enter the starting value: ');
   readln(Initial);
   write('Enter the ending value:');
   readln(final);
   for Counter:=Initial to Final do write(Counter);
end.
```

2. Run the program. Use A as the starting value and M as the ending value.

```
Enter the starting value: A
Enter the ending value: M
ABCDEFGHIJKLM
```

The capital letters "A" through "M" are printed.

3. Run the program. Use a as the starting value and x as the ending value.

```
Enter the starting value: a
Enter the ending value: x
abcdefghijklmnopqrstuvwx
```

4. Run the program. Use 1 as the starting value and 9 as the ending value.

```
Enter the starting value: 1
Enter the ending value: 9
123456789
```

Remember that numbers are characters also!

5. Run the program. Use X as the starting value and B as the ending value.

The *for* loop is not executed if the starting value is already past the ending value.

CHANGING DIRECTION Change the program so that the list is produced in descending order. This is accomplished by changing the word *to* to *downto* in the *for* statement.

1. Enter the Editor. Replace *to* with DOWNto.

```
program Alpha;
uses Crt;
var Initial, Final, Counter: char;

begin
    ClrScr;
    write('Enter the starting value: ');
    readln(Initial);
    write('Enter the ending value: ');
    readln(final);
    for Counter:=Initial downto Final do write(Counter);
    readln;
end.
```

2. Run the program. Use X as the starting value and B as the ending value.

```
Enter the starting value: X
Enter the ending value: B
XWVUTSRQPONMLKJIHGFEDCB
```

Depending on your choice of the word *to* or *downto,* the counter variable either increases or decreases each time through the loop.

3. Turn to Module 36, IoResult, to continue the learning sequence.

Module 27
FORWARD

DESCRIPTION

Use the Forward specification to allow a procedure or function definition to follow the definition of a procedure or function that references it.

Pascal requires that all procedures and functions be defined prior to their first reference in a program. In other words, as the compiler works its way through your program from the *program* statement to the final *end* statement, the first reference to any procedure or function must be the declaration of the procedure or function. For example, if procedure Purple calls procedure Pink, then the definition for Pink must be physically located prior to the definition for Purple in the program statements.

This restriction has the potential for creating a circular problem. For example, if Pink references Purple, and Purple references Pink, there is no way that they can both be first. The Forward specification solves this dilemma by allowing you to separate the declaration of a procedure from the definition of the procedure. The Forward specification allows you to declare the interface portion of a procedure or function but defer its definition until later in the program. Using this technique allows procedures and functions to have mutual references, and to be mutually recursive.

APPLICATIONS

One instance where mutually referencing procedures and functions arise is in writing error-handling routines. A procedure that manages the error handling in a program may need to write error log information to a disk file, possibly using a separate procedure to accomplish the disk write activity. In response to a user input error, the error handler procedure calls the disk write procedure to log the error. However, if the disk write procedure has a problem writing the information to the disk, it needs to call the error handler procedure. As a result, both procedures potentially need to call each other. It is impossible that they both be physically located "first" in the program. By declaring one of the procedures as *Forward*, then defining the second procedure, and following that with the definition of the forward procedure, the situation is resolved.

TYPICAL OPERATION

In this session you write a program with two mutually referencing procedures, using a *forward* declaration to resolve the requirement that a procedure or function must be declared before it is referenced in another procedure or function.

1. If you are continuing your work session from the previous module, select New from the File menu to clear the Editor workspace. Start the Editor and type the following program.

```
program dependent;
Uses Crt;
var Error: integer;

{Notice the formal parameters in the declaration}
procedure display(s:string;var Errorcode:integer);forward;
procedure Fixerror(var ErrorCode:integer);
var ch:char;
    FixErrorCode:integer;
begin
    {Statements for fixing the original error go here.}
    ErrorCode:=0;
    FixErrorCode:=0;
    Display('The error is now fixed.',FixErrorCode);
end;

{Notice that the formal parameters do not appear in the definition.}
procedure display;
begin
    If ErrorCode0 then Fixerror(ErrorCode);
    writeln(S);
end;

begin
    ClrScr;
    Error:= 1;
    display('Here is the original message.',Error);
    readln;
end.
```

2. Save the program as DEPEND and run the program.

The first call to procedure Display results in a call to Fixerror, which in turn calls Display to place "The error is now fixed." on the screen. Control then passes back to Display as the calling procedure, which then places the text "Here is the original message." on the screen. The *forward* declaration makes it possible for Display to call Fixerror and for Fixerror to call Display.

3. Turn to Module 37, Keypressed, to continue the learning sequence.

Module 28
FUNCTION

DESCRIPTION

The *function* statement takes the following form:

```
function fname : ftype;

function fname(param {,param}:paramtype

          {param {,param}:paramtype};) : ftype;
```

fname   The rules for function names are the same as the rules for variable and constant names.

ftype   The type of the result returned by a function is limited to the simple types: *integer, real, char, Boolean*, and enumerated types. A string is not a simple type. Although the system provides several string functions, you cannot write your own string functions.

param   You can use variables of any type as a parameter of a function, including string variables and structured variables such as sets, records, and arrays. You could write an integer function to return the number of *K*s in a string.

paramtype Specifies the type of the list of parameters preceding the specification. The type must be a predefined type, or it must be specified in a *type* statement. *Paramtype* cannot be a self-defining type. The type of the parameter(s) has nothing to do with the type of the function.

Turbo Pascal's built-in functions are not sufficient for solving all programming problems. Pascal lets you define your own functions as well. To define a function, Pascal requires the following items of information about it:

- The name of the function
- The type of the result returned by the function
- The parameters sent to the function and their type
- The method for determining the value of the function

A fundamental difference between a procedure and a function is that in a function, a value is assigned to the name of the function. In this way, a function name acts like a variable name. In contrast, values are not assigned to the name of a procedure.

A function is always declared before it is used. If you attempt to reference a function that is not yet defined in the program, the Compiler marks it as an error. Function definitions are placed after the program *type, const*, and *var* statements, and before the *begin* statement of the program block. The declaration of the function must physically precede any reference to the function in a program listing.

RECURSIVE FUNCTIONS A function can call other functions. A function can call a procedure. A function can call itself. When you write a function that calls itself, the technique is called recursion. Recursion is often used to simplify a series of complex operations.

APPLICATIONS

Proper use of functions and procedures is fundamental to good structured programming style. A function is a type of subprogram. The function heading specifies its interface with the outside world (possibly your main program). The program calling the function has no knowledge of how the function performs its work. It is totally insulated by the function heading. Following its heading, a function can have its own *type, const,* and *var* statements that declare variables that are local to the function. These variables can even have the same names as variables in the calling program—but not be the same variable. A function can even contain its own procedure and function definitions for procedures and functions that are local to the function and are not available anywhere else in the program.

Turbo Pascal provides you with tools to write excellent structured programs. It is possible to abuse the tools and write Pascal code that is more convoluted and confusing than the worst spaghetti BASIC, but by using the tools wisely, you can write programs that are easy to develop, document, and maintain. Two rules for writing good functions are:

- Do not perform I/O operations in functions.
- Do not modify global variables in functions. (Global variables are variables defined in the calling program, but which are not "passed" to the function in its parameter list.)

These rules are written in ink, but they are not chiseled in granite. There are times when you come up against a limitation of the computer and need to compromise. For example, memory limitations may prevent you from passing an extremely large data structure to a function. However, compromise only when necessary. The less you compromise on style, the easier your program is to document and maintain.

TYPICAL OPERATION

In this session you develop a function to compute the sum of the first N positive integers. If the function is named Nsum, the results of the function look like the following:

```
Nsum(0) = 0
Nsum(1) = 0 + 1
Nsum(5) = 0 + 1 + 2 + 3 + 4 + 5 = 15
```

To assure that the negative case is defined, assign Nsum of any negative number to 0.

```
Nsum(-5) = 0
```

This function acts on an integer and returns an integer. The declaration for the function looks like the following:

```
function Nsum (N : integer) : integer;
```

The variable N is known as a formal parameter of the function. Its type is integer. The final integer in the specification defines the type of the function as integer.

The value of the function is best computed with a loop. Because you know in advance how many times the loop must run, a *for* loop is the best loop to use.

1. If you are continuing your work session from a previous module, clear the Editor workspace. Otherwise, start Turbo Pascal.

2. Start the Editor and type the following program:

```
program Funmath;
uses Crt;
var N,Sum: integer;

function Nsum(N : integer) : integer;
var I,Total:integer;

begin
    Total:=0;
    for I:=1 to N do Total:=Total+I;
    {Define the value of the function before exiting.}
    Nsum:=Total;
end;
begin
    ClrScr;
    write('Enter an integer: ');
    readln(N);
    Sum:=Nsum(N);
    writeln('The sum of the first ',N,' integers is ',Sum,'.');
    readln;
end.
```

3. Save and run the program.

4. Type **5** and press **Enter**.

```
Enter an integer: 5
The sum of the first 5 integers is 15.
```

LOCAL VARIABLES   The program and function both make use of the variable *N*. Note that two different variables are named *N*. The first is defined in the program's *var* statement. The second is a formal parameter of the function Nsum. They are not the same variable! The variable *N*, when used in the function, is "local" to that function.

1. Place the statements

   ```
   N:=147;
   writeln('The value of N in the function is ',N);
   ```

   immediately before the final *end* statement in the function Nsum.

NOTE

Performing input or output operations in functions is poor programming practice. You do it here as a debugging aid that lets you observe the values of the variables in the function. Input or output operations in functions should be avoided in your finished programs.

```
     |        |        |
     |        |        |
     |        |        |
{Define the value of the function before exiting.}
Nsum:=Total;
N:=147;
writeln('The value of N in the function is ',N);
end;
     |        |        |
     |        |        |
     |        |        |
```

2. Run the program. Type **10** and press **Enter**.

```
Enter an integer: 10
The value of N in the function is 147
The sum of the first 10 integers is 55.
```

The assignment of 147 to N did take effect, as proven by the *writeln* statement in the function. It does not, however, affect the value of N in the main program, which remains as

10. Because N is a formal parameter of the function, any assignment to N takes effect only while that function is executing.

3. Eliminate the illustration statements from the function.

```
    |           |           |
    |           |           |
    for I:=1 to N do Total:=Total+I;
    {Define the value of the function before exiting.}
    Nsum:=Total;
end;
    |           |           |
    |           |           |
```

4. Change (as shown) all references to the parameter N to BOUND in the function.

```
function Nsum (Bound : integer) : integer;
var I,Total : integer;

begin
    Total:=0;
    for I:=1 to Bound do Total:=Total+I;
    {Define the value of the function before exiting.}
    Nsum:=Total;
end;
```

5. Run the program to verify that this change does not affect performance.

IMPLEMENTING RECURSION The Nsum function just developed can also use recursion. In this particular case, the nonrecursive definition of Nsum is probably the best. However, good examples of recursion serve as weak introductions. With that in mind, develop a new version of the function Nsum.

Nsum is a function that can be defined in terms of itself. If Nsum(0) is defined as zero, then for any N0, Nsum(N)=N + Nsum(N – 1). For example, to compute Nsum(5):

```
Nsum(5)= 5 + Nsum(4)
```

If you knew what Nsum(4) was, you could evaluate this directly, but you do know that

```
Nsum(4)= 4 + Nsum(3)
```

Expanding further, you find that

```
Nsum(3)= 3 + Nsum(2)
```

Continuing the expansion,

```
Nsum(2)= 2 + Nsum(1)
```

One final expansion yields the following:

```
Nsum(1)= 1 + Nsum(0)
```

The recursive definition of the function defines

```
Nsum(0)=0
```

Knowing that Nsum(0)=0, it is now possible to back up one step and evaluate Nsum(1) as one. Knowing that Nsum(1)=1 allows you to back up and evaluate Nsum(2) as three. Knowing that Nsum(2)=3 allows you to back up and evaluate Nsum(3) as six. Knowing that Nsum(3)=6 allows you to back up and evaluate Nsum(4) as ten. Knowing that Nsum(4)=10 allows you to back up and evaluate Nsum(5) as 15. Problem solved.

1. Start the Editor and replace the Nsum function as shown.

```
program Funmath;
uses Crt;
var N,Sum : integer;

function Nsum(Bound:integer):integer;
var I,OneLess:integer;
begin
    if Bound > 0 then
    {This part of the program handles positive numbers}
    begin
        OneLess:=Bound-1;
        {The next program step is a recursive function call}
        Nsum:=Bound + Nsum(OneLess)
    end
    else
        {This step is the one which ends the recursive function calls and
            allows the evaluation of allthe steps that were left incomplete.}
        Nsum:=0;
 end;

begin
    ClrScr;
    write('Enter an integer: ');
    readln(N);
    Sum:=Nsum(N);
    writeln('The sum of the first ',N,' integers is ',Sum,'.');
    readln;
end.
```

2. Run the program. Verify that the output is the same as the nonrecursive version of the function.

3. To provide further illustration of the flow of control in the recursive function, enter the Editor and place *writeln* statements in the function as shown:

```
function Nsum(Bound:integer):integer;
var I,OneLess:integer;
begin
    writeln('The writeln#1 value of Bound is: ',Bound);
    if Bound > 0 then
    {This part of the program handles positive numbers}
  begin
        OneLess:=Bound-1;
        {The next program step is a recursive function call}
        Nsum:=Bound + Nsum(OneLess)
    end

    else
        {This step is the one which ends the recursive function calls and
            allows the evaluation of all the steps that were left incomplete.}
        Nsum:=0;
        writeln('The writeln#2 value of Bound is: ',Bound);
    end;
```

4. Save and run the program.

5. Type **5** then press **Enter**.

```
Enter an integer: 5
The writeln#1 value of Bound is: 5
The writeln#1 value of Bound is: 4
The writeln#1 value of Bound is: 3
The writeln#1 value of Bound is: 2
The writeln#1 value of Bound is: 1
The writeln#1 value of Bound is: 0
The writeln#2 value of Bound is: 0
The writeln#2 value of Bound is: 1
The writeln#2 value of Bound is: 2
The writeln#2 value of Bound is: 3
The writeln#2 value of Bound is: 4
The writeln#2 value of Bound is: 5
The sum of the first 5 integers is 15.
```

The function behaves exactly the same as the recursive definition.

First, the writeln#1 statements track the recursive expansion of the function as was done in the above discussion. When the function is finally asked to evaluate Nsum(0), it is able to evaluate it as zero instead of instituting another recursive function call. This causes a chain reaction, enabling the evaluation of each of the preceding function calls in the reverse order of their expansion.

6. Turn to Module 47, Procedure, to continue the learning sequence.

Module 29
GOTOXY

DESCRIPTION

Turbo Pascal provides the built-in procedure *gotoxy* to allow the placement of text anywhere on the screen. The *gotoxy* procedure does not produce any output, but it specifies the position where the next *write* or *writeln* statement starts its output, or where the next *read* or *readln* places the cursor for input. The procedure has two parameters, an x-position, or horizontal value, and a y-position, or vertical value. The format of the statement is:

```
gotoxy(xpos,ypos);
```

The *gotoxy* statement moves the cursor to the position in the active text window on the screen specified by *xpos* and *ypos*. (The default text window is the entire screen. Use the *window* statement to change the active text window.)

xpos	Specifies the x-coordinate or horizontal position on the screen. It must be an integer in the range 1 . . 80 (1 . . 40 for 40-column screen modes).
ypos	Specifies the y-coordinate or vertical position on the screen. It must be an integer in the range of 1 . . 25.
gotoxy(1,1)	Places the cursor in the upper left corner of the active window. By default, this is the upper left corner of the physical screen. If you use the *window* command to change the active window, *gotoxy*(1,1) places the cursor in the upper left corner of the window.
gotoxy(80,25)	Places the cursor in the lower right corner of the screen if the screen is in an 80-column text mode and you have not used the *window* command to change the size of the screen. If the screen is in a 40-column text mode, *gotoxy*(40,25) places the cursor in the lower right corner of the screen.

If you happen to be working with one of the 40-column text modes, do not use a horizontal value greater than 40.

APPLICATIONS

The use of *gotoxy* is the foundation for control of interactive screen displays. Successive use of the *write* and *writeln* statements allow only sequential output on a line-by-line basis. Using *gotoxy* to position the cursor allows placement of text for output, as well as positioning of the cursor for input at any point on the screen.

TYPICAL OPERATION

As an example of the use of the *gotoxy* procedure, create a program which randomly places graphics characters on the screen.

Recall that the function *Random*(num) returns a random integer greater than or equal to zero and less than *num*.

The function *Keypressed* is a Boolean function which returns a value of *True* when a key has been pressed on the keyboard, and *False* if no key has been pressed. In the example, a *repeat* loop is used to allow the program to continue until a key is pressed on the keyboard.

The most interesting graphics characters are found between the ASCII values of 127 and 255.

1. If you are continuing from a previous module, close all open Editor windows and open a new Editor window. Otherwise, start Turbo Pascal.

2. Create program Fill as shown.

```
program Fill;
uses Crt;
var symbol:char;
    x,y,foreground,background:integer;

begin
    Textmode(C80);
    randomize;
    repeat
        x:=1+Random(80);
        y:=1+Random(24);
        foreground:=Random(16);
        background:=Random(8);
        symbol:=chr(Random(127)+128);
        Textcolor(foreground);
        Textbackground(background);
        Gotoxy(x,y);
        write(symbol);
    until keypressed;
end.
```

3. Save the program as FILL. (You need this program again in the Window module.)

4. Run the program.

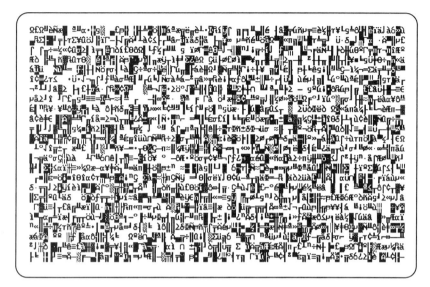

The screen is filled with randomly selected characters in random positions.

5. Press a key to stop the program and press **Enter** to return to the Turbo Pascal environment.

6. Turn to Module 75, Window, to continue the learning sequence.

Module 30
GRAPHICS UNIT

DESCRIPTION

You need a supported graphics adapter and monitor to use the techniques in this module. Turbo Pascal supports the following graphics standards:

- IBM Color Graphics Adapter (CGA)
- IBM Multiple Color Graphics Adapter (MCGA)
- IBM Enhanced Graphics Adapter (EGA)
- IBM Video Graphics Array (VGA)
- IBM 8514/A Graphics Adapter
- Hercules Graphics Adapter
- AT&T 400 Graphics Adapter
- IBM 3270 PC Graphics Adapter

Any adapter that is fully compatible with one of the supported adapters is also supported. A color monitor is suggested, but a black and white monitor is acceptable. None of the activities in this module works with the IBM Monochrome display and Monochrome Display Adapter.

The computer graphics screen is made of dots arranged in rows and columns. Each of the supported graphics adapters has different specifications for the number of rows, the number of columns, and the number of colors. The original IBM Color Graphics Adapter provides 200 rows of dots and 320 columns of dots, for a total of 64,000 dots. Each of these dots, or pixels, can be one of four different colors, the background color plus three additional colors from the current palette. At the other end of the spectrum, the VGA standard provides 480 rows and 640 columns of dots in 256 colors.

With the exception of the AT&T Graphics Adapter and the IBM 8514/A adapter, Turbo Pascal can automatically detect the graphics hardware present in the system when the program is run. You do not have to compile separate versions of your programs for each graphics variant. The simplest way to start using graphics is with the *InitGraph* procedure. Use the syntax

```
InitGraph(GraphDriver, GraphMode, DrivePath)
```

where *GraphDriver* is an integer variable with the value 0. This procedure automatically detects the graphics hardware present and sets the default (maximum resolution) graphics mode. *GraphDriver* and *GraphMode* are integer parameters, and *DrivePath* is a string. The Graphics unit predefines a number of constants corresponding to the values for *GraphDriver* and *GraphMode* that are either sent to or returned from the *InitGraph* procedure. The predefined constants associated with *GraphDriver* are:

Detect	= 0	IBM8514	= 6
CGA	= 1	HercMono	= 7
MCGA	= 2	ATT 400	= 8
EGA	= 3	VGA	= 9
EGA64	= 4	PC3270	= 10
EGAMono	= 5	CurentDriver	= –128

The EGA values, 3 through 5, require further explanation. The EGA card can be connected to either an EGA color monitor or a monochrome monitor. The *EGA* and *EGA64* values correspond to the color monitor applications; the *EGAMono* value corresponds to an EGA adapter connected to a monochrome monitor. EGA adapters made by companies other than IBM contain 256K of memory. IBM manufactures EGA cards with 64K, 128K, and 256K of memory. The *EGA64* value is designed for use with IBM EGA cards with only 64K of graphics memory installed.

Each graphics driver supports one or more graphics modes. When you use autodetection, the mode is automatically set to the highest available numeric value. When you call *InitGraph* with a value for *GraphDriver* other than 0, you must also specify a valid graphics mode. The modes you use with *InitGraph* and the modes returned by *InitGraph* are integers that correspond to the following predeclared constants:

CGAC1	= 0 320 x 200 resolution; red, yellow, green; 1 page
CGAC2	= 2 320 x 200 resolution; cyan, magenta, white; 1 page
CHAHi	= 3 640 x 200 resolution; 1 page
MCGAC1	= 0 320 x 200 resolution; red, yellow, green; 1 page
MCGAC2	= 1 320 x 200 resolution; cyan, magenta, white; 1 page
MCGAMed	= 2 640 x 200 resolution; 1 page
MCGAHi	= 3 640 x 480 resolution; 2 colors; 1 page
EGALo	= 0 640 x 200 resolution; 4 pages
EGAHi	= 1 640 x 350 resolution; 16 colors; 2 pages
EGA64Lo	= 0 640 x 200 resolution; 16 colors; 1 page

EGA64Hi	= 1 640 x 350 resolution; 4 colors; 1 page
EGAMonoHi	= 0 720 x 350 resolution; 64K=2 pages, 256K=4pages
HercMonoHi	= 0 740 x 348 resolution; 2 pages
ATT400C1	= 0 320 x 200 resolution; red, yellow, green; 1 page
ATT400C2	= 1 320 x 200 resolution; cyan, magenta, white; 1 page
ATT400Med	= 2 640 x 200 resolution; 1 page
ATT400Hi	= 3 640 x 400 resolution; 1 page
VGALo	= 0 640 x 200 resolution; 16 colors; 4 pages
VGAMed	= 1 640 x 350 resolution; 16 colors; 2 pages
VGAHi	= 2 640 x 480 resolution; 16 colors; 1 page
VGAHi2	= 3 640 x 480 resolution; 2 colors; 1 page
PC3270Hi	= 0 720 x 350 resolution; 1 page
IBM8514Lo	= 0 640 x 480 resolution; 256 colors
IBM8514Hi	= 1 1024 x 768 resolution; 256 colors

There are two situations where you may want to override the autodetection feature. The first situation is the use of the AT&T Graphics Adapter or the IBM 8514/A. These adapters, although not autodetected, are still supported. Calling *InitGraph* with *GraphDriver* having a value of 2 and *GraphMode* a valid graphics mode for the AT&T driver allows your program to run on this graphics device. The second situation is that you may decide to use a graphics driver other than the one that is autodetected. For example, you may want a high-resolution device to use one of the graphics modes of a compatible low-resolution device. For example, the CGA driver can be used with the CGA, EGA, and VGA hardware. You may also want to specify a graphics resolution other than the maximum resolution available for the device.

The procedure *DetectGraph(GraphDriver, GraphMode)*, where *GraphDriver* and *Graph Mode* are integer variable parameters, provides manual detection of the graphics hardware. You can use this procedure to determine the hardware configuration, then allow your program to determine the specific graphics driver and graphics mode to use when calling *InitGraph*.

COLOR SELECTION   Colors in graphics operate differently than colors for text. When in text mode, different parts of the screen could contain text of different colors. In graphics mode, the number of colors available is dependent on the graphics hardware. For example, on the IBM CGA, only four colors are available at any one time. The remaining three colors are selected from a "palette." There are four palettes available. Each palette contains three colors. These three colors, plus the background color, make a total of four colors available on the screen at one time.

Color number:	0	1	2	3
Palette 0	Background	Green	Red	Brown
Palette 1	Background	Cyan	Magenta	LightGray
Palette 2	Background	LightGreen	LightRed	Yellow
Palette 3	Background	LightCyan	LightMagenta	White

The colors are numbered 0-3. Color "0" is the background color. Colors 1, 2, and 3 depend on which palette is selected. This highly restrictive palette is specific to the IBM CGA and certain modes of the AT&T400. The EGA and VGA adapters allow total flexibility in the specification of color palettes in their high resolution modes. If you change the palette after a drawing is created, the colors of the drawing change to match the new palette.

The Graphics unit predeclares a number of constants that are useful in manipulating colors. These constants are:

Black	= 0	*DarkGray*	= 8
Blue	= 1	*LightBlue*	= 9
Green	= 2	*LightGreen*	= 10
Cyan	= 3	*LightCyan*	= 11
Red	= 4	*LightRed*	= 12
Magenta	= 5	*LightMagenta*	= 13
Brown	= 6	*Yellow*	= 14
LightGray	= 7	*White*	= 15

The procedures and functions used in manipulating the palette are as follows:

GetPalette(Palette) is a function that returns a variable of type *PaletteType*, a predefined type in the graphics unit. The *PaletteType* parameter is an untyped variable that is predefined as:

```
const Maxcolors = 15;
type PaletteType = record
        Size : byte;
        Colors : array[0..MaxColors] of shortint;
     end;
```

Each short integer value in the *Colors* array is the color number of that particular drawing color. For example, if Colors[2]=4, then anything drawn with color 2 would appear red on the screen because color 4 is red.

SetAllPalette(Palette) is a procedure that allows simultaneous changes to multiple drawing colors in the current palette. The parameter is of the predeclared type *PaletteType*:

```
const Maxcolors = 15;
type PaletteType = record
        Size : byte;
        Colors : array[0..MaxColors] of shortint;
      end;
```

Each short integer in the *Colors* array determines the actual color of that drawing color. Assigning a value of –1 to an element in the *Colors* array retains the previous value.

SetPalette(ColorNum,Color) is a procedure that allows you to change the color of a single drawing color in a palette. *ColorNum* is a word, and *Color* is a byte. For example, to change drawing color number 1 to magenta, use the procedure call *SetPalette(1,Magenta)*

The manipulation of colors and palettes becomes confusing quickly. For example, in the case of a 16-color EGA palette, the default palette assigns each drawing number its respective color number. Therefore, drawing a line with color 3 draws a cyan line. However, if you change the value of the drawing color 3 to 1 from the default of 3, the line changes color from cyan to blue. In that case, drawing color 3 refers to actual color 1, which is blue.

ADDRESSING THE SCREEN Turbo Pascal provides a rectangular coordinate system for accessing the screen. The upper left point on the screen is (0,0), and the lower right point is dependent on the hardware and selected graphics driver. With the *CGAC1* or *CGAC2* graphics drivers, the lower right point is (319,199). With the *CGAHi* driver, it is (639,199). With the *VGAHi*, driver it is (639,479).

The hard way to deal with the differences in graphics capabilities is to try to remember them all and deal with them separately. The easy way is to let the computer do (almost) all the work. The Turbo Pascal Graphics unit provides two functions for determining the maximum X and Y coordinates of the graphics screen.

GetMaxX returns the maximum X coordinate.

GetMaxY returns the maximum Y coordinate.

The center point of the screen, therefore, is (GetMaxX/2,GetMaxY/2). Write your programs to compute the actual points "on the fly" to achieve maximum portability across different graphics hardware systems.

USING GRAPHIC WINDOWS Turbo Pascal does graphics windows. The window defines the active area on the screen for graphics. All commands refer to a coordinate system inside the current window. The upper left point of the window is always (0,0).

SetViewPort(X1,Y1,X2,Y2,Clip)

> Specifies the active graphics window. The x-axis is the horizontal axis, and the y-axis is the vertical axis. (X1,Y1) specifies the upper left corner of the window and (X2,Y2) specifies the lower right corner of the window. The default setting is the entire screen. The Boolean variable *Clip* specifies whether drawings are clipped at the viewport boundaries. *SetViewPort* moves the current pointer to (0,0).

GetViewSettings(ViewPort)

> This procedure returns a variable (ViewPort) of the type *ViewPortType*, which is predeclared as

```
type ViewPortType = record
                        x1, y1, x2, y2, : word;
                        Clip : boolean;
                    end;
```

> The points (x1,y1) and (x2,y2) are the physical coordinates of the viewport limits.

Clearing the Screen The *ClrScr* procedure works only for clearing the text screen. It does not clear the graphics screen.

ClearViewPort

> This procedure clears the graphics viewport with the color set in *Palette(0)*.

ClearDevice

> This procedure clears the entire physical screen. It resets the settings for the current pointer, palette, color, and viewport to their defaults.

Current Pointer Some of the drawing procedures make use of the concept of a *current pointer (CP)* in carrying out drawing commands. The CP is similar to the current location of the cursor in the text screen modes. There are procedures and functions specifically for manipulating the current pointer without drawing anything.

GetX

> This integer function returns the x coordinate of the current pointer relative to the viewport.

GetY

> This integer function returns the y coordinate of the current pointer relative to the viewport.

MoveTo(X,Y)

> Moves the current pointer to (X,Y) relative to the current viewport. Does not draw anything on the screen.

MoveRel(Dx,Dy)

> Moves the current pointer from its current location a distance of *Dx* units in the x-axis and *Dy* units in the y-axis relative to the current viewport. Does not draw anything on the screen.

DRAWING   Turbo Pascal provides procedures to plot points and draw lines, arcs, bars, and circles in the rectangular coordinate system.

Line Styles   The lines produced by the *Arc, Circle, DrawPoly, Line, LineTo,* and *Rectangle* procedures are user definable. You can set the linetype to a predefined pattern, define your own line style, and inquire as to the current line pattern and thickness.

SetLineStyle(LineStyle, Pattern, Thickness)

> Determines the style of lines used in the Arc, Circle, DrawPoly, Line, LineTo, and Rectangle procedures. All parameters have the data type *word*. Several constants are defined by the Graph unit to make working with line styles easier. They are:
>
> | | |
> |---|---|
> | SolidLn | = 0 |
> | DottedLn | = 1 |
> | CenterLn | = 2 |
> | DashedLn | = 3 |
> | UserBitLn | = 4 |
>
> Styles 0 . . 3 are predefined line styles. Style 4 produces a line as defined by the bit pattern of *Pattern*. Each bit in *Pattern* corresponds to a pixel. If the bit is on in *Pattern*, the pixel is on, if the bit is off in *Pattern*, the pixel is off.
>
> Two predefined constants are available for use as the *Thickness* parameter.
>
> | | |
> |---|---|
> | NormWidth | = 1 |
> | ThickWidth | = 3 |

GetLineSettings(LineInfo)

This procedure returns *LineInfo*, having the predefined type *LineSettingsType* as follows.

```
type LineSettingsType = record
                LineStyle : word;
                Pattern   : word;
                Thickness : word;
            end;
```

The values for *LineStyle*, *Pattern*, and *Thickness* are interpreted the same as the corresponding values in *SetLineStyle*.

Drawing Basic Shapes   The following procedures draw dots, lines, rectangles, polygons, arcs, circles, elipses, and polygons.

PutPixel(X,Y,Color)

Places a single point on the screen at the coordinates (X,Y). *Color* is selected from the current palette. The parameters X and Y are integers. *Color* is a *word*.

Line(X1,Y1,X2,Y2)

Draws a line between the points (X1,Y1) and (X2,Y2) in the selected color. All parameters are integer expressions. The style and thickness of the line is determined by the current settings for *SetLineStyle* and *SetColor*. The current pointer is not changed.

LineRel(Dx,Dy)

Draws a line from the current drawing pointer (CP) to a point specified by the x displacement and y displacement. The style and thickness of the line is determined by the current settings for *SetLineStyle* and *SetColor*. The current pointer is moved to the last point drawn.

LineTo(X,Y)

Draws a line from the current drawing pointer (CP) to the point (*X,Y*). The style and thickness of the line is determined by the current settings for *SetLineStyle* and *SetColor*. The current pointer is moved to the last point drawn.

Arc(X,Y,StartAngle,EndAngle,Radius)

Draws an arc or partial circle. The point (*X,Y*) specifies the starting point for the arc. *StartAngle* and *EndAngle* are specified in degrees and specify the number of degrees in the arc. The radius of the arc is specified by *Radius*. The arc is drawn in the current drawing color.

Circle(X,Y,Radius)

> Draws a circle with the centerpoint at *(X,Y)* and a radius as specified by *Radius*. The circle is drawn in the current color. *X* and *Y* are integers; *Radius* is a word.

Ellipse(X,Y,StAngle,EndAngle,XRadius,YRadius)

> Draws an ellipse (or portion of an ellipse) in the current color. *X* and *Y* are integers and specify the center point of the ellipse. *StAngle* and *EndAngle* are words and specify the starting and ending angles. (StAngle=0 and *EndAngle*=359 produces a complete ellipse.) *XRadius* and *YRadius* are words and specify the X and Y radius for the ellipse.

DrawPoly(NumPoints,PolyPoints)

> Draws the outline of a polygon. *NumPoints* specifies the number of vertices in the polygon plus one. (Drawing a pentagon requires six points.) *PolyPoints* specifies the x and y coordinates of the vertices. The first and last points are identical. For example, to draw a rectangle,

```
const Rectangle : array[1..5] of Pointtype =
                   ((x :  50 ; y:  50),
                    (x :  50 ; y:100),
                    (x :100 ; y:100),
                    (x :100 ; y:  50),
                    (x :  50 ; y:  50));
begin
    |   |
    DrawPoly(5,Rectangle);
    |   |
end.
```

Filling Areas You may draw filled shapes using the *FillPoly, PieSlice, Bar,* or *3DBar* procedures. You may also construct the shape with a continuous outline and then fill it with *FloodFill.* To fill any shape, first draw the shape outline with a single color. Make sure there are no gaps in the outline. Then use the *FloodFill* procedure to fill the shape.

FillPoly(NumPoints,PolyPoints)

> Draws a filled polygon. *NumPoints* specifies the number of verticies in the polygon plus one. (Drawing a pentagon requires six points.) *PolyPoints* specifies the x and y coordinates of the vertices. The first and last points are identical. For example, to draw a filled rectangle,

```
const Rectangle : array[1..5] of Pointtype =
                   ((x :  50 ; y:  50),
                    (x :  50 ; y:100),
                    (x :100 ; y:100),
                    (x :100 ; y:  50),
                    (x :  50 ; y:  50));
```

```
begin
    |     |
    DrawPoly(5,Rectangle);
    |     |
end.
```

The polygon is automatically filled with the current color using the current pattern.

FloodFill(X,Y,BorderColor);

The point *(X,Y)* can be any point inside the shape. *BorderColor* is the color of the shape outline. The shape is filled with the current color and current pattern.

FINDING OUT THE GRAPHICS STATUS   Several functions allow you to determine the status of the graphics screen.

GetX

The integer function *GetX* returns the current X coordinate of the current pointer.

GetY

The integer function *GetY* returns the Y coordinate of the current pointer.

GetPixel(X,Y)

The word function *GetPixel* returns the color number of the dot at *(X,Y)*.

APPLICATIONS

Turbo Pascal provides the tools to write graphics programs that automatically configure themselves for use on a wide variety of graphics display devices. It requires additional effort to write graphics programs that are truly portable, but the effort is well spent.

When calculating positions on the screen, make use of the *GetMaxX* and *GetMaxY* functions to determine relative positions on the screen. Instead of making use of your knowledge of the size of various screens and having separate code to support each, write one generic set of program statements. For example, you can describe the center point of the screen as *(GetMaxX div 2, GetMaxY div 2)*. If you want to place a circle in the center of the screen with a diameter of 50 percent of the screen height, you could use a statement such as

```
Circle(GetMaxX div 2, GetMaxY div 2, GetMaxY div 4);
```

to accomplish the feat. The first parameter specifies the X coordinate as halfway across the screen. The second parameter specifies the Y coordinate as halfway down the screen. The third parameter specifies the radius as 25 percent of the vertical height of the screen.

If you want to save a screen of graphics for later use, as was done with the text windows, you can use the same technique. However, instead of saving 4000 bytes of memory, you must save considerably more. The CGA adapter uses 16K bytes of memory, EGA uses either 64K or 128K depending on the mode, and VGA uses up to 256K of memory.

TYPICAL OPERATION

In this session you create a program to place an exploded pie chart on the screen using color graphics. The parameters for the sample piechart are:

- The background is blue.
- The main chart section occupies 75 percent of the area.
- The secondary (exploded) chart section occupies 25 percent of the area.
- If the graphics device and mode support color, differentiate the areas by color. If not, differentiate the areas by pattern.

1. If you are continuing your work session, clear the Editor workspace. Otherwise, start Turbo Pascal.

2. Start the Editor and type the following program.

```
program PieChart;
uses Graph;
    var ch:char;
    GraphDriver, GraphMode, CenterX, CenterY, Radius: integer;
begin
    {"Detect" is declared as a constant with value 0 in the GRAPH unit.
    This allows Turbo Pascal to automatically determine your graphics
    hardware system.}
    GraphDriver:=Detect;
    {Change the path in the following statement to match your system's
    directory structure.}
    InitGraph(GraphDriver,GraphMode,'c:\tp6\bgi');
    {"GetMaxX" and "GetMaxY" are functions defined in the GRAPH unit. The
    following two statements determine the centerpoint of the screen.}
    CenterX:=GetMaxX div 2;
    CenterY:=GetMaxY div 2;
    {Compute a radius for the piechart.}
    Radius := GetMaxY div 3;
    {If this is a color system set the color for the pie slice. If it
    is a monochrome system, then modify the patterns instead.}
    {"GetMaxColor" is a function defined in the GRAPH unit.}
    If GetMaxColor > 2 then SetColor(1) else SetFillStyle(3,1);
    {Set the start angle for the pieslice at 0 and the ending angle at 270.}
    PieSlice(CenterX, CenterY, 0, 270, Radius);
    If GetMaxColor 2 then SetColor(2) else SetFillStyle(6,1);
    {Move the center point to the right and down 5 pixels. Set the start
    angle at 270 and continue to 360 as the ending angle.}
    PieSlice(CenterX+5, CenterY+5, 270, 360, Radius);
    {Wait until Enter is pressed}
```

```
        Readln;
   end.
```

3. Save the program as PIECHART.PAS.

4. Run the program.

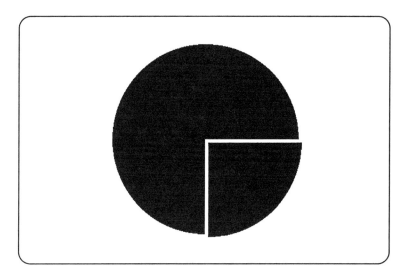

5. Press a key to return to the Turbo Pascal environment.

6. Turn to Module 59, Sound and NoSound, to continue the learning sequence.

Module 31
HELP MENU

DESCRIPTION

The Help menu is the gateway to Turbo Pascal's online help system. The Help system displays five options:

Contents   Displays a table of contents for the online help system.

Index   Displays an alphabetical index of Turbo Pascal options, commands, functions, reserved words, and predeclared identifiers.

Topic search   Displays a topical index of information about Turbo Pascal or information about a particular command, depending on the position of the cursor in the current Editor window.

Previous topic   Switches you into the help system at the point where you were previously located in the help system.

Help on help   Displays information about using the online help system.

APPLICATIONS

The actions of the Topic Search option on the Help menu depend on the position of the cursor in the current Editor window. If the cursor is located on a Turbo Pascal command when you select Topic Search (either from the Help menu or by pressing Ctrl-F1), the help system immediately displays a dialog box showing information about the command, complete with a Pascal example. You can use the Copy example command on the Edit menu to copy the example from the help system and then use the Paste command on the Edit menu to paste the sample statements into your program.

The online help system is the handiest source of information about the exact syntax to use for a Turbo Pascal command — certainly easier than finding the information you need in the maze of printed materials that comprise the manual set for Turbo Pascal.

TYPICAL OPERATION

In this session you practice using the commands that appear on the Help menu.

1. Begin the session with the program SIMPLE.PAS, which you created in Module 2, in the Editor window.

2. Press **F1** and Turbo Pascal displays a dialog box that describes the use of the Editor.

3. Press the **Down Arrow, PgDn, Up Arrow**, and **PgUp** keys to read through the information. Then press **Esc** to close the Help window.

4. Press **Alt-H** to display the Help menu, then type **C** to display the Contents dialog box.

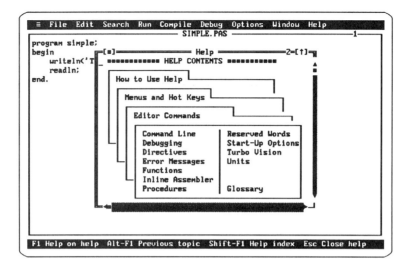

5. Press **Tab** until Editor Commands is highlighted in the dialog box and press **Enter.** The following dialog box is displayed.

6. Press **Tab** until Cursor-movement commands is highlighted in the dialog box and press **Enter.** The following dialog box is displayed.

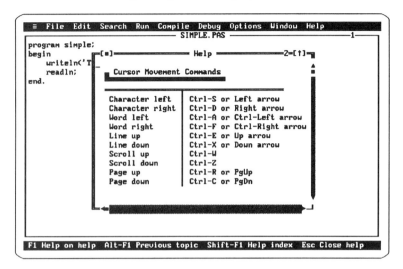

7. Press **Esc** to close the Help window.

8. Move the cursor under the word writeln in the Editor window, then press **Ctrl-F1**. The following dialog box appears on the screen.

9. Press **Down Arrow** until the example appears in the window, as shown in the following display.

```
 ≡  File  Edit  Search  Run  Compile  Debug  Options  Window  Help
─────────────────────────── SIMPLE.PAS ───────────────────────────1──
program simple;
begin          ┌─[■]──────────── Help ═══════════════2=[↑]─┐
    writeln('T │                                           │
    readln;    │   { Example for Readln and Writeln}       │
end.           │                                           │
               │   var                                     │
               │     s : String;                           │
               │   begin                                   ■
               │     Write('Enter a line of text: ');       │
               │     ReadLn(s);                             │
               │     WriteLn('You typed: ',s);              │
               │     WriteLn('Hit <Enter> to exit');        │
               │     ReadLn;                                │
               │   end.                                     │
               │                                            │
               │                                            │
               │                                            │
               └◄───■■■■■■■■■■■■■■■■■■■■■■■■■■■───────────►─┘
─────────────────────────────────────────────────────────────────────
 F1 Help on help  Alt-F1 Previous topic  Shift-F1 Help index  Esc Close help
```

10. Press **Alt-E** to display the Edit menu; then type **e** to select Copy example.

11. Press **Esc** to close the Help window.

12. Move the cursor following the *end* statement in the program in the Editor window.

13. Press **Alt-E** to display the Edit menu, then type **P** to paste the copy of the clipboard (containing the example) into the Editor window.

```
 ≡  File  Edit  Search  Run  Compile  Debug  Options  Window  Help
┌─[■]──────────────────────── SIMPLE.PAS ═══════════════════════1=[↕]─┐
│program simple;                                                      ▲
│begin                                                                │
│    writeln('This is as simple as it gets!');                        │
│    readln;                                                          │
│end.                                                                 │
│                                                                     │
│                                                                     │
│{ Example for Readln and Writeln}                                    │
│                                                                     │
│var                                                                  │
│  s : String;                                                        │
│begin                                                                │
│  Write('Enter a line of text: ');                                   │
│  ReadLn(s);                                                         │
│  WriteLn('You typed: ',s);                                          │
│  WriteLn('Hit <Enter> to exit');                                    │
│  ReadLn;                                                            │
│end.                                                                 │
│                                                                     │
└──── 6:1 ────◄───────────────────────────────────────────────────►──┘
 F1 Help  F2 Save  F3 Open  Alt-F9 Compile  F9 Make  F10 Menu
```

The best programming techniques frequently come from modeling the examples of other good programmers. The online examples in the help system are excellent models to use as a basis for developing your own Turbo Pascal programs.

14. Press **Alt-X** to quit Turbo Pascal. Type **N** to not save the changes to SIMPLE.PAS.

15. Turn to Module 63, System Menu, to continue the learning sequence.

Module 32
IF

DESCRIPTION

The *if* statement allows the programmer to control the performance of program statements depending on the value of a *Boolean* variable or expression. When *Boolean expression* evaluates as *True*, the statement or statements following *then* are executed. When *Boolean expression* is *False*, the statement or statements following *then* are skipped. If an *else* clause is present in the *if* structure, the statements following the *else* clause are executed only if *Boolean expression* is False, otherwise they are skipped.

Simple *if* statement:

```
if Boolean expression then statement;

if Boolean expression then statement else statement;
```

Compound *if* statement:

```
if Boolean expression then statement;
if Boolean expression then
begin
    statement;
    statement;
        |    |
    statement
end
else begin
    statement;
    statement;
        |    |
    statement
end;
```

Boolean expression	A Boolean constant, variable, or relation.
statement	Any Pascal statement, including another *if* statement.

COMPOUND STATEMENTS   Many times it is necessary to have a group of statements performed together. It is possible to repeat the same *if* condition for each statement, but Pascal provides a simpler way. Enclosing a group of statements between the reserved words *begin* and *end* creates a compound statement in Pascal. You can use a compound statement any place you use a simple statement. You can also have compound statements within compound statements.

Pascal provides several statements to alter the execution of a program while it is running. Many of these techniques are based on the use of Boolean variables. A Boolean variable has two possible values: *True* and *False*. Boolean values are assigned in two ways. If DONE is declared as a Boolean variable in your program, the statement "Done:=True;" assigns the value *True* to DONE. The second way to assign a value is through the use of a Boolean expression.

BOOLEAN RELATIONS The comparisons available to form Boolean expressions using integer, real, char, and string expressions are as follows:

=   equal to

<>   not equal to

>   greater than

>=   greater than or equal to

<   less than

<=   less than or equal to

The following operators are available to form Boolean expressions:

not   negation

and   conjunction

or   union

Boolean operators have an order of precedence. Operations using *not* are performed first, followed in order by *and*, then *or*. Parentheses are used to alter the order of precedence.

If you define TEST as a Boolean variable:

TEST:= 5<10;	Assigns *True* to TEST because 5<10 is a true statement.
TEST:= 3 >17;	Assigns *False* to TEST because 17 is greater than 3.
TEST:= 3>1 and 5>6;	Assigns *False* to TEST. Although 3>1 is true, both parts of an AND operation must be true to make the statement true. 5>6 is false, therefore, the entire statement is false.
TEST:= 3>1 OR 5>6;	Assigns *True* to TEST. Only one of the expressions in an OR comparison must be true to make the entire statement true.
TEST:= 5=5;	Assigns the value *True* to TEST, because five is equal to itself.

TEST:= NUM=17	If NUM=17 is a true statement, *True* is assigned to TEST. If NUM is not equal to 17, then *False* is assigned to TEST. This statement does *not* assign the number 17 to NUM. Do not confuse the assignment operator (:=) and the Boolean equal sign (=).

THE *ODD* FUNCTION   Turbo Pascal provides a Boolean function to test whether an integer is odd or even. The following function returns a Boolean value:

Odd*(i)*   *i* must be an integer. Returns *True* if *i* is odd, *False* if *i* is even.

APPLICATIONS

The *if* statement is useful for allowing a Pascal program to select between two possible courses of action. Through the use of nested *if* statements, a Pascal program can choose among several possible actions.

For example, a payroll program might have a section to compute regular wages as Payrate * Hours and overtime wages as Payrate * Hours * 1.5. Assuming all variables are properly declared and have appropriate values, the following code segment performs the computation of wages:

```
if Hours<=40 then Pay:=Hours * Payrate
    else Pay:= 40 * Payrate + (Hours-40) * Payrate * 1.5;
```

In general, the semicolon is used to separate Pascal statements. Note that the semicolon is always incorrect immediately prior to an *else* statement.

TYPICAL OPERATION

In this session you write a coin-toss program. Use the Random function to generate a random integer. Use the *odd* function to determine whether the number is even or odd. Display "Heads" if the number is odd, "Tails" if the number is even.

1. If you are continuing from a previous module, clear the Editor workspace. Otherwise, start Turbo Pascal from the DOS prompt.

2. Start the Editor and type the following program:

```
program Cointoss;
uses Crt;var Coin: word;

begin
    ClrScr;
    Randomize;
    Coin:=Random(50000);
```

```
    If Odd(Coin) then write('Heads')
        else write('Tails');
    readln;
end.
```

3. Run the program.

```
Heads
```

Of course, the odds are 50-50 that your results are different.

4. Run the program several times to verify that there are two possible outcomes.

5. Turn to Module 7, Case, to continue the learning sequence.

Module 33
IMPLEMENTATION

DESCRIPTION

Use the reserved word *implementation* to begin the private portion of a unit definition. The implementation part of a unit contains the constants, types, variables, and procedures that are local to the unit and therefore inaccessible to the calling program or unit. It contains the definitions of the procedures whose declarations and formal parameters are located in the interface portion of the unit. It also contains a closing begin-end group that serves as initialization code for the unit.

APPLICATIONS

Constants, types, variables, and procedure headings that are shared with the calling portion of the program are placed in the interface portion of a unit. The implementation portion of the unit is hidden from the calling program.

In developing programs, developers frequently first concentrate on making the program work, then work on making the program faster and more asthetically pleasing. In a properly constructed unit, this is possible through changing only the contents of the implementation part of the unit. The benefit of this strategy is that there is no possibility of creating an unwanted side effect in the calling program.

A *var* statement in the interface portion of a unit creates a variable that is global both to the unit and to the calling program. A *var* statement in the implementation portion of a unit creates a variable whose scope is limited to the unit.

Data types that are used by the calling program are frequently defined in the interface portion of the unit. Data types that are used only within the unit are defined in the implementation portion of the unit.

When you have initialization activities that must be performed in a unit, place a begin-end group at the end of the unit for these program statements. A unit to perform windowing might contain, for example, a variable to keep track of how many screens of information were stored in a data structure. Initialize the variable in the begin-end group at the close of the implementation section of the unit.

TYPICAL OPERATION

In this session you add the implementation section of the unit you began in the Interface module.

1. Continue your work session directly from the Interface module, or load the unit MESSAGE.PAS into the Editor workspace.

```
Unit Message;

Interface
Procedure DisplayMessage(S:String);
```

2. Add the data structures required to save and restore a text window on the screen. (These techniques were presented in the Move module if you need to review them.)

```
Unit Message;
Uses Crt;
Interface;
DisplayMessage(S:String);
Implementation
uses Crt;
type image = array[1..4000] of byte;
var screen : image absolute $B800:$0000; {Use $B000:$000 for monochrome.}
    screenkeep : image;
    XPosition, YPosition : byte;
```

There are three actions that must be performed. First, the contents of the current screen must be saved. Second, you must display the message in a window on the screen. Third, you must restore the previous screen image. Writing the unit in a highly modular fashion allows you the option of coming back later and extending it, for example, to display different special-use window types. As a result, the implementation of the unit is best structured as three procedures: one procedure to perform each of the three actions.

3. Add the procedure definitions as shown.

```
Implementation
type image = array[1..4000] of byte;
var screen : image absolute B800:0000; {Use B000:000 for monochrome.}
    screenkeep : image;

procedure screensave;
begin
    screenkeep:=screen;
    XPosition:=WhereX;
    YPosition:=WhereY;
end;

procedure screenrestore;
begin
    screen:=screenkeep;
    window(1,1,80,25);
```

```
        GotoXY(XPosition,YPosition);
    end;

    procedure displaymessage;
    begin
        screensave;
        window(15,5,65,10);
        Textcolor(white);
        Textbackground(red);

        ClrScr;
        Gotoxy(10,2);
        write(s);
        Gotoxy(10,4);
        write('Press any key to continue');
        readln;
        screenrestore;
    end;

    begin
    end.
```

The procedures "screensave" and "screenrestore" are local to the implementation section of the unit. The calling program does not know that they exist or have any way of finding out that they exist. The only procedure visible to the calling program is procedure displaymessage. Notice that instead of using the *move* statement, as was demonstrated in the Move module to save and restore the screens, the array variables are moved with an assignment statement. The use of the assignment statement for this kind of move operation is more understandable than using the move statement. Notice also that in addition to saving and restoring the contents of the screen, the XY coordinate position of the text cursor is saved by calling the *WhereX* and *WhereY* functions from the Crt unit.

The *end* statement followed by a period is mandatory at the close of a unit. The corresponding *begin* statement is optional. If the unit required initialization code, it would be placed in the closing begin-end group. Code in the initialization section of the unit is executed before the first executable statement in the main program. A possible enhancement of this program would allow for multiple, overlapping windows. If you used a linked list to save the list of saved screens, the initialization code would be used to establish the linked list with a *new* statement.

    4. Save the unit.

A unit can't be run. It only provides support procedures to develop host programs. Therefore, to test the unit it is necessary to create a calling program.

    5. Select New from the File menu. Return to the Editor and type the following program.

```
program Test;
uses Crt, Message;
var i : integer;
```

```
begin
   ClrScr;
   For i := 1 to 24 do
   write('This is a line of text that is written repeatedly to the screen');
   Displaymessage('Hello there, this is the message!');
   gotoxy(24,25);
   write('Press Enter to end the program.');

   readln;
end.
```

6. Save the program. Name it TEST.PAS.

7. Select Make from the Compile menu.

8. Select Run from the Run menu. The lines of text appear briefly on the screen before the window opens and displays the message.

9. Press **Enter** to continue the program.

The screen is restored as expected.

10. Press **Enter** to end the program.

11. Turn to Module 44, Object, to continue the learning sequence.

Module 34
INTERFACE

DESCRIPTION

The definition of a unit is broken into two parts: the interface part and the implementation part. The interface contains the constants, types, variables, functions, procedures, and objects that are maintained in common with the calling program. A *type* statement in the interface portion of a unit makes the type available to the calling program. A *const* statement in the interface portion of a unit makes the constant available to the calling program. Variables declared in the interface of a unit are global to the calling program. Including the header and formal parameters of a procedure or function makes it available to the calling program.

APPLICATIONS

The interface describes the parts of the unit that are visible to a program (or unit) making use of the unit's features. The implementation contains the exact description of how the feature is performed. This division provides you with the ability to revise the implementation of a particular feature, for example, to make it run faster or to use less memory, without requiring that you modify the programs that use the unit.

The interface should contain only the definition of constants, types, variables, procedures, functions, and objects that you want to share with the calling program. Generally, you want to provide as clean an interface as possible between the unit and the calling program. Any data type, variables, constants, procedures, function, or objects that are created exclusively to implement the action and are not required for communictions with the calling program should be defined in the implementation portion of the unit instead of the interface section.

TYPICAL OPERATION

In this session you define the interface portion for a unit that places a message on the screen in a dialog box.

1. Start Turbo Pascal, or select New from the File menu to clear the Editor and begin a new work session.

2. Type the following unit.

    ```
    Unit Message;
    Interface
    Procedure DisplayMessage(S:String);
    ```

3. Save the file as UNITMES.

4. Turn to Module 33, Implementation, to continue the learning sequence.

Module 35
INTR

DESCRIPTION

```
Intr(Number,Result)
```

The *intr* procedure is located in the *DOS* unit. It issues the software interrupt specified by the integer value *Number*. *Result* contains the information returned by the interrupt. *Result* must be declared having a type of *Registers*. The *Registers* type is declared in the *Crt* unit with the following definition:

```
type Registers = record
                   case integer of
                     0: (AX,BX,CX,DX,BP,SI,DI,DS,ES,Flags: word);
                     1: (AL,AH,BL,BH,CL,CH,DL,DH: byte);
                   end;
```

APPLICATIONS

Many of the sophisticated features of IBM PCs and compatibles are accessed through a system of software interrupts. In IBM DOS versions 2.0 or later, this documentation is located in a separate DOS technical reference manual. In early versions of PC-DOS and in some compatible manufacturers' MS-DOS, the software interrupt system is documented as part of the basic DOS documentation.

The software interrupt system provides the facility for manipulation of the video display, advanced disk access, and writing "terminate and stay resident" programs, such as Borland's Sidekick™.

TYPICAL OPERATION

In this session you create a program to determine the display adapter type installed on the computer. On the IBM PC, bits 4 and 5 of the equipment status word designate the display configuration of the computer. If both bits are 1, a monochrome display is installed. The combination 01 designates a 40 x 25 display, and 10 designates an 80 x 25 display. The bit pattern 00 indicates there is no display adapter attached to the machine.

The equipment status word is accessed through software interrupt 17.

1. If you are continuing your work session, clear the Editor workspace. Otherwise, start Turbo Pascal.

2. Start the Editor and type the following program.

```
program Monitor;
uses Crt,Dos;
var Result : Registers;
      Code : Integer;
begin

    ClrScr;
    Intr(17,Result);
    Code:=Result.AX and $0030;
    Case Code of
        $0020 : writeln('80 x 25 Color Display');
        $0010 : writeln('40 x 25 Color Display');
        $0030 : writeln('Monochrome Display');
    end;
end.
```

3. Save and run the program.

```
80 x 25 Color Display

Press any key to return to Turbo Pascal
```

Of course, your screen is different if you have a different hardware configuration.

4. Turn to Module 39, MsDOS, to continue the learning sequence.

Module 36
IORESULT

DESCRIPTION

Normally, the Turbo Pascal system handles all I/O errors. However, the way the system handles errors is to abort the program and display the Program Counter. This is not generally an acceptable error-handling method for serious software projects. Using the I compiler directive, you instruct the system to allow the Pascal program to handle its own errors.

The system provides a predeclared identifier, *IoResult*, that is set each time an input or output operation is performed. When an I/O operation completes successfully, *Ioresult* is set to zero. When a problem occurs, *IoResult* is set to a nonzero value. Use *IoResult* in combination with the {$I+} compiler directive to implement your own error-handling routines.

IORESULT VALUES The possible values of *IoResult* follow. Notice that the values are printed here in decimal notation.

00 The I/O operation completed successfully.

02 File not found. There is no existing file in the current directory matching this filename.

03 Path not found. The path you specified is invalid or specifies a subdirectory that does not exist.

04 Too many open files. DOS only allows eight open files on your system at one time. You may raise this number with a statement such as FILES=20 in your CONFIG.SYS file on your boot disk. In any event, your program is limited to no more than 15 open files.

05 File access denied. There are several possible reasons for this message.

- Disk directory full. You are trying to *rewrite* a file, and there is no more room in the disk directory.
- You attempted to *reset* or *append* a read-only file.
- You attempted to *rename* an existing file to the name of an existing file or directory.
- You attempted to *erase* a directory or read-only file.
- You attempted to *Mkdir* on a device or to create a duplicate directory.
- You attempted to remove a nonempty directory.

- You attempted to *read* or *blockread* a file that is not open for reading.

- You attempted to *write* or *blockwrite* a file that is not open for writing.

06 Invalid file handle. DOS is confused. You may have somehow corrupted the file variable.

12 Invalid file access code. The value of *filemode* is invalid.

15 Invalid drive number. The drive number provided to *GetDir* is invalid.

16 Cannot remove current directory. You attempted to perform a *RmDir* operation on the current directory.

17 Cannot rename across drives. You attempted to rename a file to a name referencing another disk drive.

100 Disk read error. You tried to read past the end of a typed file.

101 Disk write error. Probably caused by a full disk. The error may occur when a *write, writeln, blockwrite,* or *flush* perform disk output; the error can also occur when *read, readln,* or *close* flush the output buffer prior to performing their operation.

102 File not assigned. You must use the *assign* statement for this file before you perform any operation on the file.

103 File not open. You must *rewrite* or *reset* the file before you can perform other operations on the file.

104 The file is not open for input. There are three possible ways to generate this error: 1) You are trying to read from a file that has not been enabled for reading by a prior *reset* or *rewrite*. 2) You are trying to read from a text file that was opened with *rewrite* and is therefore an empty file. 3) You are trying to read from an output-only device, such as *Lst*.

105 The file is not open for output. There are three possible ways to generate this error: 1) You are trying to write to a file without opening it with a prior *reset* or *rewrite*. 2) You are trying to write to a text file which was opened with *reset*. 3) You are trying to write to an input-only device, such as Kbd.

106 There is an error in the numeric format. The string read from a text file, or the keyboard, does not conform to the rules for forming the type of numeric value being read.

APPLICATIONS

You can intercept I/O (Input/Output) errors in the program instead of letting these errors abnormally end the program and return you to the operating system by turning off Pascal's error handling and providing your own error-handling routine. *IoResult* is reset on every input and output statement. One common trap to avoid is illustrated in the code segment below:

```
    |           |
var Radius : Real;
    |           |
{$I-}
readln(Radius);
If IoResult=106 then
begin
    writeln('The format of the radius is incorrect');
    writeln('The value of I/O result is:',IoResult);
end;
{$I+}
    |           |
```

Assume that when this program is run, the user types "THREE" as the value for Radius. Because I/O checking is off, *IoResult* is set to 16 (Error in numeric format) and processing is allowed to continue. (You are responsible for handling the error. If you ignore the error, your program results are unpredictable.) The first *writeln* statement places a descriptive message on the screen. Assuming that there is no problem writing the error message, *IoResult* is reset to 0. The second *writeln* statement displays the value of *IoResult* based on the success of the *writeln* operation, not the failure of the *readln* operation.

The preferred technique is immediately to assign *IoResult* to an integer variable. This assignment puts the value of *IoResult* in a safe place where it remains unchanged. Use the integer variable as the basis for all error code comparisons in the error-handling routine.

You must tell the Compiler that you wish to do your own error handling by including the Compiler I/O check option, *{$I }*. If you specify nothing, the Compiler assumes you want it to generate I/O checking code, *{$I+}*. When you wish to do your own checking, change the Compiler switch to *{$I-}* before the I/O statement. In general, you only want to turn off I/O checking around a single statement or small group of statements that generate I/O errors you are prepared to handle. At other times, leave I/O checking on so the system can handle unpredictable errors. You can use the I compiler directives *{$I+}* and *{$I-}* as many times as you like in your program.

TYPICAL OPERATION

Display the result of *IoResult* after reading a number with an illegal numeric format by improving the code segment discussed.

1. If you are continuing your work session, clear the Editor workspace. Otherwise, start Turbo Pascal.

2. Start the Editor and type the following program.

```
program Checkit;
uses Crt;
var Radius : Real;
    ErrorCode : Integer;

begin
    ClrScr;
    write('Enter the value of the radius: ');
    {$I-}
    readln(Radius);
    ErrorCode:=Ioresult;
    {$I+}
    If Errorcode=106 then
    begin
        writeln('The format of the radius is incorrect.');
        writeln('The value of I/O result is: ',ErrorCode);
    end;
    readln;
end.
```

3. Press **Alt-F** and type **S**. Type **CHECKIT** as the program name and press **Enter**.

4. Run the program. You are prompted: "Enter the value of the radius:"

5. Type **Four** and press **Enter**.

```
Enter the value of the radius:  Four
The format of the radius is incorrect.
The value of I/O is 106

C:\TP>
```

The error-handling routine correctly identifies the error. Note that this error-handling routine is primitive in that it only identifies one error. Furthermore, the process ends with the error's identification, there is no provision for error correction. A more complete use of *IoResult* in the construction of an error handler is included in the Typical Operation section of the Repeat module.

6. Turn to Module 51, Repeat, to continue the learning sequence.

Module 37
KEYPRESSED

DESCRIPTION

The *keypressed* function is a Boolean function that allows you to determine if a key is waiting to be read from the keyboard. The function does not actually perform a read operation, it only allows you to know that information is waiting for processing.

Keypressed　　　　　Boolean function that returns *True* if a key has been pressed on the keyboard, and *False* if a key has not been pressed.

APPLICATIONS

The most useful application of the *keypressed* function is to poll the keyboard for user input. The *read*, *readln*, and *readkey* statements halt program execution to wait for input. Many times you want program execution to continue until the user presses a key—then respond to the keyboard input.

The *keypressed* function alerts you that the user has pressed a key. You then use *readkey* to determine which key was pressed.

Use this technique for a demonstration program that follows a predefined script of screens, unless a customer interrupts it by pressing a key on the keyboard. Use the technique for writing a spreadsheet that continues to allow the user to move the cursor and type data, interrupting a recalculation.

TYPICAL OPERATION

In this session you write a short program loop that generates random numbers until a key is pressed. When a key is pressed, the loop exits.

1. If you are continuing your work session from the previous module, clear the Editor workspace. Otherwise, start Turbo Pascal.

2. Start the Editor and type the following program:

```
program MakeRand;
uses Crt;
var   i: word;

begin
```

```
    ClrScr;
    Randomize;
    Repeat
        i:=Random(65535);
        writeln(i);
    until keypressed;
end.
```

3. Run the program.

4. Press a key to stop the program.

Use the techniques of this program anytime you need to keep a program operating until the user decides to stop the action.

5. Turn to Module 66, TextColor, to continue the learning sequence.

Module 38
MOVE

DESCRIPTION

The *move* procedure copies a range of memory to another range of memory. No checking is done for what memory is moved or where it is moved to. The types of data located in *source* and *destination* are irrelevant. Turbo Pascal provides no protection against overwriting important areas of memory, such as your program, other data, the Turbo Pascal System, or the Disk Operating System. Therefore, *move* is a dangerous operation. However, *move* is also exceptionally fast.

```
move(source,destination,bytes);
```

source   Specifies the starting location of the memory moved by the operation.

destination   Specifies the starting location of the area in memory *source* that is moved.

bytes   Specifies the number of bytes moved by the operation.

APPLICATIONS

The *move* operation is extremely useful for rapidly moving large amounts of data in memory. The most common application of the technique is for saving images and performing animation.

When you clear a window on the screen, the previous contents of the window are erased. One of the most common applications of windows, however, is to interrupt a program with an error message or an optional task, and then to resume the program. If you want to restore the previous screen and resume a program, it is necessary to save the contents of the screen so that the original display can be restored.

Accomplishing this task is easy with Turbo Pascal. Be warned, however, that the method is "tricky." It violates the rules of "good" programming practice, and it takes advantage of the machine-specific technique that the IBM PC uses to produce memory-mapped text screen displays. The technique must be modified for use with machines that are not totally compatible with the IBM PC.

TYPICAL OPERATION

Use the *move* operation to save and restore a screen image.

1. Load the file WINDOWS.PAS used in Module 75, Window Menu.

2. Save the file as RESTORE.PAS.

You need two variables to accomplish a screen save. One variable points to the actual location of the video screen in memory. The other variable is used as a storage location.

3. Declare SCREEN as an absolute variable of type IMAGE, located at the address of your computer's display adapter. Make the declaration local to Openwindow. Use the *move* procedure to save and restore the screen.

   - If you have an IBM Monochrome display or a Hercules graphics card, use the declaration

     ```
     var Screen: image absolute $B000:0000;
     ```

   - If you have an IBM or compatible color graphic display CGA, EGA, or VGA, use the declaration

     ```
     var Screen: image absolute $B800:0000;
     ```

4. Modify procedure Openwindow to save the screen in Screenkeep.

   ```
   procedure OpenWindow;
   type image=array[1..4000] of byte;
   var screen: image absolute $B800:0000;
       screenkeep: image;

   begin
       {Save the screen contents with a move statement.}
       move(screen,screenkeep,4000);
       window(15,5,65,10);
       Textcolor(white);
       Textbackground(blue);
       ClrScr;
       Gotoxy(10,2);
       write('On a clear day, I can see forever.');
       readln;
       {Reset the screen to a full screen of white on black.}
       window(1,1,80,25);
       {Restore the screen contents with a move statement.}
       move(screenkeep,screen,4000);
       Textcolor(white);
       Textbackground(black);
       readln;
   end;
   ```

5. Save and run the program.

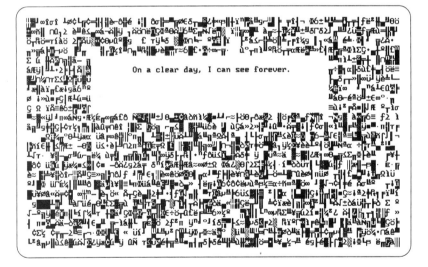

6. Press **Spacebar** to open the window.

On a clear day, I can see forever.

7. Press **Enter** to restore the contents of the screen.

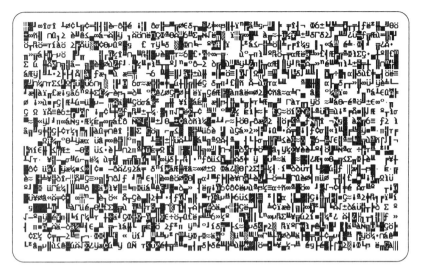

The screen is restored to exactly the condition it was prior to the creation of the screen window. The techniques of this module can be combined in a number of ways to produce an excellent user interface for the programs that you write.

8. Press **Enter** to return to the integrated environment.

9. Turn to Module 57, Set, to continue the learning sequence.

Module 39
MSDOS

DESCRIPTION

One important class of software interrupts is the DOS services, accessed through interrupt 21. This category of operations is used so frequently, it has its own procedure devoted to it. The *MsDOS* procedure is located in the *DOS* unit.

```
MsDOS(Result)
```

Result is a record data structure in the form

```
type Registers = record
                   case integer of
                     0: (AX,BX,CX,DX,BP,SI,DI,DS,ES,Flags: word);
                     1: (AL,AH,BL,BH,CL,CH,DL,DH: byte);
                   end;
```

which, conveniently, is predefined by the *DOS* unit.

The number of the required DOS service is placed in the high byte of the AX register. Depending on the specifications for the particular DOS service, information may also need to be placed in other registers. When the *MsDOS* procedure returns to the program, the values in the record structure are updated to reflect the results of the DOS service.

APPLICATIONS

The DOS services are documented in the *IBM PC-DOS Technical Reference Manual* and the MS-DOS documentation distributed by some compatibles manufacturers. Although the individual DOS services can be accessed through the *Intr* procedure using interrupt number 21, the preferred method is to access DOS through the *MsDOS* procedure.

TYPICAL OPERATION

In this session you use DOS service $2A to get the system date from within a Turbo Pascal program.

1. If you are continuing your work session, clear the Editor workspace. Otherwise, start Turbo Pascal.

2. Enter the Editor and type the following program:

```
program Date;
uses Crt,DOS;
var result:registers;
    Day,Month,Year:integer;

begin
    ClrScr;
    Result.AX:=$2A00;

    MsDOS(Result);
    Day:= lo(Result.DX);
    Month:= hi(Result.DX);
    Year:=Result.CX;
    writeln('Today''s date is ',Month,'-',Day,'-',Year);
    readln;
end.
```

3. Save the program as MYDATE, then run the program.

```
Today's date is 4-15-1991
```

4. Turn to Module 70, Unit, to continue the learning sequence.

Module 40
NAMING

DESCRIPTION

All names and statements in Turbo Pascal are built from the Turbo Pascal character set. This character set contains the following letters and symbols:

Letters and numbers:

A B C D E F G H I J K L M N O P Q R S T U V W X Y Z
a b c d e f g h i j k l m n o p q r s t u v w x y z
0 1 2 3 4 5 6 7 8 9

Turbo Pascal makes no distinction between uppercase and lowercase letters.

Special symbols:

Turbo Pascal creates some special symbols out of pairs of standard symbols:

>	greater-than sign	^	caret
(	left parenthesis	<	less-than sign
)	right parenthesis	;	semicolon
[	left bracket	'	single quote
]	right bracket	#	number sign
{	left brace	$	dollar sign
}	right brace	@	at sign
,	comma	:=	assignment operator
:	colon	<>	not-equal-to relation
+	plus	<=	less-than-or-equal-to relation
-	minus	>=	greater-than-or-equal-to relation
*	asterisk	(.	may be used instead of the left bracket
/	slash	(*	may be used instead of the left brace
=	equal sign	*)	may be used instead of the right brace

Other Characters Turbo Pascal can process any of the 255 ASCII characters as data or as parts of literals; but these characters do not form part of the Pascal language.

Reserved Words Reserved words are built into Turbo Pascal. Their meaning cannot be changed. A complete list of reserved words is included in Appendix B. You may not use any of these words as names for constants, variables, programs, procedures, functions, or objects.

Standard Identifiers Turbo Pascal provides a number of predeclared identifiers for constants, variables, types, procedures, and functions. You can redefine any of these names to suit the purposes of your program, but it means the loss of that program feature. These identifiers are best left with their original meaning.

CREATING NAMES In Turbo Pascal you provide names, sometimes called identifiers, for program elements such as data types, constants, variables, procedures, functions, and the program itself. The rules for the creation of all names in Turbo Pascal are the same:

- Names must start with a letter (A-Z).
- All other characters in the identifier must be letters (A-Z), numbers (0-9), or an underscore(_). All characters in the name are significant, including the underscore.
- An identifier can be any length, but only the first 63 characters matter.
- Identifiers must not be the same as a Pascal reserved word. Pascal does not differentiate between uppercase and lowercase characters in identifiers. The following names are all identical: TOTAL, total, Total, ToTaL. This feature is used to improve the readability of names. For example, the name TOTALCOST is more readable written as TotalCost, capitalizing the first letter of each word within the variable. The underscore could also be used to improve readability as in TOTAL_ COST or Total_Cost. Remember that the underscore is a significant character in a name. In other words, while TOTAL_COST and Total_Cost are the same name (the difference between uppercase and lowercase is ignored in names), TOTALCOST and TOTAL_COST are completely different names.

Examples of valid names include: COST, SUM, PAYRATE, TOTAL, SUM1, K3425, ThisIsALongPascalName.

Examples of invalid identifiers include:

4thQuarter	(starts with a number)
Pay#24	(includes a special character)
Write	(Pascal reserved word)
Total Pay	(includes a space)

Notice that the restriction against using reserved words as names does not mean that names cannot have reserved words contained in them.

ReadInteger, WriteReal, CaseWise, NewObject, and FileWrite are all legal names in Turbo Pascal—even though they contain reserved words.

Turn to Module 72, Var, to continue the learning sequence.

Module 41
NEW

DESCRIPTION

Pascal provides a way for a program to create new data structures of unspecified and unlimited (except for the physical size of the computer's memory) size.

When storing information in the computer's memory, it is sometimes difficult to know exactly how much information is going to be used when the program is written. When writing programs with matrices, the *array* data structures were declared sufficiently large to accommodate the problems of that section. However, there is no way to change the absolute upper limit of an array's size except by compiling the program again.

Data structures that are created under program control are sometimes referred to as dynamic data structures. The individual data items cannot be referenced directly. They can only be referenced in terms of another variable, a pointer.

To define a pointer data type, follow the symbol ^ with the type identifier of the variable type referenced by the pointer variables of this type.

```
type pointertype = ^vartype;
     vartype     = anytype;
```

pointertype   Specifies a type name for pointers to *vartype*.

vartype   Specifies a type name for the data structure.

anytype   Any Turbo Pascal type, including structured types, can be used to construct dynamic data structures.

To use space in dynamic memory (also referred to as the heap) for data referenced by pointers, declare a variable as

```
var varname : pointertype;
```

then use the *new* statement to perform the actual allocation of memory.

```
new(varname);
```

The predefined constant *nil* is compatible with all pointer types. It indicates a pointer that points nowhere.

To use referenced variables and pointers it is necessary to declare them. Every pointer is tied to a specific base type. In other words, a pointer to integer is a different data type than a pointer to a record. The only operations allowed on pointers are assignment and comparison. You cannot perform arithmetic with pointers. You cannot assign the value of a pointer of one base type to a pointer of another base type.

To declare Intpoint as a pointer to integer, write

```
var Intpoint : ^integer;
```

The caret (^) before the word "integer" means that Intpoint is a pointer to integer variables. The pointer Intpoint can now be used to dynamically reference integer variables. Intpoint refers to the pointer itself and Intpoint^ refers to the location it points to.

The variable that Intpoint points to is not defined by the declaration of the pointer. The variable itself is always defined separately using the *new* statement. For example,

```
new(Intpoint)
```

creates a new integer variable. Contrary to what you might think, this variable is not named Intpoint. In fact, it doesn't have a name. It can only be referred to by its pointer. To assign a value to the variable you could write:

```
Intpoint^=1776;
```

This assignment places the number 1776 in the location pointed to by Intpoint.

APPLICATIONS

When working with lists of items, you have used the array structure. The array data structure has several limitations. These are:

- The array has a fixed size which is established when the program is written.
- When a new item is inserted into the middle of a sorted array, you make room for the new element by moving every element in the array beyond the insertion point toward the end of the array.
- When an item is deleted from the middle of a sorted array, you fill the deletion hole by moving every element in the array past the deletion point toward the beginning of the array.
- When you are finished with the information in an array, there is no way to make the memory used by the array available for other information.

The linked list addresses all these limitations. The linked list is made possible by records and pointers. To construct a linked list, you start with a pointer to the first record in the list. To maintain a linked list of names and addresses, you might use the declaration:

```
type Person = record
```

```
            Name     : string[30];
            Address  : string[30];
            City     : string[16];
            State    : string[2];
            ZipCode  : string[9];
            Link     : ^person;
          end;

   var Head, Keep, Entry : ^Person;
```

where the record contains a pointer, in this case named Link, that can be used to point to the next element in the list.

These declarations create a structure that looks like this:

At the start of the program there are no variables of type Person. To create the first element in the list, use the statement

```
   new(Entry);
```

This statement creates one record of type Person. It also causes the pointer variable Entry to point to this record. The structure looks like this:

At this point you assign values to the record with statements such as:

```
        Entry^.Name:='Donald Brown';
        Entry^.Address:='1828 Broadway';
        Entry^.City:='Denton';
        Entry^.State:='TX';
        Entry^.ZipCode:='76201';
```

You can also use the *with* statement in the same way you use it with ordinary records. The equivalent set of statements using the with statement is:

```
with Entry^ do
begin
    Name:='Donald Brown';
    Address:='1828 Broadway';
    City:='Denton';

    State:='TX';
    ZipCode:='76201';
end;
```

Each time you need to add an element to the list, you use the *new* statement to create a new record. Pascal does not impose any limit on the number of times you can use *new* to create an additional storage location. If you use *new* enough times, you eventually run out of memory in the computer. But that is a limitation of the computer, not a limitation of the Pascal programming language. The problem is solved by adding more memory to the computer. It does not require a change in the Pascal program.

If at this point you use the statement:

```
new(Entry);
```

you create the structure:

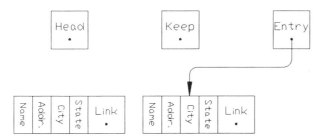

and there is no way to access the first entry in the list. This is the reason that the variable Head is declared as a pointer to Person. By storing the pointer to the start of the list in Head you can create a new element in the list and not lose the previous element. The statement

```
Head:=Entry;
```

creates the structure:

Now that Entry is no longer needed to point to the first item in the list, it can be used to create a second element in the list. Now the statement:

        new(Entry);

creates the structure:

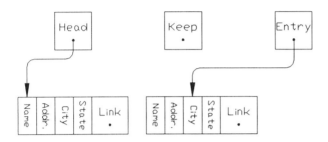

After adding the information portion of the record, you are ready to create the third entry. Again, take care not to leave any records hanging and inaccessible. It is now time to create the first link in the linked list by making the Link in the first element point to the second element in the list. The statement:

        Head^.Link:=Entry;

accomplishes this, creating the structure:

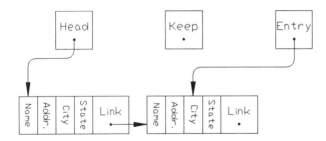

Now to create the third element in the list. Although there is a link to the second element, it is cumbersome to follow the chain of links through the list to make the last item in the list point to the next item. It is now apparent that it is best to perform this operation with three pointers. Place the pointer for the current (second) element in Keep:

        Keep:=Entry;

creating the following structure:

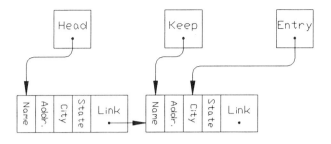

Now use the statement

```
new(Entry);
```

to create an additional element.

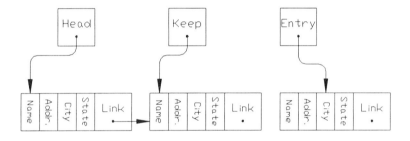

Complete the link of the third element into the list with the statement

```
Keep^.Link:=Entry;
```

making the structure:

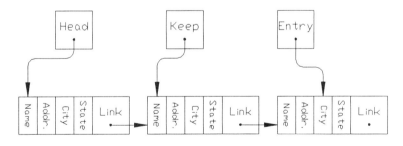

The statements used to add the fourth element, and each element after that, are the same as for the third element. For each additional element, first store the value of the pointer to the end of the list in Keep.

```
Keep:=Entry;
```

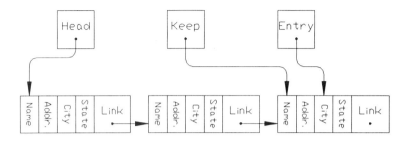

Next, create a new element for the list.

        new(Entry);

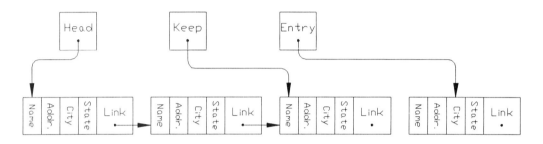

Assign data to the information part of the new record, and complete the link of the element into the list with the statement:

        Keep^.Link:=Entry;

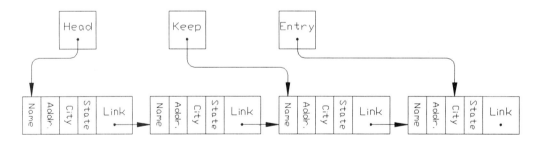

You repeat this sequence of steps as many times as necessary to add entries to the list.

POINTING NOWHERE When all the elements are added to the list, the pointer in the last element in the list has nowhere to point. Leaving it undefined is not appropriate. Turbo Pascal provides the value *nil* to assign to a pointer that points nowhere. You can perform a comparison such as Head = *nil* to determine whether the list has any members.

The pointer Link in the last position in the list has nowhere to point. Instead of letting it remain undefined, assigning the value *nil* to the pointer allows your program to check to see when the end of the list has been reached. At the end of the list creation, a statement such as

```
Entry^.Link:=nil;
```

provides a well-defined end node for the linked list.

It is now possible to check and see if an element is the last element in the list. The relation *Entry^.Link = nil* can be used in a *repeat* or *while* loop or in an *if* statement to determine whether the current element in the list is the last.

MULTIPLE-LINK LISTS   It is possible to create a linked list with more than one link. For example, a club secretary might need to print membership lists in two different orders. For example, membership lists are printed in alphabetical order by name. Mailing labels for the club newsletter are printed in Zip code order. Instead of having two copies of the list, you can have one copy of the list with two sets of links. The structure for the record could look like this:

```
type Person = record
                Name    : string[30];
                Address : string[30];
                City    : string[16];
                State   : string[2];
                Zipcode : string[9];
                NameLink: ^Person;
                ZipLink : ^Person;
              end;

var Head,Keep,Entry : ^Person;
```

Each record now contains two links: NameLink is a pointer linking to the next item in order by name, ZipLink is a pointer linking to the next item by Zip code. Instead of having just one Head pointer, there must be two pointers: one pointing to the first item in order by Name, and one to the first item by Zip code.

TYPICAL OPERATION

In this session you implement a simple linked list. You create a linked list, insert elements into the list, delete from the list, and print the list.

Although a linked list does not have to be kept in any particular order, one of the powerful features of a linked list is the ease with which items can be added to and deleted from the list while maintaining the order.

As an illustration of working with linked lists, develop a program to work with a linked list of integers. The same techniques work with any record construction. The program needs to support these three main features, each of which can be implemented with a procedure:

- Adding an integer to the list
- Removing an integer from the list
- Printing the list in order

Although you have seen that creating and maintaining a linked list requires three pointers, there is no need to make them global variables. A reasonable program structure for this program is to implement each of the major functions of the program, insertion, deletion, and printing as a procedure. Each of the procedures, Insert, Delete, and Print, needs as a parameter a pointer to the start of the list. The Insert and Delete procedures need the value to be added to or deleted from the list.

1. Start the Editor, create the program heading, define the data structure, and outline the program as shown. (Later steps in this typical operation develop each of the procedures shown in the following program outline.)

```
program Dynamic;
uses Crt;
type Point = ^Item;
     Item = record
                 Information:integer;
                 Link       :Point
            end;

var head:Point;
    Choice:char;
procedure Insert(var Top:Point);
begin
end;

procedure Delete(var Top:Point);
begin
end;

procedure Print(Top:Point);
begin
end;

begin
end.
```

Even though the procedures could make use of the fact that Head is a global variable, it is much cleaner to pass this variable to the procedures and let the procedures work only with local variables. Because Insert and Delete may need to perform their operations at the start of the list, it is necessary to pass the pointer to the start of the list as a var parameter.

However, printing the list should not modify the list in any way. Therefore, use a value parameter to pass the pointer to the top of the list to Print.

Next expand the main program *begin/end* group into a complete main program section. Use a *case* statement to select the operation to perform.

2. Enter the structure of the main program.

```
begin
    Head:=nil;
    repeat
      ClrScr;
      writeln('Perform which operation?');
      writeln('I : Insert an element');
      writeln('D : Delete an element');
      writeln('P : Print the list');
      writeln('Q : Quit the program');
      writeln('Press the letter of your choice  ');
        Choice:=Readkey;
        Choice:=Upcase(Choice);
        ClrScr;
        case Choice of
            'I': Insert(Head);
            'D': Delete(Head);
            'P': Print(Head)
        end;
    until Choice ='Q';
end.
```

The assignment of the pointer Head to *nil* begins the program by creating an empty linked list.

INSERTING INTO A LINKED LIST   Next, develop the insert procedure. Inserting elements into a linked list is a matter of creating a new item and moving some pointers. Look at the case of a linked list of the structure:

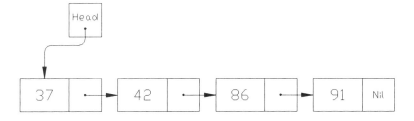

To insert an item into the list, first create the item. As an example, insert the integer 50 into this list.

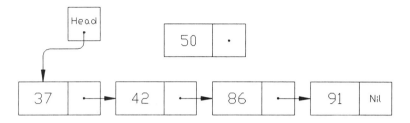

Next, reset the pointer in the second item (value 42) so that it points to the inserted item. Then set the pointer in the inserted item (value 50) so that it points where the second item (value 42) used to point.

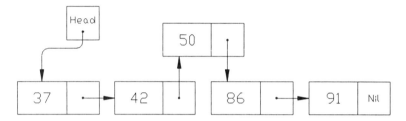

This assignment completes the insertion. Now, implement the operation in Pascal.

3. Complete the Insert procedure as shown.

```
procedure Insert(var Top:Point);
var Entry,Back,Next:Point;
    Found : Boolean;
begin
    {Create a new location and assign a value.}
    new(Entry);
    write('What value should be added to the list? ');
    readln(Entry^.Information);
    {Scan the list to find the insertion point.}
    Back:=nil;
    Next:=Top;
    Found:=false;
    while (Next <> nil) and not Found do
    if Next^.Information > Entry^.Information then
        Found:=true
    else

    begin
        Back:=Next;
        Next:=Next^.Link
    end;
    Entry^.Link:=Next;
    {Handle the case of insertion at the head of the list.}
    if Back = nil then Top:=Entry else Back^.Link:=Entry;
end;
```

The first phase of the procedure creates a new dynamic variable and accepts the value from the keyboard. Next, you find the location where the element should be inserted. The procedure scans the linked list until an element is found that is greater than the value to be inserted.

At the start of the search there is no previous entry in the linked list. Therefore, the pointer Back is initialized to *nil*. The procedure considers that it is also possible to perform an insertion at the beginning or end of the list. There is also no guarantee that there are any elements in the list. In fact, the first time the procedure is called, there definitely won't be any items in the list. Therefore, the Next pointer is set to point to the Top of the list.

It is necessary to keep track of whether an item greater than the item to be added has been found. A Boolean variable accomplishes this. It is initialized to *False* at the start of the search.

A *while* loop is used to scan the list. The terminating conditions of the loop are either:

- *next=nil*, meaning that the end of the list has been reached.
- *Found=true,* meaning the place for the insertion has been found within the list.

At the conclusion of this loop, Back points to the element before the added element and Next points to the element after the added element.

At this point you must consider the special case of adding an element at the beginning of the linked list. If the element is the first element in the list, it is necessary to modify the pointer Top. Otherwise, you modify the Link pointer of the previous element in the list. Remember that the value of Back was set to *nil* at the beginning of the search. If the value of Back is *nil* at the end of the search, it means that this is the first element in the list.

DELETING AN ELEMENT FROM A LINKED LIST Deleting an entry from a linked list is a matter of locating the element and resetting one pointer. Consider the linked list:

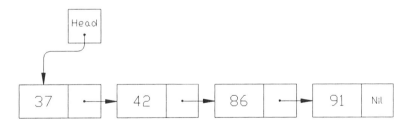

To delete the value 86 from the list, simply move the pointer from the second item to the fourth item.

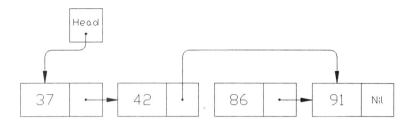

The value 86 is now bypassed anytime you follow the links through the list. There is still a link from 86 to 91, but because there is no way to get to the item with value 86, that link is not important. Now, implement the process in Pascal.

4. Complete the Delete procedure as shown.

```
procedure Delete(var Top:Point);
var Back,Next:Point;
    Found:boolean;
    Value:integer;

begin
    write('What value should be deleted from the list? ');
    readln(Value);
    {Check to see if you must delete the first element in the list.}
    if Top^.Information = value then
        Top:=Top^.Link
    else
    begin
        Back:=Top;
        Next:=Top^.Link;
        Found:=false;
        while (Next <> nil) and not Found do
        begin
            if Next^.Information = Value then
            begin
                Found:=true;
                Back^.Link:=Next^.Link;    {Reset the link}
            end
            else
            begin
                Back:=Next;
                Next:=Next^.Link
            end;
        end;
    end;
end;
```

Just as adding an element at the beginning of a linked list is a special case, so is deleting the first element in a linked list. Therefore, the first step is to check to see if it is the first element in the list that requires deletion.

The next step is to find the element in the linked list. Of course, you must be sure to take care of the case where the user requests the deletion of something not in the list. A *Boolean* variable Found can keep track of whether or not the item is actually in the list. Once you can guarantee that it is not the first element that is being deleted, you can initialize the pointer Back to the top of the list. The pointer variable Next is set to the value of the pointer of the first element in the list (which could be *nil*).

A *while* loop is used to scan the linked list and locate the position for the deletion. Then you change the links.

If the element is not in the list, Found never becomes true and the *while* loop exits when *next* equals *nil*. In this case, nothing is changed and the procedure exits without doing anything.

PRINTING A LINKED LIST   Printing a linked list is simply a matter of following the links and printing each element as it passes. Because the pointer to the top of the list is passed as a value parameter, it can be safely destroyed in the printing process. It would be possible to implement the Print procedure using a local variable to transverse the list, as shown in the following listing.

```
procedure Print(Top:Point);
var Current:Point;
begin
    Current:=Top;
    while Current <> nil do
    begin
        writeln(Current^.Information);
        Current:=Current^.Link
    end;
    gotoxy(28,24);
    write('Press Enter to continue.');
    readln;
end;
```

However, the use of Current in the preceding implementation is not necessary. The procedure can be implemented more simply as shown in the following step.

   5. Complete the Print procedure as shown.

```
procedure Print(Top:Point);
begin
  while Top <> nil do
    begin
        writeln(Top^.Information);
        Top:=Top^.Link
    end;
    gotoxy(28,24);
    write('Press Enter to continue.');
    readln;
end;
```

The procedure uses a *while* loop to travel across the linked list. Testing the relation *Top<>nil* at the top of the loop prevents encountering an error condition if the list is empty.

6. Save the program as DYNAMIC and run the program.

```
Perform which operation?
I :Insert an element
D :Delete an element
P :Print the list
Q :Quit the program
Press the letter of your choice:_
```

7. Type **I** for Insert.

```
What value should be added to the list? _
```

8. Type **9842** and press **Enter**.

```
Perform which operation?
I :Insert an element
D :Delete an element
P :Print the list
Q :Quit the program
Press the letter of your choice:_
```

9. Select **Insert** and enter **17** to test whether insertion at the beginning of the list works.

10. Select **Insert** and enter **32** to test whether insertion in the middle of the list works.

11. Select **Insert** and enter **10375** to test whether insertion at the end of the list works.

12. Select **Insert** and enter **32** to test insertion of a duplicate value in the list.

13. Select **Insert** and enter **50**.

14. Type **P** to print the list.

```
17
32
32
50
9842
10375
Press ENTER to continue.
```

Verify for yourself that all the numbers appear in the correct order.

15. Press **Enter** to return to the Main menu.

16. Type **D** for Delete.

```
What value should be deleted from the list?
```

17. Type **17** and press **Enter** to test deletion at the beginning of the list.

18. Select **Delete** and enter **10375** to test deletion at the end of the list.

19. Select **Delete** and enter **50** to test deletion in the middle of the list.

20. Select **Delete** and enter **32** to test deletion of a duplicate item.

21. Type **P** to print the list.

```
32
9842
```

All the functions of creating and maintaining a list now work. The procedures of this section can be changed to handle any sort of linked list of records. This is done by modifying the type declaration of the record to specify different information fields.

22. Turn to Module 20, Dispose and Mark/Release, to continue the learning sequence.

Module 42
NUMBERS

DESCRIPTION

If you have a fundamental hatred of mathematics, feel free to skip this module. However, a basic understanding of how Pascal deals with numbers can make your programming easier.

INTEGERS Integer numbers are expressed in either whole-number decimal or hexadecimal notation. An integer expressed in decimal notation must consist of only the digits 0 through 9. It must not either contain or end with a decimal point. An integer expressed in hexadecimal form begins with a dollar sign ($) and is followed by the hexadecimal digits 0 through 9 and A through F. The decimal integer range in Turbo Pascal depends on the particular integer data type used.

REALS Real numbers are expressed in either decimal or exponential notation. The decimal point is used to identify a real number expressed in decimal format. A real number written in exponential notation has two parts, a mantissa and an exponent. The first part of the number is interpreted as the mantissa. The letter E is used to separate the mantissa from the exponent. The number is interpreted as the mantissa times 10 raised to the power of the exponent.

EXAMPLES The following illustrate the use of valid and invalid numbers.

34   Interpreted as a decimal integer.

21,621   Invalid. Commas are not allowed in any numbers.

$22   Interpreted as a hexadecimal integer.

$1A90   Interpreted as a hexadecimal integer.

3E4   Interpreted as a real number, 3×10^4 or 30000.

1.234E5   Interpreted as a real number, 1.234×10^5 or 123400.

17.4   Interpreted as a real number.

APPLICATIONS

It is entirely an accident of biology that our number system is based on the number 10. Ten fingers made a useful basis for the development of a system of arithmetic. Computers, however, do not have fingers and toes. Digital computers operate on the principle of the presence or absence of an electrical voltage. If a voltage is present, it is interpreted as the number 1. If no voltage is present, it is interpreted as the number 0. Because there are two possibilities, this is referred to as base 2, or binary, arithmetic.

BINARY NUMBER SYSTEM   Binary arithmetic uses only the digits 0 and 1 to represent numbers. If 1 is added to 0 the result is 1. Adding 1 and 1 does not give 2 because the digit 2 does not exist in binary arithmetic. 1 plus 1 gives 10. 10 plus 1 gives 11. 11 plus 1 gives 100.

When working with base 10 arithmetic, the system you have grown up with, the rightmost digit in a number is referred to as the units place, the next digit as the tens place, followed by the hundreds place, the thousands place, the ten thousands place, the hundred thousands place, the millions place, and the ten millions place. These place values correspond to the first eight powers of 10.

$$10^0=1$$
$$10^1=10$$
$$10^2=100$$
$$10^3=1000$$
$$10^4=10,000$$
$$10^5=100,000$$
$$10^6=1,000,000$$
$$10^7=10,000,000$$

A similar system holds true for binary arithmetic. Because binary arithmetic is based on the number 2, each place corresponds to a power of 2. The first eight places are:

$$2^0=1$$
$$2^1=2$$
$$2^2=4$$
$$2^3=8$$
$$2^4=16$$
$$2^5=32$$
$$2^6=64$$
$$2^7=128$$

Therefore, the binary number 10110110 can be written as:

$$1*2^7 + 0*2^6 + 1*2^5 + 1*2^4 + 0*2^3 + 1*2^2 + 1*2^1 + 0*2^0$$

which reduces to

$$128 + 32 + 16 + 4 + 2$$

which reduces to 182.

While computers work well with binary numbers, they are difficult for humans to read, much less work with. However, converting base 2 numbers to base 10 all the time is cumbersome. Computer scientists have developed a compromise that makes it easier for humans to work with machine arithmetic. Although at first it might look like it makes the whole situation more difficult, it turns out that the easiest solution is to represent everything in base 16! In base 16, the units place represents the numbers 0 through 15, the second digit is the 16s place (16^1), the third digit is the 256s place (16^3), etc. Base 16 arithmetic is referred to as hexadecimal arithmetic.

One minor problem is that our number system does not have any more digits after reaching 9. Therefore, to represent the numbers 11 through 15 in base 16, we use the letters A-F where

A	=	10
B	=	11
C	=	12
D	=	13
E	=	14
F	=	15

Counting in base 16, therefore, proceeds 0, 1, 2, 3, 4, 5, 6, 7, 8, 9, A, B, C, D, E, F, 10, 11, 12, 13, etc.

What makes base 16 so convenient is that it is possible to convert easily between base 2 and base 16 and back again. The equivalency between base 2, base 10, and base 16 looks like this:

BASE 10	BASE 2	BASE 16
0	0000	0
1	0001	1
2	0010	2
3	0011	3
4	0100	4
5	0101	5
6	0110	6
7	0111	7
8	1000	8
9	1001	9
10	1010	A
11	1011	B
12	1100	C
13	1101	D
14	1110	E
15	1111	F

The advantage of working in base 16 is the ability to do the base 2 to base 16 conversion one base-16 digit at a time. As an example, convert the binary number 1011010001011100101000101011011 into hexadecimal.

The first step is to write the number in groups of four binary digits:

0101 1010 0010 1110 0101 0001 0101 1011

Notice that because the number of digits in the number is not evenly divisible by four that a leading zero is added at the beginning of the number.

The second step is to translate each group of four binary digits into its hexadecimal equivalent:

0101	=	5
1010	=	A
0010	=	2
1110	=	E
0101	=	5
0001	=	1
0101	=	5
1011	=	B

The full number is then written as 5A2E515B hexadecimal. You can see that even a large number such as this can be converted from binary to hexadecimal without any fancy arithmetic.

Conversion from hexadecimal to binary works in a similar fashion. For example, to convert the hexadecimal number 3B3F to binary, first find the four-digit binary equivalent of each hexadecimal digit:

3	=	0011
B	=	1011
3	=	0011
F	=	1111

The final binary number is 0011 1011 0011 1111. Again, the conversion is made without any complicated arithmetic.

INTEGER REPRESENTATION Integers are represented in the computer's memory as a 16-bit (2-byte) binary quantity. The first (leftmost) binary digit is interpreted as a sign. If this bit is 0, the number is positive. If this bit is 1, the number is negative. The largest positive number is, therefore, written as 0111111111111111 in binary, which converts to 7FFF in hexadecimal, or 32767 in decimal. The data type byte is stored as an 8-bit (1-byte) binary quantity interpreted as a positive value (no sign bit). The smallest value of a byte is 00000000 and the largest 11111111 in binary, which converts to FF in hexadecimal, or 255 in decimal.

REAL REPRESENTATION   Turbo Pascal represents a real number in 48 bits (6 bytes) of memory. The mantissa occupies 40 bits, and the exponent occupies eight bits. The co-processor based numeric types use from 32 to 80 bits to represent real numbers depending on the type.

TYPICAL OPERATION

In this session you use the *writeln* statement to write several numeric values on the screen.

1. Clear the current program from the Editor workspace by pressing **Alt-F** (File) and typing **N** (New).

2. Type the following program.

```
program Number;
uses Crt;
begin
    ClrScr;
    writeln(34);
    writeln($22);
    writeln($1A90);
    writeln(3E4);
    writeln(1.234E5);
    writeln(17.4);
    readln;
end.
```

3. Press **Alt-F** to drop down the File menu; then type **S** to save the program. Type **numbers** as the filename and press **Enter**.

4. Press **Alt-R** and **Enter** to run the program.

```
34
34
6800
  3.0000000000E+04
  1.2340000000E+05
  1.7400000000E+01
```

Notice that all integers are printed in whole number decimal format. All hexadecimal values are converted to decimal. All real numbers are displayed in exponential notation. Printing real numbers in the more familiar decimal format is discussed in the Writeln module.

5. Press **Enter** to display the Turbo Pascal Main menu.

6. Turn to Module 4, Arithmetic, to continue the learning sequence.

Module 43
NUMERIC FUNCTIONS

DESCRIPTION

Pascal provides a number of functions to help you develop programs. Functions are much like variables and constants because they are used in numeric expressions in the same way as a variable or constant. They are also like constants and variables by having a type. A function has a name and usually requires you to specify one or more arguments or parameters. The name of the function can be used in a mathematical expression or a *write* statement in the same way you use the name of a variable, a constant, or a numeric literal. You provide input to the function through arguments. These are values that are placed in parentheses and separated by commas immediately after the function name. The function considers the inputs and then returns a single value. The value returned has a particular type. Some functions only return integers, some only return reals. Other functions can return either integer or real results. If you give them an integer as input, they produce an integer as output. If you give them a real as input, they produce a real as output.

Abs(*x*)	Returns the absolute value of *x*. *x* may be integer or real.
Arctan(*x*)	Returns the trigonometric arctangent of *x*. *x* may be either real or integer and is expressed in radians.
Cos(*num*)	Returns the cosine of *num*. *num* may be either an integer or a real number. The result is always real.
Exp(*x*)	Raises the constant *e* to the power *x*. This is the inverse of the Ln(*x*) function. *x* may be real or integer.
Frac(*x*)	Returns the fractional part of *x*. It is equal to *x*-Int(*x*).
Int(*x*)	Returns the integer part of *x*.
Ln(*x*)	Computes the natural (base *e*) logarithm of *x*. Ln(*x*) is the inverse of the Exp(*x*) function. *x* may be real or integer.
Pi	Returns the value of π.
Random	Returns a real number greater than zero and less than one. Notice that this function does not have any arguments.
Random(*num*)	*Num* must be a integer (0..65535). The function returns a integer less than *num*.

Sin(x)	Computes the trigonometric sine of x. x may be real or integer and is expressed in radians.
Sqr(x)	Computes the square of x. x may be real or integer.
Sqrt(x)	Computes the square root of x. x may be real or integer.
Round(x)	Converts a real value to an integer by rounding. x must be real.
Trunc(x)	Converts a real value to an integer by ignoring the digits to the right of the decimal point. x must be real.

APPLICATIONS

The predeclared numeric functions provide you with a method of performing many numeric operations without the tedium of deriving formulas and procedures yourself.

The trigonometric functions include only the sine and cosine functions, but these provide the basis for construction of all trigonometric functions. For example, to assign Y the tangent of X, take advantage of the fact that the tangent is equal to the sine divided by the cosine and write the Pascal statement as

```
Y:=sin(X)/cos(x);
```

If your applications require additional trigonometric functions, create them as user-defined functions with the Turbo Pascal Function statement.

TYPICAL OPERATION

In this session you use the logarithmic functions to perform multiplication and exponentiation.

WORKING WITH LOGARITHMS   Before computers were invented, logarithms were often used to perform mathematical calculations. The procedure for multiplying two numbers using logarithms is:

- Convert the numbers to their logarithms.
- Add the logarithms.
- Compute the antilogarithm (exponential) of the sum.

Write a general purpose multiplication program to multiply two real numbers. Perform the multiplication by both direct multiplication and the use of logarithms. Use the natural logarithm function.

1. Start Turbo Pascal or clear the Editor workspace. Enter the Editor and create program LOGS as shown in the following display.

```
program Logs;
uses Crt;
var X,Y,Product,LogProduct:real;

begin
    ClrScr;
    write('Enter a value for X: ');
    readln(X);
    write('Enter a value for Y: ');
    readln(Y);

    LogProduct:= Ln(X) + Ln(Y);
    LogProduct:= Exp(LogProduct);

    Product:= X * Y;

    Writeln('The product using logarithms is    : ',LogProduct);
    writeln('The product using multiplication is: ',Product);
    readln;
end.
```

2. Save the program with the filename LOGS.PAS.

3. Run the program. Use a value of 7 for X and 8 for Y.

```
Enter a value for X: 7
Enter a value for Y: 8
The product using logarithms is    :   5.6000000000E+01
The product using multiplication is:   5.6000000000E+01
```

4. Run the program again. Experiment with various values for X and Y.

It is possible that you may discover values for X and Y that do not yield identical products. Remember that real arithmetic has limited precision. Performing the same calculation in two different ways has the potential for producing different answers. The difference would be small but would prevent a test for equality between the numbers from returning a value of true.

PERFORMING EXPONENTIATION   In reading the module on arithmetic operators, you may have noticed that an operator for exponentiation was conspicuous by its absence. In any event, Pascal does not provide an operator for performing exponentiation. However, it is possible to compute the power of a number using the intrinsic numeric functions. The easiest way to compute a power is to use a logarithmic function and an exponential function. Turbo Pascal provides the functions Ln and Exp, based on the natural logarithms.

To compute a power, first multiply the logarithm of the number by the exponent. Then compute the exponential of the result.

5. Select New from the File menu, then enter the Editor. Create the program as shown.

```
program Power;
uses Crt;
var Number, Exponent, Result : real;

begin
    ClrScr;
    Exponent:=18;
    Number:=4.79;
    Result:=Exp(Ln(Number)*Exponent);
    Writeln(Result);
    readln;
end.
```

6. Save the file as POWER and run the program.

```
1.7621352601E+12
```

7. Press **Enter** to return to the integrated system.

The result, of course, is a very large number. To verify that the procedure actually works, try out one you know for sure, such as computing 12 to the second power.

8. Modify the program to compute 12 squared.

```
program Power;
uses Crt;
var Number, Exponent, Result : real;

begin
    ClrScr;
    Exponent:=2;
    Number:=12;
    Result:=Exp(Ln(Number)*Exponent);
    Writeln(Result);
    readln;
end.
```

9. Save and run the program.

```
1.4400000000E+02
```

10. Press **Enter** to return to the integrated system.

You know the result, 144, is correct. You can use this logarithmic computation technique anytime you need to compute a power.

11. Turn to Module 8, Character Functions, to continue the learning sequence.

Module 44
OBJECT

DESCRIPTION

An object is a Turbo Pascal programming structure that extends the definition of the *record* data type to include not only data fields, but the methods, or procedures, that are used to manipulate the data. In defining an object type, the data portion of the object defintion must preceed the method (procedure and function) portion of the definition. For example, in the following definition of an object,

```
type Place = object
        X, Y : word;
        procedure Initialize(XPos,YPos : word);
        procedure ChangeLocation(XDisplacement,YDisplacement : integer);
        function XLocation : word;
        function YLocation : word;
    end;
```

the portions of the defintion could not be changed to place either of the procedures before the definition of X and Y.

The procedure and function headings in an object definition (its methods) are like the procedure and function headings in the interface portion of a unit. The definitions are there, but the details of the implementation are specified separately.

Remembering the similarity between an object's methods and a record's data fields makes it easy to understand that the complete name of the methods in the "place" object are Place.Initialize, Place.ChangePlace, and Place.WhereIsIt. The methods are then defined in the usual manner. For example, procedure Place.WhereIsIt might be defined as

```
procedure Place.ChangeLocation(XDisplacement,YDisplacement : integer);
begin
    X:=X+XDisplacement;
    Y:=Y+YDisplacement;
end;
```

Notice that the variables X and Y actually refer to Place.X and Place.Y. An object method is surrounded by an implied *with* statement allowing direct reference to the data fields within the object. This invisible parameter, referred to as *self* may also be used explicitly when program complexity creates the potential for confusion. Using the *self* parameter, the procedure could be defined as follows:

```
procedure Place.ChangeLocation(XDisplacement,YDisplacement : integer);
begin
    Self.X:=X+XDisplacement;
    Self.Y:=Y+YDisplacement;

end;
```

It is seldom necessary to use the *self* parameter, but in those rare cases that you need it, it is there.

APPLICATIONS

The graphics-based user interface that has become popular in computer programs poses significant new challenges for program developers. In many programs, the graphics interface represents over 90 percent of the program development effort. While the problems of graphics-oriented programs can be solved with traditional programming paradigms, the intensity of effort involved in graphics programming was largely responsible for the development of object-oriented programming.

Object-oriented programming, sometimes appreviated OOP, provides a new way of expressing the solutions to programming problems, a way that is similar to the way we think about problems in real life. Object-oriented programming has three main properties:

- Encapsulation. Combining the definition of data with the procedures and functions (methods) that operate on the data.
- Inheritance. A group of objects can be defined in a heirarchy where each descendent object inherits the properties of its ancestor object.
- Polymorphism. A method or procedure with a single name that is shared among heirarchial objects, with each object having its own special version of the method that is unique to the needs of that particular object.

You have seen how the unit structure helps to hide the workings of a program by segregating the fine details of the process in the implementation section of the unit. Using objects allows you to combine both data definitions and procedures in a single structure, called an object, that hides both the details of the data representation and the details of the procedures from the calling program. A correct use of objects provides you with an increased ability to reuse portions of your previously developed program code as you develop programs.

With inheritance, you do not need to redefine the common properties of an object. For example, consider a "window" as an object, with properties consisting of a position on the screen, a foreground color, and a background color. To define a scroll-bar for the window it is not necessary to start from scratch. You can define a scroll-bar as a descendent of the "window" object, with the additional property of having a position indicator in the window.

Polymorphism allows you to define a procedure, or method, for a class of objects, but to implement it differently for each object in the class. For example, if you developed an object heirarchy consisting of points, circles, and squares in a graphics program, you might have a "Move" method for changing their location. Polymorphism allows you to define "Move" as a method that is applicable to all objects of a class, but to implement it differently for each type of object. In this example, you would likely use a slightly different technique to implement point movement, circle movement, and square movement. Polymorphism allows you to refer to the action as "Move," but to define it independently for each object. Without polymorphism, you would need procedures such as MovePoint, MoveCircle, and MoveSquare—and it would be your responsibility as a programmer to keep track of when the use of the appropriate procedure was called for. Polymorphism of object methods allows you to transfer that responsibility to the Pascal compiler. Although standard Pascal has no provision for you to write your own polymorphic procedures, the *write* statement is an excellent example of a system-provided polymorphic procedure. The *write* procedure adapts its operation to compensate for data of any type. The polymorphism of Turbo Pascal objects allows you as a programmer to write your own polymorphic procedures.

Objects and units make an excellent match. Defining objects inside units is an excellent way to implement object-oriented programming. Declare the object type in the interface portion of the unit and specify the details of the method implementation in the implementation portion of the unit. This strategy provides you with an easy way to reuse objects from program to program.

The powerful program designs of an object-oriented approach are not limited to graphics applications. Objects lend themselves to alternative expressions of other problems as well. For example, a "customer" could be defined as an object in a database program. The object's methods would possibly be used to change information about the customer, and to send bills or other notices to the customer.

TYPICAL OPERATION

In this session you create an object definition for a location and a ball. This is a natural application for the foundation of a graphics object library.

1. Enter the following unit in the Turbo Pascal Editor.

```
Unit ScrnObj;
interface
type Place = object
        X, Y : word;
        procedure Initialize(XPos,YPos : word);
        procedure ChangeLocation(XDisplacement,YDisplacement : integer);
        function XLocation : word;
        function YLocation : word;
    end;
```

```
implementation

Uses Graph;
procedure Place.Initialize;
begin
    X:=XPos;
    Y:=YPos;
    Moveto(X,Y);
end;

procedure Place.ChangeLocation;
begin
    X:=X+XDisplacement;
    Y:=Y+YDisplacement;
    Moveto(X,Y);
end;

function Place.XLocation;
begin
    XLocation:=X;
end;

function Place.YLocation;
begin
    YLocation:=Y;
end;

end.
```

Notice that the definition of the object type is located in the interface portion of the unit and that the specification of the methods is located in the implementation portion of the unit.

A circle is typically defined in terms of a center point and a radius. Next you create an additional object, a ball, through the process of inheritance. (Naming the object "Ball" avoids confusion with the Circle procedure in the Graph unit.)

2. Add the following statements to the interface portion of the unit as shown to create a definition for circle.

```
Unit ScrnObj;
interface
type Place = object
        X, Y : word;
        procedure Initialize (XPos,YPos : word);
        procedure ChangeLocation (XDisplacement,YDisplacement : integer);
        function XLocation : word;
        function YLocation : word;
    end;

    Ball = object(Place)
        Radius : word;
        procedure Initialize (XPos,YPos,Size: word);
        procedure ChangeLocation (XDisplacement,YDisplacement : integer);
```

```
        end;
```

Implementation

Although not explicitly repeated, the variables X and Y from Place are present in the definition of Ball. Because Location is a Place, all of the fields in Place are inherited by circle.

Ball also inherits Place's methods: Initialize, ChangeLocation, XLocation, and YLocation. The definitions of XLocation and YLocation are acceptable as they are inherited. However, the definitions of Initialize and ChangeLocation must be different. Therefore, the functions XLocation and YLocation are not repeated in the definition of Ball. However, by including declarations for Initialize and ChangeLocation the inherited definitions from Place are overridden. Next, add the definitions for Ball.Initialize and Ball.ChangeLocation to the Implementation portion of the unit.

3. Add the statements as shown to the Implementation portion of the unit.

```
function Place.YLocation;
begin
    YLocation:=Y;
end;

procedure Ball.Initialize;
begin
    Place.Initialize(XPos,YPos);
    Radius:=Size;
    SetColor(White);
    X:=XPos;
    Y:=YPos;
    Circle(X,Y,Radius);
end;

procedure Ball.ChangeLocation;
begin
{Redraw the circle in the background color at the old
location to make it disappear.}
    SetColor(Black);
    Circle(X,Y,Radius);
    X:=X+XDisplacement;
    Y:=Y+YDisplacement;
    SetColor(White);
    Circle(X,Y,Radius);
end;

end.
```

4. Save the unit as SCRNOBJ.PAS.

5. Select New from the File menu and type the following program.

```
program ObjDemo;
uses Crt,Graph,ScrnObj;
Const Wait = 5;
var i,GraphDriver,GraphMode : integer;
    ABall   : ball;
begin
    GraphDriver:=Detect;
    InitGraph(GraphDriver,GraphMode,'');
    ABall.Initialize(GetMaxX div 2, GetMaxY div 2, GetMaxY div 20);
    For i:=1 to GetMaxY div 2 do
    begin
        ABall.ChangeLocation(1,1);
        Delay(Wait);
    end;
    For i:=1 to GetMaxY do
    begin
        ABall.ChangeLocation(-1,-1);
        Delay(Wait);
    end;
For i:=1 to GetMaxY div 2 do
begin
    ABall.ChangeLocation(1,1);
    Delay(Wait);
end;
end.
```

6. Save the program as OBJDEMO.PAS, then run the program. The ball appears in the center of the screen, moves downward and to the right, back to the upper left corner, then returns to the center of the screen. You are returned to the integrated environment at the end of the program.

7. Turn to Module 73, Virtual, to continue the learning sequence.

Module 44
OPTIONS MENU

DESCRIPTION

Press Alt-O to drop down the Options menu.

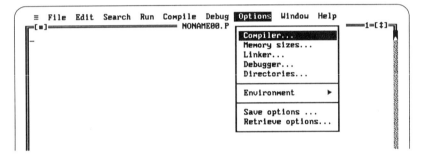

Selecting Compiler from the Options menu displays a screen of compiler options. These options are equivalent to the Compiler directives discussed in Module 11, Comments and Compiler Directives.

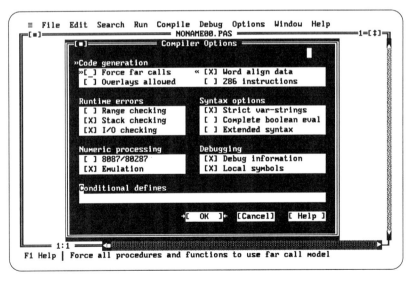

Selecting Memory sizes displays the Memory sizes dialog box.

Selecting Linker from the Options menu displays the Linker dialog box.

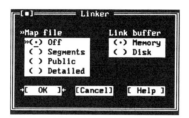

The Map file option allows the creation of a map file. The map file is created in one of three ways:

Segments   Shows memory segment information inluding start and stop segments, names, and sizes.

Publics   Shows all the segment information plus public and global symbol names, addresses, and program entry points.

Details   Contains all information in the Segments and Publics options, plus line numbers and module tables.

The Link buffer is normally set to memory, providing shorter compile times. However, when compiling large programs, you may run out of memory. In this case, set the Link buffer to Disk. The Disk setting slows down the compile/link operation but provides more memory space for the compiler to perform its work.

The Environment Options screen allows you to modify behavior of the integrated environment.

Selecting the Preferences Environment option displays the following dialog box.

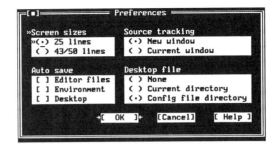

You may specify the number of lines available on the text screen. You may not specify any more lines than are supported by your hardware. All hardware systems support the default 25 line display. On an EGA system you may optionally display 43 lines of text. A VGA system is additionally capable of a 50 line display.

The Auto save feature automatically saves the selected files whenever you run your program or use the DOS Shell function from the File menu.

Selecting the Editor Environment option displays the following dialog box.

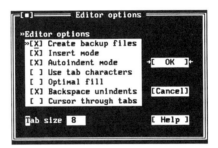

Here you specify the creation of backup files, whether the Editor starts in Insert mode, the use of autoindentation, whether tabs or spaces are placed in the source file, the behavior of the Backspace key, and the behavior of the cursor in a tab field. The size of the tab field is changed from its default of 8 characters by typing a new value in the provided field.

Selecting the Mouse Environment options displays the following dialog box.

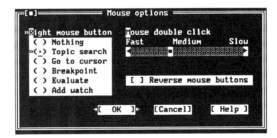

Here you specify the action performed by the right mouse button, adjust the mouse double click speed, and have the option of reversing the behavior of the left and right mouse buttons.

Selecting the Startup Environment options displays the following dialog box.

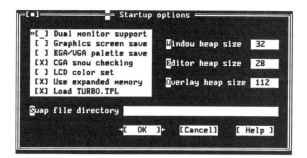

Here you adjust memory allocated within the integrated environment, specify dual-monitor support, adjust the colors for use on an LED display, and specify the location for a temporary swap file. On a system with RAM to spare, placing the swap file on a RAM disk can speed things up.

Selecting the Colors Environment option displays the following dialog box.

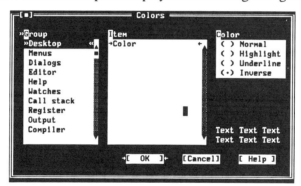

Here you adjust the color choices used within the integrated environment to suit your personal preferences.

The Save options and Retrieve options display the standard Turbo Pascal file selection dialog boxes.

The Save Options command saves your Compiler, Environment, and Directories options in a file. The default file is TURBO.TP. When you start Turbo Pascal, the system automatically sets its options to match the settings in TURBO.TP. You may also save your options in a file with another filename.

The Retrieve Options command allows you to set the Compiler, Environment, and Directories options from a filename that you previously created with the Save Options command.

Turn to Module 46, Printer Unit, to continue the learning sequence.

Module 46
PRINTER UNIT

DESCRIPTION

The Printer unit provides a simple method for producing output on a printer. Add the name of the Printer unit to the list of units in the Uses statement at the beginning of the program as shown in the following statements:

```
Uses Printer;
```

or

```
uses Crt, Printer;
```

or

```
uses Crt, Printer, Graphics;
```

The position of the Printer unit in the list of units that you use is not important.

Then add the specification for the standard file *Lst* at the beginning of each *writeln* statement for *writeln* statements whose output should appear on the printer.

The Printer unit provides access only to printers connected to LPT1:, the first parallel printer port.

APPLICATIONS

Turbo Pascal provides two methods for accessing a printer. The first method is to use the Printer unit. The limitation of this method is that it works only with printers connected to LPT1:, although you can use the DOS MODE command to redirect the output of LPT1: to a COM port. However, for access to the second and third parallel printer ports or to write a program that allows the user to specify the output device, you need to use the second method. The second method uses the *assign* statement to associate a Pascal filename with the DOS printer, *rewrite* the file, then perform the printing. This method is illustrated in Module 53, Rewrite.

TYPICAL OPERATION

In this session you modify the program created in Module 78, Write and Writeln, to place its output on the printer instead of on the screen.

NOTE
You must have a printer connected to your system to perform the activities in this session.

1. Start Turbo Pascal and open WRITE.PAS, created in Module 78, Write and Writeln.

2. Add *Printer* to the *uses* statement as shown.

```
program WriteFormats;
uses Printer, Crt;

var X, Y, Z:  real
    i, j, k:  integer;
    S, T, R:  string[255];
    B      ;  Boolean;
```

Use the Editor search and replace feature to replace the opening parenthesis in each *writeln* statement with the pattern (Lst,. The replacement is simplified because the only left parentheses in this program occur in the *writeln* statements you need to change.

3. Press **Ctrl-Q** and type **A** to start the replace operation.

4. Type **(** and press **Tab** to specify the replacement of the left parenthesis.

5. Type **(Lst,** (make sure you type the comma) to specify the replacement string.

6. Select global replacement and change all. Notice the following screen:

```
  ≡  File  Edit  Search  Run  Compile  Debug  Options  Window  Help
┌─[■]═══════════════════════════ WRITE.PAS ═══════════════════════════1=[↕]┐
│   ClrScr;                                                                  ▲
│   i:=2+3;                                                                  │
│   j:=27350 - 21845;                                                        │
│   k:=I × 2 + 1;                                                            │
│   X:=2/3;                                                                  │
│   Y:=3.14159 × 5 × 5;                                                      │
│   Z:=X + Y;                                                                │
│   S:='The cow jumped';                                                     │
│   T:= ' over the moon.';                                                   ■
│   R:=S+T;                                                                  │
│   B:=True;                                                                 │
│   writeln(Lst,'The value of I is: ',i:2);                                  │
│   writeln(Lst,'The value of J is: ',j:2);                                  │
│   writeln(Lst,'The value of K is: ',k:2);                                  │
│   writeln(Lst,'The value of X is: ',x:2:3);                                │
│   writeln(Lst,'The value of Y is: ',y:2:4);                                │
│   writeln(Lst,'The value of Z is: ',z:2:5);                                │
│   writeln(Lst,'The value of R is: ',r:2);                                  │
│   writeln(Lst,'The value of B is: ',b:2);                                  │
│   readln;                            █                                     │
│ end.                                                                       ▼
└─*── 28:17 ═══◄█───────────────────────────────────────────────────────►──┘
  F1 Help  F2 Save  F3 Open  Alt-F9 Compile  F9 Make  F10 Menu
```

Increase the field width from 2 to 30 to right-justify the output on the printer. Use the Editor replace feature for this change.

7. Press **Ctrl-Q** and type **A** to start the replace operation.

8. Type **:2** as the string to find and press **Tab**.

9. Type **:30** as the replacement string.

10. Select change all without confirmation as the options and press **Enter**.

NOTE

When working with the Turbo Pascal Editor, there are often several acceptable strategies for performing a task. There is no single correct method of editing. The correct method is the one that is easiest for you and that produces the correct result with the least effort.

```
  ≡  File  Edit  Search  Run  Compile  Debug  Options  Window  Help
┌─[■]═══════════════════════ WRITE.PAS ═══════════════════════1═[↕]┐
│     ClrScr;                                                       ▲│
│     i:=2+3;                                                        │
│     J:=27350 - 21845;                                             │
│     k:=I × 2 + 1;                                                 │
│     X:=2/3;                                                       │
│     Y:=3.14159 × 5 × 5;                                           │
│     Z:=X + Y;                                                     │
│     S:='The cow jumped';                                         │
│     T:= ' over the moon.';                                       │
│     R:=S+T;                                                       │
│     B:=True;                                                      │
│     writeln(Lst,'The value of I is: ',i:30);                     │
│     writeln(Lst,'The value of J is: ',J:30);                     │
│     writeln(Lst,'The value of K is: ',k:30);                     │
│     writeln(Lst,'The value of X is: ',x:30:3);                   │
│     writeln(Lst,'The value of Y is: ',y:30:4);                   │
│     writeln(Lst,'The value of Z is: ',z:30:5);                   │
│     writeln(Lst,'The value of R is: ',r:30);                     │
│     writeln(Lst,'The value of B is: ',b:30);                     │
│     readln;                █                                     ▼│
│end.                                                               │
├─┼── 28:43 ══◄■■■■■■■■■■■■■■■■■■■■■■■■■■■■■■■■■■■■■■■■■■■■■■■■►     │
└ F1 Help  F2 Save  F3 Open  Alt-F9 Compile  F9 Make  F10 Menu ────┘
```

11. Save the program and run it.

```
    The value of I is:                                  5
    The value of J is:                               5505
    The value of K is:                                 11
    The value of X is:                              8.667
    The value of Y is:                            78.5397
    The value of Z is:                           79.20642
    The value of R is:          The cow jumped over the moon.
    The value of B is:                               TRUE
```

The output appears on the printer.

12. Press **Enter** to return to the integrated environment.

13. Turn to Module 48, Read and Readln, to continue the learning sequence.

Module 47
PROCEDURE

DESCRIPTION

Pascal lets you define your own procedures as a method of extending the Pascal language. Procedures, like functions, are a type of subprogram. There are, however, fundamental differences between procedures and functions that determine which is most appropriate for use in each situation:

- The name of a function is used as a value in an expression. You reference a function by using the function name as a value. The name of a procedure does not have a value. The name of a procedure never appears as part of an arithmetic or string expression.

- A function returns exactly one value, which must be a simple type. (Turbo Pascal also allows a function to return a string value.) A procedure may return any number of values. It may perform an I/O operation and return no values; it may return a single value integer value; it may return two integers, three reals, a string, and an array. It is totally flexible in the number and type of the values returned.

The general form for a procedure declaration is as follows:

```
procedure pname;

procedure pname({var} param {,param}:paramtype

             {;{var} param {,param}:paramtype});
```

pname	The rules for procedure names are the same as the rules for variable and constant names.
param	You can use variables of any type as a parameter of a procedure, including string variables.
paramtype	Specifies the type of each preceding parameter. The type must be a Turbo Pascal predefined type or previously defined in a *type* statement. The type definition never appears in the procedure heading. For example, specifying a type of *integer* is acceptable. Specifying a type of *string[40]* is unacceptable. You must, instead, first define a type, such as "STRING40," in a *type* statement, then specify String40 as the parameter type in the procedure definition.

var   The reserved word *var*, when used in the declaration part of a procedure, signifies that the actual variable is sent to the procedure. When the parameter is preceded by the word *var*, any modifications made to the variable in the procedure automatically modify the value of the variable in the calling program, procedure, or function. When the *var* specification does not precede the parameter name, only the value of the variable is sent to the procedure. Any modifications made to the parameter within the procedure apply only to a local copy of the variable, and they do not modify the value of the variable in the calling program, procedure, or function.

A procedure is always declared before it is used. If you attempt to reference a procedure that is not yet defined in the program, the Compiler marks it as an error. Procedure definitions are placed with the function definitions: after the program *type*, *const*, and *var* statements, and before the *begin* statement of the program block. Procedures and functions should be arranged in the order that makes the program easiest to understand, remembering that the declaration of every procedure and function must physically precede any reference to the procedure or function in a program listing.

CALLING PROCEDURES   To use a procedure in a program, follow the name of the procedure by the names of the actual parameters enclosed in parentheses. (The *formal parameters* are the names used in the procedure declaration and the procedure definition. The *actual parameters* are the values sent to the procedure when the procedure is called.) You must place the actual parameters in the same order as the formal parameters. Turbo Pascal uses the order of the parameters to keep track of which actual parameter corresponds to which formal parameter.

PARAMETERS   There are two types of formal parameters available for use in procedures. The first type of parameter is a "value" parameter. A value is sent into the procedure, but any modification made to the variable within the procedure does not have any effect outside of the procedure. Recall that in program Funmath (Module 28, Function), you assigned the number 147 to N inside a function. When you printed the value from the main program, the assignment had no effect. When you use a value parameter only a copy of the value is sent to the procedure. A value parameter acts like a one-way door—a value is sent into the procedure, but no changes to the value are sent back out from the procedure. The second type of parameter is var (short for "variable") parameter. While the value parameter sent information on a one-way passage into the function, a var parameter passes information both ways. Any changes made inside the procedure are also reflected in the main program.

THE V COMPILER DIRECTIVE   Pascal requires that any variable sent to a procedure or function have the same type as the formal parameter listed in the definition. Pascal is rigid in its interpretation of type. Strictly speaking, a string[40] is a different data type than a *string[50]*. For data passed as value parameters, Turbo Pascal relaxes this strict typing restriction and allows you to ignore the defined length of strings when using them as parameters to functions and as value parameters to procedures. However, Turbo Pascal strictly enforces string type matching when passing strings as var parameters. Many programmers find this level of type checking excessive. Turbo Pascal, therefore, allows you to use the compiler directive {$V–} to turn off the strict type checking for string length when strings are used as var parameters. You are warned, however, that when strict type checking is not in effect that you may possibly modify memory you did not intend, possibly destroying data or program code. When operating with {$V–} in effect, never make assumptions about the length of a string variable. Always use the *Length* function to determine the length of the string.

RECURSIVE PROCEDURES   A procedure can call other procedures. A procedure can use a function. A procedure can call itself. When you write a procedure that calls itself, the technique is called "recursion." Recursion is often used to simplify a series of complex operations.

APPLICATIONS

Together with functions, procedures provide the basis of good structured programming style. A procedure is a type of subprogram. The procedure heading specifies its interface with the outside world, which may be your main program, a function, or another procedure. The program calling the function has no knowledge of how the procedure performs its work. It is totally insulated by the procedure heading. Following its heading, a procedure can have its own *type*, *const*, and *var* statements that declare variables that are local to the procedure. These variables can even have the same names as variables in the calling program. If they are specified with *var*, the location of the variable in the procedure corresponds to the location of the variable in the calling program, and any modifications are reflected in changes in the calling program's variables. If not specified with *var*, the values are stored in a completely different portion of the computer's memory; any changes made are effective only until the procedure terminates. A procedure can contain its own procedure and function definitions for procedures and functions that are local to the procedure and are not available anywhere else in the program.

As with functions, you can use procedures to clarify your programs and make them easily maintainable, or you can use them to confuse, obfuscate, and confound anyone trying to understand what you have written—including yourself after even a remarkably short break. Some guidelines for writing good procedures include:

- Parameters which only send information into a procedure should be declared as value parameters. Do not declare a parameter as a *var* parameter unless you intend to modify it inside the procedure.

- Use global variables with extreme caution. It is always preferable to pass the variable as a *var* parameter. If you must modify a global variable in a procedure, clearly comment your use of the global variable with a comment statement at the start of the procedure.

- Make each procedure less than one page in length. The mind has a difficult time understanding procedures longer than a single page. If one procedure must be longer, break it into two or more procedures that are both local to a single large procedure. The large procedure is then nothing more than a call to each local procedure.

These are guidelines, not absolute rules. However, experienced programmers find that by following these guidelines their programs are easier to develop, debug, document, and maintain.

TYPICAL OPERATION

In this session you use a procedure to change all the characters in a string to uppercase characters. The UpCase function converts a character to uppercase. The first version of the program uses only a single *var* parameter, which is used both to send the input to the procedure and receive the output from the procedure. In the process, the original string is destroyed.

1. If you are continuing your work session from the previous module, clear the Editor workspace. Otherwise, start Turbo Pascal.

2. Start the Editor and type the following program.

```
{$v-}
program StringProcedure;
uses Crt;
type BigString = String[255];
var Sentence : Bigstring;

procedure UpString(var Target:Bigstring);
var i: integer;
    Work : string[255];
    NextChar: string[1];
begin
    Work:='';
    for i:=1 to length(Target) do
    begin
        {Extract the next character from the string.}
        NextChar:=Target[i];
        {Convert the character to uppercase.}
        NextChar[1]:=UpCase(NextChar[1]);
        {Concatenate the character to the work string.}
        Work:=Work+NextChar;
    end;
    Target:=Work;
end;

begin
```

```
      ClrScr;
      Write('Type a string for conversion: ');
      Readln(Sentence);

      Upstring(Sentence);
      Writeln(Sentence);
      Readln;
   end.
```

Notice the statement

```
      NextChar[1]:=Upcase(NextChar[1]);
```

The Upcase function is a character function. NextChar is defined as a string. Remember that a string with a length of 1 is different from a character. The expression Upcase(NextChar) would produce a compiler error because of the type mismatch. However, each individual position in a string is a character. By using the array notation to explicitly refer to the first character of NextChar as NextChar[1], you can effectively work around this type conflict.

3. Save the program as STRING and run the program. You are prompted: "Type a string for conversion:."

4. Type **This is a test of string conversion.** and press **Enter**.

```
    Type a string for conversion: This is a test of string conversion.
    THIS IS A TEST OF STRING CONVERSION.
```

The string is assigned to the variable Sentence. Sentence is used as the actual parameter passed to procedure UpString. UpString refers to the variable as Target, but because Target is a var parameter, all changes to Target are automatically reflected in Sentence. When the procedure terminates, control passes back to the calling point in the program, and the *writeln* statement displays the value of Sentence on the screen.

CHANGING PROCEDURES   One of the great advantages of using procedures is that the main program does not have to consider the details of the internal operation of procedures. The only point of importance is the type and ordering of the parameters. This allows you to make changes in a procedure without making changes in the program using the procedure.

It is a simple matter to eliminate the use of the temporary variable NextChar from the procedure by combining several simple steps into one complex step.

1. Modify the procedure as shown on line 13. Notice that because you make no changes in the procedure heading there are no changes required in the main program.

```
{$v-}
program StringProcedure;
uses Crt;
type BigString = String[255];
var Sentence : Bigstring;

procedure UpString(var Target:Bigstring);
var i : integer;
    Work : string[255];
begin
    Work:='';
    for i:=1 to length(Target) do Work:=Work+Upcase(Target[i]);
    Target:=Work;
end;

begin
    ClrScr;
    Write('Type a string for conversion: ');
    Readln(Sentence);
    UpString(Sentence);
    Writeln(Sentence);
    readln;
end.
```

2. Save and run the program. Type **A penny saved is a penny earned.** and press **Enter**.

```
Type a string for conversion: A penny saved is a penny earned.

A PENNY SAVED IS A PENNY EARNED.
```

Notice that the operation of the program is unchanged.

USING VALUE PARAMETERS   In many situations you must not destroy the values provided to a procedure. In this session you modify the UpString procedure to accept the source string as a value parameter and then return the converted string with a *var* parameter.

1. Modify the procedure and the program as shown.

```
{$v-}
program StringProcedure;
uses Crt;
type BigString = String[255];
var Sentence, ConvertedSentence : Bigstring;

procedure UpString(Source:Bigstring; var Target:Bigstring);
```

```
var i : integer;
begin
    Target:='';
    for i:=1 to length(Source) do Target:=Target+Upcase(Source[i]);
end;

begin
    ClrScr;
    Write('Type a string for conversion: ');
    Readln(Sentence);
    UpString(Sentence,ConvertedSentence);

    Writeln(Sentence);
    Writeln(ConvertedSentence)
end.
```

Notice that when UpString is called, only Sentence has a value.

2. Run the program. Type **My dog has fleas.** and press **Enter**.

```
Type a string for conversion: My dog has fleas.
My dog has fleas.
MY DOG HAS FLEAS.
```

To demonstrate more clearly the protection that the use of value parameters provide against unwanted procedure side effects, change the procedure definition to explicitly modify the value of Source in the procedure.

3. Enter the Editor and add the assignment statement modifying Source to the procedure as shown.

```
{$v-}
program StringProcedure;
uses Crt;
type BigString = String[255];
var Sentence, ConvertedSentence : Bigstring;

procedure UpString(Source:Bigstring; var Target:Bigstring);
var i : integer;
begin
    Target:='';
    for i:=1 to length(Source) do Target:=Target+Upcase(Source[i]);
    Source:='I want a pickle and mayonnaise sandwich';
end;

begin
    ClrScr;
    Write('Type a string for conversion: ');
    Readln(Sentence);
    UpString(Sentence,ConvertedSentence);
```

```
        Writeln(Sentence);
        Writeln(ConvertedSentence);
        Readln;
    end.
```

4. Run the program. Type **My DOS has bugs.** and press **Enter**.

```
Type a string for conversion: My DOS has bugs.
My DOS has bugs.
MY DOS HAS BUGS.
```

Notice that changing the value of Source in the procedure has absolutely no effect on the value of Sentence. Source is a value parameter; any changes made to its value are local to the procedure where the changes are made. When the procedure finishes, the changes disappear.

5. Press **Ctrl-F7**, type **Sentence,** and press **Enter** to add Sentence as a watch variable.

6. Press **Ctrl-F7**, type **ConvertedSentence**, and press **Enter** to add Converted Sentence as a watch variable.

7. Press **Alt-R** and type **T** to begin step tracing the program with the Turbo Debugger.

8. Repeatedly press **F7** and observe the values of Sentence and ConvertedSentence as the program and procedure execute. (While tracing the *for* loop in the procedure, you may want to press **Down Arrow** and then press **F4** to skip the details of the for loop.) Notice that modifications to Target in the procedure change the value of ConvertedSentence. Notice that modifications to Source in the procedure do not affect the value of Sentence.

NOTE

A value parameter acts as a one-way door only passing a copy of data into a procedure. Any modifications made to the data in the procedure is discarded at the end of the procedure. A var parameter acts as a two-way door. The actual data (not just a copy) is sent to the procedure. Any changes made in the procedure are retained when the procedure ends.

9. Turn to Module 27, Forward, to continue the learning sequence.

Module 48
READ and READLN

DESCRIPTION

The *read* and *readln* procedures are the input procedures in Turbo Pascal. They are used for both keyboard input and disk input. The general format for the procedures is as follows:

```
read ({filename,} variable {,variable});
readln ({filename,} variable {,variable});
```

filename   If you do not include a value for *filename*, the input is accepted from the default DOS input device. This is usually the system console, or keyboard, but can be any input device or file if you have used the DOS I/O redirection facilities to change DOS's default input device. If you specify a value for *filename*, it can be either a Turbo Pascal predefined system file or a disk file.

variable   This is any Turbo Pascal variable. The operation of the *read* and *readln* statements varies slightly with different variable types.

STANDARD INPUT FILES   By default, Turbo Pascal opens two predefined files, *input* and *output*. These are assigned to the DOS file handles corresponding to the keyboard and screen, unless you use DOS I/O redirection to change things around. If you use the *Crt* unit in your program, *Crt* changes the meaning of *input* and output and does not allow DOS I/O redirection. If you want DOS I/O redirection with the *Crt* unit, you must specifically enable it.

DOS Input   This input file by default is assigned to the DOS standard input device CON:. Under most circumstances, this device is the DOS keyboard, with automatic echoing of each character typed on the screen. It may be redirected by DOS. No keyboard editing is available with this device. (This means the Backspace key does not work.)

CRT Input   Normally, this device is the keyboard, and each character typed is automatically echoed to the screen. Unlike the DOS Input device, the *Crt Input* device provides buffered input. This means that each *read* or *readln* from the keyboard is first read into a buffer area where line editing facilities are available. When Enter is pressed, the values are transferred to the Pascal program variables.

EOF AND EOLN Turbo Pascal provides two predefined Boolean values *Eof* (end-of-file) and *Eoln* (end-of-line) to assist in control of read operations. Your program can test the value of *Eof* and *Eoln* to determine the status of the input file. *Eof* and *Eoln* by themselves refer to the default input device or file. *Eof(filename)* and *Eoln(filename)* refer to the end-of-file and end-of-line for the file designated by *filename*. *Eof* is defined for all files. *Eoln* is defined only for text files.

CHECKEOF The *Crt* unit contains a predefined variable, *CheckEof*, that controls the reaction of Turbo Pascal to typing Ctrl-Z from the keyboard. By default, *CheckEof* is *False*, and Ctrl-Z has no effect when typed. If you assign *CheckEof* the value *True*, then pressing Ctrl-Z during a *read* or *readln* statement generates an end-of-file condition, setting *Eof* to *True*.

READING CHAR DATA When the input variable is a *char* variable, *read* accepts a single character from the keyboard or input file. Eoln is signaled by the carriage return character or *Eof* becoming true. *Eof* is signalled by Ctrl-Z or by the physical end of a disk file. If the input file is a disk file, the determination is based on the next character in the file (the one after the character that is read). If the input source is a device, the determination is based on the character that is read.

Placing yourself in the position of the computer helps to understand the different strategies for input from disk files and device files. When working on a disk file, the computer has the capability to "peek" ahead and examine the next character in the disk file. When accepting input from the keyboard, the computer does not have the capability to peek into the user's mind and determine the next character that will be typed at the keyboard. Therefore, the rules are different for determining *Eof* and *Eoln* when working with disk files and when working with devices, such as the keyboard.

READING STRING DATA When the input variable is a string, *read* accepts the number of characters specified as the maximum length of the string in its declaration, unless *Eof* or *Eoln* is reached first. *Eoln* is set by a carriage return (pressing Enter on the keyboard), and *Eof* is set by the character Ctrl-Z or by reaching the physical end of a disk file.

READING NUMERIC DATA When the input variable is an integer or real data type, *read* expects a string of characters forming the legal definition of a number. Integer data contain an optional leading sign, followed by one or more digits 0 through 9. Real data may be expressed in either decimal form, or in scientific notation using the E format notation to separate the exponent from the mantissa. The string of characters must not be longer than 30. Turbo Pascal determines the end of a numeric value when it finds a blank, a tab, a carriage return, or Ctrl-Z. When reading a disk file and the number terminates with a space or tab, the next *read* operation continues with the next character in the file. When reading all devices and files, *Eoln* (end-of-line) is true if the string ends in a carriage return or tab, and *Eof* (end-of-file) is true if the string ends with Ctrl-Z.

If *Eoln* or *Eof* is true at the beginning of a *read* operation for numeric variables, no change is made in the value of the variable. This would be the case if you press only Enter or Ctrl-Z without typing any digits when providing numeric input.

INPUT EDITING FEATURES   When using the *Crt Input* device, Turbo Pascal provides the capability to edit the input line at the keyboard. When using *Crt Input*, each line is read into an input buffer. When the input line is terminated, by pressing Enter or Ctrl-Z, the line is passed to the *read* or *readln* statement for processing. Prior to pressing Enter or Ctrl-Z, you can use the following editing features to modify your input.

Backspace   Backspaces the cursor one position and deletes the character in that position.

Ctrl-S   Same meaning as Backspace.

Del   Has no effect.

Esc   Erases the entire line.

Ctrl-X   Same meaning as Esc.

Ctrl-D   Recalls one character from the last input line.

Enter   Ends the input line. Sets *Eoln* to true. When used with the *readln* statement, a carriage-return/line-feed sequence is echoed to the screen. When used with *read*, the carriage-return/line-feed sequence is not echoed.

Ctrl-Z   If *CheckEof* is True: Ends the input line. Sets Eof to true. As a result, if there are fewer values on the input line than there are variables in the *read* parameter list, any *char* variables are set to Ctrl-Z, strings are set to the empty string, and numeric variables are unchanged. If *CheckEof* is false (the default), then Ctrl-Z is ignored.

DIFFERENCES BETWEEN READ AND READLN   The operation of *read* and *readln* are essentially the same, with several minor differences:

- The terminating carriage return (pressing Enter for keyboard input) is not echoed to the screen by the *read* statement. It is echoed as a carriage-return/line-feed sequence by the *readln* statement.

- The *readln* statement forces the next *read* or *readln* statement to begin accepting data from the next line or the next record, in the case of a disk file.

- The *readln* statement can be used without parameters. Specifically, the statement

```
readln;
```

    performs no input. It only forces subsequent input to begin on a new line or from the next record in a disk file.

APPLICATIONS

The concept of a *text file* is central to understanding data input in Turbo Pascal. A *text file* is any file or device which contains or produces the characters found in the extended ASCII character set. It can be either a physical file, such as a disk file, or a logical (imaginary) file representing a character oriented device, such as the keyboard or a modem.

If the first variable name in the parentheses following the *read* or *readln* statement is the name of a text file, the file is used as the source of the data. If the first variable name is not a text file, the default file Input is used as the source of data.

Using the DOS *Input* and *Output* devices, instead of the *Crt* unit's *Input* and *Output* devices, allows you to write programs that support full DOS I/O redirection and piping for the construction of programs such as DOS filters. (The programs SORT.EXE and MORE.COM on your DOS disk are examples of DOS filters. A further discussion of DOS I/O facilities is available in the *DOS Manual*, the *DOS Technical Reference Manual* and Wordware Publishing's *Illustrated MS/PC-DOS* or *Illustrated MS-DOS 5.0*.)

When writing programs using the keyboard for input, good programming style dictates accepting only one variable per *read* or *readln* statement. Expecting users to type multiple responses on a line, separated by blanks, is simply asking too much of the program user. The only time you should have more than one variable input per *read* or *readln* statement is when reading data from a disk file where the format of the data is guaranteed.

When using the *read* statement with a single *char* variable, the user does not have to press Enter after typing the character. This technique is useful for writing choice menus, such as the Turbo Pascal Main menu.

When you want to maintain absolute control over the keyboard, reacting to each key as it is pressed, allowing for program control of all function keys, shift keys, lock keys, control keys, and alternate key combinations, use the *Keypressed* and *Readkeys* functions instead of *read* or *readln*.

TYPICAL OPERATION

In this session you accept both character and numeric data from the keyboard. You use both the DOS *Input* device and the *Crt* unit *Input* device.

NUMERIC INPUT   In the first program in this session, you use the *readln* statement to provide numeric input to a program for calculating the diameter, circumference, and area of a circle.

1. Start Turbo Pascal, or clear the Editor workspace if you are continuing from the previous module.

2. Enter the Editor and type the following program.

```
program Circles;
uses Crt;
var Radius, Diameter, Circumference, Area:real;

begin
    ClrScr;
    write('Type the measure of the radius, then press Enter: ');
    readln(Radius);
    Diameter:= Radius * 2.0;
    Circumference:= Diameter * Pi;
    Area:= Pi * Radius * Radius;
    writeln('The radius of the circle is:',Radius:10:5);
    writeln('The diameter of the circle is:',Diameter:10:5);
    writeln('The circumference of the circle is:',Circumference:10:5);
    writeln('The area of the circle is:',Area:10:5);
    readln;
end.
```

The *write* statement informs the user of what is required. The *readln* accepts the input.

3. Save the file as CIRCLES and run the program.

```
Type the measure of the radius, then press Enter:
```

The computer stops when it comes to the *readln* statement and waits for you to enter a value.

4. Type **23** and press **Enter**.

```
Type the measure of the radius, then press Enter: 23
The radius of the circle is:   23.00000
The diameter of the circle is:   46.00000
The circumference of the circle is: 144.51326
The area of the circle is:   1661.90251
```

5. Press **Enter** to return to the integrated environment.

To use the program again with a new value, run it again. Notice that the computer does not have to recompile your program.

6. Press **Alt-R** and **Enter** for Run.

```
Type the measure of the radius, then press Enter:
```

7. Type **0.3** and press **Enter**.

```
Type the measure of the radius, then press Enter: 0.3
The radius of the circle is:   0.30000
The diameter of the circle is: 0.60000
The circumference of the circle is:   1.88496
The area of the circle is:   0.28274
```

8. Press **Enter** to return to the Turbo Pascal environment.

CHAR INPUT WITH READLN Numbers are not the only elements entered from the keyboard. Characters are also entered. Input of characters is done in the same way as input of numbers. Character entry permits greater flexibility in program input. A variable of type *char* is useful for providing short answers. In your use of the Turbo Pascal system, you have used single-character input to select items from drop-down menus.

9. Clear the Editor workspace. Enter the Editor and use the *program* statement to name the new program SHORT. Declare the variable "C" to be *char* data. Input a value for the variable "C" with the *readln* statement. Display the value of "C" with the *writeln* statement.

```
program Short;
uses Crt;
var C:char;

begin
    ClrScr;
    write('Type a character, then press Enter: ');
    readln(C);
    writeln('The character you typed was ',C);
    readln;
end.
```

10. Run the program.

```
Type a character, then press Enter:
```

11. Type **K** and press **Enter**.

```
Type a character, then press Enter: K
The character you typed was K
```

12. Press **Enter** to return to the integrated environment.

The computer responds exactly as expected, echoing your letter onto the screen.

13. Run the program again.

```
Type a character, then press Enter:
```

14. Type the number **8** and press **Enter**.

```
Type a character, then press Enter: 8
The character you typed was 8
```

Remember that numbers are also characters.

15. Press **Enter** to return to the Turbo Pascal menu.

16. Run the program again. Type the plus sign, **+** and press **Enter**.

Letters, numbers, and special symbols are all valid input to a *char* variable.

KEYBOARD INPUT OF STRING VARIABLES You can enter string values from the keyboard using the *readln* statement.

17. Clear the Editor workspace. Enter the Editor and name the program INSTRING. Declare Sentence as a variable of type *string*. Input Sentence from the keyboard using the *readln* statement and display it on the screen using *write*.

```
program Instring;
uses Crt;
var Sentence : string;

begin
    ClrScr;
    writeln('Type a sentence, then press Enter.');
    readln(Sentence);
    writeln('Your sentence is: ');
    write(Sentence);
    readln;
end.
```

18. Run the program. The screen prompts:

```
Type a sentence, then press Enter.
```

19. Type **One small step for a man, one giant leap for mankind!** and press **Enter**.

```
Type a sentence, then press Enter.
One small step for a man, one giant leap for mankind!
Your sentence is:
One small step for a man, one giant leap for mankind!
```

The string is echoed on the screen by the *writeln* statement.

USING READLN WITH I/O REDIRECTION In this program you use the input redirection facility to read a line from a disk file and type it on the screen. First, use the Turbo Pascal Editor to create a data file containing a single line of text. Then use the Editor to create a program to read a string from the DOS input device and display it on the screen. Compile the program into an EXE file, and use the DOS I/O redirection facility to specify the program input.

20. Save the INSTRING file and clear the Editor workspace.

21. Use the Editor to create the following line of text.

    Have an absolutely normal day!

22. Press **Alt-F** to drop down the File menu, then type **A** for Save As.

23. Type **MESSAGE.TXT** as the name and press **Enter.**

24. Open a new Editor window.

25. Enter the Editor and create the following program:

```
program Transfer;
var Sentence: String;

begin
    readln(Sentence);
    writeln(Sentence);
end.
```

Notice that this program does not make use of the *Crt* unit. As a result, the default *Input* and *Output* files are assigned to the DOS input/output devices and are redirectable.

NOTE

It is possible to use the *Crt* unit and still make use of the redirectable version of *Input* and *Output*. To accomplish this, include the following statements in your program:

```
Assign(Input,'');Reset(Input);
Assign(Output,'');Rewrite(Output);
```

These statements are explained more fully in their respective modules.

26. Save the program as TRANSFER.

27. Press **Alt-C** to drop down the Compile menu.

28. Type **D** for "Destination," changing the destination of the compiled program to the disk.

29. Press **Alt-F9** to compile the program.

NOTE

Don't worry if the numbers for memory are different on your screen. This is hardware- and software-dependent information and varies with your exact configuration.

30. Press **Enter** to display the Compile menu.

31. Quit Turbo Pascal by pressing **Alt-X**; you are returned to the DOS prompt.

32. Type **TRANSFER** and press **Enter**.

```
C>TRANSFER
```

The program waits for your input. Because you did not specify an input file, the program looks to the keyboard for input.

33. Type **This is me typing at the keyboard.** and press **Enter**.

```
C>TRANSFER
This is me typing at the keyboard.
This is me typing at the keyboard.

C>_
```

The program accepts your input from the default input device, which is the keyboard (with concurrent character echo to the screen). Pressing Enter forces *Eoln* to true, terminating the *readln* statement. The output is placed on the default output device.

Now use the DOS input redirection symbol, <, to specify MESSAGE.TXT as the source of input for the program.

34. Type **TRANSFER <MESSAGE.TXT** and press **Enter**.

```
C>TRANSFER <MESSAGE.TXT
Have an absolutely normal day!

C>_
```

The program looks to the file MESSAGE.TXT as the input file, reads the value for Sentence, and displays the value on the screen.

35. If you have a printer, type **TRANSFER <MESSAGE.TXT> LPT1:** and press **Enter**.

Your printer prints the following.

```
        Have an absolutely normal day!
```

You have now constructed a DOS filter and used it to read from the keyboard and from a disk file. You have used it to display text on the screen and the printer.

36. Continue the learning sequence with Module 49, Readkey.

Module 49
READKEY

DESCRIPTION

The *Readkey* function returns a *char* value corresponding to the key pressed on the keyboard. For standard characters, *Readkey* returns the character value. For special keys such as the function keys, control key combinations, alt key combinations, shift keys, etc., the function returns a null character (#0). A second call to *Readkey* then returns the keyboard scan code associated with the key.

The following table shows the keyboard return code for each key on the keyboard pressed alone and in combination with the Shift, Ctrl, and Alt keys. Both single-character and double-character return codes are shown. Where no code is shown, the key combination is inaccessible.

	Alone		Shifted		Ctrl		Alt	
F1	00	59	00	84	00	94	00	104
F2	00	60	00	85	00	95	00	105
F3	00	61	00	86	00	96	00	106
F4	00	62	00	87	00	97	00	107
F5	00	63	00	88	00	98	00	108
F6	00	64	00	89	00	99	00	109
F7	00	65	00	90	00	100	00	110
F8	00	66	00	91	00	101	00	111
F9	00	67	00	92	00	102	00	112
F10	00	68	00	93	00	103	00	113
←	00	75	52		00	115	00	178
→	00	77	54		00	116	00	180
↑	00	72	56		00	160	00	175
↓	00	80	50		00	164	00	183
Home	00	71	55		00		00	174
End	00	79	49		00	117	00	182
PgUp	00	73	57		00	132	00	176
PgDn	00	81	51		00	118	00	184

	Alone		Shifted	Ctrl		Alt	
Ins	00	82	48	00	165	00	185
Del	00	83	46	00	166	00	186
Esc	27		27	27			
BackSp	8		8	127			
Tab	9		00	15			
Enter	13		13	10			
A	97		65	1		00	30
B	98		66	2		00	48
C	99		67	3		00	46
D	100		68	4		00	32
E	101		69	5		00	18
F	102		70	6		00	33
G	103		71	7		00	34
H	104		72	8		00	35
I	105		73	9		00	23
J	106		74	10		00	36
K	107		75	11		00	37
L	108		76	12		00	38
M	109		77	13		00	50
N	110		78	14		00	49
O	111		79	15		00	24
P	112		80	16		00	25
Q	113		81	17		00	16
R	114		82	18		00	19
S	115		83	19		00	31
T	116		84	20		00	20
U	117		85	21		00	22
V	118		86	22		00	47
W	119		87	23		00	17
X	120		88	24		00	45
Y	121		89	25		00	21
Z	122		90	26		00	44
[	91		123	27			
\	92		124	28			
]	93		125	29			
'	96		126				
0	48		41			00	129
1	49		33			00	120
2	50		64	00	3	00	121

	Alone	Shifted	Ctrl		Alt	
3	51	35			00	122
4	52	36			00	123
5	53	37			00	124
6	54	94	30		00	125
7	55	38			00	126
8	56	42			00	127
9	57	40			00	128
*	42		00	114	00	
+	43	43			00	
–	45	95	31		00	130
=	61	43			00	131
,	44	60				
/	47	63				
;	59	58				

Unlike *read* and *readln*, *readkey* does not echo keyboard input to the screen. If you want the input echoed to the screen, add a *write* statement to your program code.

APPLICATIONS

The *read* statement does not behave exactly like the input statement that makes the Turbo Pascal menu system work. When you use the *read* statement, the user must press Enter after typing the input. Turbo Pascal provides the *Readkey* function as part of the *Crt* unit to accept input one keystroke at a time instead of one line at a time.

Good program design often dictates that the user be able to interact with a program by pressing a single key on the keyboard. For example, when you interact with the Turbo Pascal integrated environment, you make selections from the menu by pressing a single key. *Read* and *Readln* do not allow your program to react to the special keys on the computer keyboard. The *Readkey* function is the preferred method of determining that the user has pressed a function key, cursor control key, or other special key. The following program segment is useful in identifying keys other than the standard typing keys. Use this technique as the basis of a full-featured screen editing routine.

```
InChar:=Readkey;
    if InChar <> #0 then SpecialKey := False
else begin
    SpecialKey := True
    InChar:=Readkey;
end;
```

The only way that *Readkey* can generate a code of #0 is when a special key is pressed. In this program fragment, if Readkey returns a nonzero value, processing continues following the program fragment. If the value returned by *Readkey* is #0, another call to *Readkey* returns the scan code of the key. In this case, the Boolean variable SpecialKey is set to true, and InChar contains the scan code for the function key. It is up to your program then to determine what action is appropriate when SpecialKey is True, based on the scan code in InChar.

TYPICAL OPERATION

1. Start Turbo Pascal, or clear the Editor workspace if you are continuing your work session.

2. Load the program SHORT.PAS, created in the Read and Readln module.

```
program Short;
uses Crt;
var c:char;

begin
    ClrScr;
    write('Type a character, then press Enter: ');
    readln(C);
    writeln('The character you typed was ',C);
    readln;
end.
```

3. Change the first *readln* statement to a *Readkey* statement. Change the first *write* statement to display only "Type a character."

```
program Short;
uses Crt;
var c:char;

begin
    ClrScr;
    write('Type a character: ');
    C := readkey;
    writeln('The character you typed was ',C);
    readln;
end.
```

4. Run the program.

```
Type a character _
```

5. Type **P**.

```
Type a character The character you typed was P
```

The program did not require you to press Enter before accepting your input. As a result, the cursor was not repositioned at the start of the next line. The second line of output is displayed immediately following the first line.

It is not necessary to use a *readln* statement to move the cursor to the next line. You can add a *writeln* statement to accomplish the same thing.

6. Add a *writeln* statement after the *readkey* statement.

```
program Short;
uses Crt;
var c:char;

begin
    ClrScr;
    write('Type a character: ');
    C := readkey;
    writeln;
    writeln('The character you typed was ',C);
    readln;
end.
```

7. Save the program as SHORT.

8. Run the program, responding with the character **q**.

```
Type a character
The character you typed was q
```

9. Press **Enter** to return to the integrated environment. Save the program.

The program output is now the same as it was before. In using the *readkey* function, you have saved the program user an additional keystroke.

10. Turn to Module 43, Numeric Functions, to continue the learning sequence.

Module 50
RECORD

DESCRIPTION

The *record* is a structured data type allowing the association of data of different types within a single structure. An array of strings could be used to represent the names of players on a football team. An array of integers could be used to represent player salaries. However, a two-dimensional array cannot be used to represent both names and salaries because all elements in an array must be of the same type. Real numbers and strings are not compatible types. The *record* data structure provides the structured solution. The format for the definition of a record is:

```
type typename = record fieldlist end;
```

typename   Specifies the name of the new record type.

fieldlist   A sequence of identifiers and types, separated by semicolons specifiying the fields in the record.

For example, using the definition

```
type player = record
                LastName : String[30];
                Salary   : Real
              end;
```

a team can be defined as

```
var team : array[1..40] of player;
```

providing a data structure that fits the way you think about the data.

The individual elements of a record are called fields. In your program, you refer either to a single field or to the entire record. In creating a program using employee records, you might construct a type definition such as

```
type person = record
                LastName  : String[20];
                FirstName : String[10];
                SocialSec : String[9];
                Payrate   : Real;
                Deductions: Integer
              end;
```

and use the new type definition to create a variable called NewHire,

```
var NewHire : person;
```

One way to specify the individual fields in a record-type variable is to separate the name of the variable and the name of the field with a period. In a program to accept values for the individual fields in NewHire, you could use a series of statements such as

```
   |          |            |
write('Enter the Lastname: ');
readln(NewHire.Lastname);
write('Enter the Firstname: ');
readln(NewHire.Firstname);
   |          |          |
```

Another method to refer to the individual fields of a record variable is to nest the references inside a *with* statement. The previous example could be written as

```
with NewHire do
begin
      |          |          |
   write('Enter the Lastname: ');
   readln(Lastname);
   write('Enter the Firstname: ');
   readln(Firstname);
      |          |          |
end;
```

Inside the *begin/end* group, all references to LastName, FirstName, SocialSec, Payrate, and Deductions are assumed to refer to the fields in NewHire.

There are two ways to assign the value of one record variable to another record variable: you either assign the fields one at a time, or you assign the entire structure in a single assignment statement. If the program has the declaration

```
var NewHire, Trainee : person;
```

you can use the statements

```
Trainee.LastName     :=NewHire.LastName;
Trainee.FirstName    :=NewHire.FirstName;
Trainee.SocialSec    :=NewHire.SocialSec;
Trainee.Payrate      :=NewHire.Payrate;
Trainee.Deductions   :=NewHire.Deducations;
```

or use the single statement

```
Trainee := Newhire;
```

to accomplish exactly the same task. Using the assignment statement on the entire data structure accomplishes several worthwhile goals at the same time:

- It requires less typing, therefore is less likely to contain errors.
- It hides the details of the operation, making the statement easier to read.
- It compiles and executes faster.

Unfortunately, Turbo Pascal does not support the comparison of structured data types. For instance, the following statement is not allowed:

```
if NewHire = Trainee then write ('They are the same person.');
```

You must perform all comparison operations between structured data by individually comparing each simple data element in the structure.

APPLICATIONS

Use a record data structure anytime you need to associate data of different types in a single structure. Common applications are found anytime you must maintain information about people or things. A parts inventory program is built on records containing information about part number, part description, cost, sales price, reorder level, and reorder quantity. A school's student record system contains information about names and addresses, but it also contains real-number data such as gradepoints. Each of these applications is ideal for a record-based data structure.

You have created a text file and a file of integers on a disk. A typed file of integers or real numbers is useful for only a limited range of problems. Most problems require that many different kinds of information be stored. The record is the data structure that allows multiple data types to be placed in a single structured data type. As a result, the "file of record" is one of the most useful file types when constructing general purpose information files.

TYPICAL OPERATION

In this session you manipulate the text screen of the computer using memory-mapped video techniques. First you fill the screen with characters, then you change the attributes of the characters. The text screen of the IBM PC occupies 4000 bytes of memory. Each character position on the screen is represented by two bytes. The first byte specifies the ASCII code for the character; the second byte contains an attribute code, specifying such items as the color and intensity of the character. In Module 38, Move, an Array of byte is used to represent the screen memory. A more appropriate data structure is an Array of two-byte records.

```
type position = record
                  ASCII : char;
                  Code  : byte
```

```
                  end;
       image = array[1..2000] of position;

   var screen : image;
```

This data structure allows easy-to-understand manipulation of the contents of the screen.

1. If you are continuing your work session, clear the Editor workspace. Otherwise, start
    Turbo Pascal.

2. Type the following program.

```
program Video;
type position = record
                     ASCII : char;
                     Code  : byte;
                 end;
     image = array[1..2000] of position;
var screen : image absolute $B800:0000;
                     {Use $B000:0000 for a monochrome monitor}
     index, color:integer;

begin
    for index:=1 to 2000 do screen[Index].ASCII :='+';
    for Color := 0 to 255 do
        for Index := 1 to 2000 do
            Screen[Index].Code := Color;
    readln;
end.
```

3. Save the program as VIDEO then run the program.

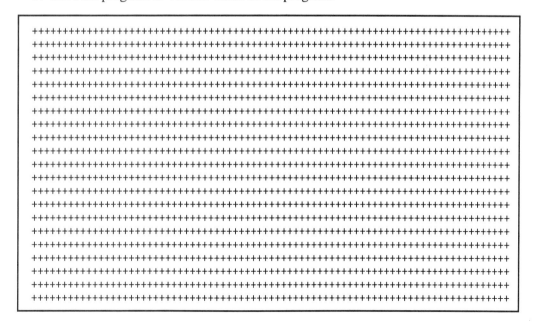

All 256 possible color combinations are shown on the screen in rapid succession.

4. Press **Enter** to restore the Turbo Pascal environment.

5. Turn to Module 77, With, to continue the learning sequence.

Module 51
REPEAT

DESCRIPTION

The *repeat* statement repeatedly executes a single statement or a group of statements *until* a condition you specify becomes true. In the compound form of the statement, notice that the words *begin* and *end* are not used to group the statements that make up the loop. The grouped statements are set off only by the words *repeat* and *until*, which define the scope of the loop.

```
repeat statement until condition;

repeat
    statement;
    statement;
     |   |
    statement
until condition;
```

statement is any legal Pascal statement.

condition is a Boolean expression.

The operation of the *repeat* loop is as follows:

- The statement or group of statements making up a repeat loop is executed.
- The *condition* is evaluated. If *condition* is false, the execution continues at the *repeat* statement, and the statements comprising the loop are executed again. If *condition* is true, the program continues with the next statement.

Because *condition* is evaluated at the bottom of the loop, a repeat loop is always executed at least one time. If *condition* never becomes true, the loop executes forever.

APPLICATIONS

The *repeat* loop is ideally suited for constructing a loop that must be executed at least one time, but it is impossible to determine in advance exactly how many executions are necessary.

One ideal application for the *repeat* loop is the construction of input error-handling routines. The input operation must always be performed at least once, but there is no way of knowing in advance exactly how many tries it is going to take the user before the input is correct.

The *repeat* looping structure allows you to perform a *read* or *readln* operation over and over until the condition *IoResult = 0* is true.

The *repeat* loop is ideal for conducting searches. For example, in searching a string for a particular character, you could use a *for* loop to examine each character in the string, beginning at the first character, and using the *Length* function to determine the last character in the string. However, it is more efficient to end the search when either of two conditions is true—either you reach the end of the string, or you find the target character. Upon finding the target, there is little reason to continue the search.

TYPICAL OPERATION

In this session you use the *repeat* statement to build on the error-handling control technique developed in the IoResult module. You then use the *repeat* loop to construct a random-number guessing game.

ERROR HANDLING WITH A REPEAT LOOP   The *repeat* statement forms the ideal foundation for the construction of error-handling routines.

1. If you are continuing your work session, clear the Editor workspace with the New command from the File menu. Otherwise, start Turbo Pascal.

2. Start the Editor. Press **Ctrl-K** and type **R** to read a file.

3. Type **CHECKIT.PAS** and press **Enter** to specify the program developed in the IoResult module.

```
program Checkit;
uses Crt;
var Radius : Real;
    ErrorCode : Integer;

begin
    ClrScr;
    write('Enter the value of the radius: ');
    {$I-}
    readln(Radius);
    ErrorCode:=Ioresult;
    {$I+}
    If Errorcode=106 then

    begin
        writeln('The format of the radius is incorrect.');
        writeln('The value of I/O result is: ',ErrorCode);
    end;
    readln;
end.
```

4. Modify the program as shown, enclosing the input and error checking routine in a *repeat* loop.

```
program Fixit;
uses Crt;

var Radius : Real;
    ErrorCode: Integer;

begin
    repeat
        ClrScr;
        write('Enter the value of the radius: ');
        {$I-}
        readln(Radius);
        ErrorCode:=IoResult;
        {$I+}
        If ErrorCode=16 then
        begin
            writeln('The format of the radius is incorrect.');
            writeln('The value of I/O result is: ',ErrorCode);
            writeln('Press Enter to Continue.');
            readln;
        end;
    until ErrorCode=0;
    writeln('The value of the radius is: ',Radius);
    readln;
end.
```

5. Save the program as FIXIT then run the program. You are prompted "Enter the value of the radius:"

6. Type **Seven** and press **Enter**.

```
Enter the value of the radius: Seven
The format of the radius is incorrect.
The value of I/O result is: 106
Press Enter to Continue.
```

7. Press **Enter**. You are again prompted to enter the value of the radius.

8. Type **7** and press **Enter**.

```
Enter the value of the radius: 7
The value of the radius is:    7.0000000000E+00
```

The *repeat* loop repeats the input operation until the operation is completed successfully.

CONSTRUCTING A GUESSING GAME   In this game, you accept guesses until the player either makes a correct guess or exceeds the maximum number of guesses allowed. Because you cannot predict in advance how many guesses a player will take, and because the player must always take at least one guess to get the answer, this is an ideal application for a *repeat* loop.

In many programs, especially game programs and simulations, you need to have the computer select options in an unpredictable way. These selections are done easily using random numbers.

Recall that if you need a random real number,

```
Random
```

is a function that returns a real value which is greater than or equal to zero and less than 1.00. If you need a random integer,

```
Random(num) -> 0<=n<65535
```

returns a positive integer less than *n*.

A simple game program for guessing high-low numbers illustrates this operation. The computer selects a number between one and 100. You must guess the correct number in six guesses or less. The computer tells you whether each guess is higher or lower than the target number.

In this game the range of the computer's number is a minimum value of one and a maximum value of 100. The random-number function *Random(num)* returns a value between zero and the function argument. Therefore, the expression *Random(101)* returns a value between one and 100.

The game player has six chances to guess the number correctly. Therefore, the main control structure should be a loop that ends when either five guesses have been tried or the correct number is guessed. The five possible guesses might incorrectly lead you to code this loop using a *for* statement. Although there will not always be six guesses to enter, the loop must always be executed at least once to enter the first guess, which may solve the puzzle. A *repeat* statement is a natural choice when the loop must be executed at least once but you do not know the exact number of times.

1. Clear the Editor workspace and type the program as shown:

```
program HiLow;
uses Crt;
var Target, Count, Guess: integer;

begin
   ClrScr;
```

```
    Randomize;
    Target:=Random(101);
    Count:=0;

    repeat
        Count:=Count+1;
        Write('I am looking for a number between 1 and 100. ');
        readln(Guess);

        if GuessTarget then
           writeln('Your guess is too low.')
        else
            if GuessTarget then
                writeln('Your guess is too high.')
            else writeln('Your guess is just right.');
    until (Count=6) or (Guess=Target);
    if GuessTarget then
    begin
        writeln('Too many guesses. You lose.');
        writeln('The correct number is ',target,'.');
    end;
    readln;
end.
```

The guessing routine rewards the player for winning. One final statement is necessary to inform the player that too many guesses were required.

2. Save the program as HILOW then run the program several times. Verify that the computer's choice of a number is not predictable.

3. Turn to Module 69, Type, to continue the learning sequence.

Module 52
RESET

DESCRIPTION

To process an existing file, first use the *assign* statement to make the association between the program filename and the DOS filename. Then use the *reset* statement to initialize the file for processing.

```
reset (filevar, recsize)
```

The disk file assigned to the file variable *filevar* with a prior *assign* statement is prepared for processing, and the file pointer is set to the beginning of the file.

Filevar must refer to the name of an existing disk file. If the file does not exist, an I/O error occurs.

Recsize is an optional specification used only for untyped files. It specifies the record length in bytes. If omitted, the record length defaults to 128 bytes.

APPLICATIONS

To use an existing file as a source of input:

- Declare *filevar* in a *var* statement.
- Associate *filevar* with a DOS file or device with the *assign* statement.
- Use the *reset* statement to set the file pointer at the first position in the file.

Reset may also be used with a file that is currently open. If the file is already open, the file pointer is repositioned at the beginning of the file.

If *filevar* is empty, as in the statements

```
Assign(Device,'');
Reset(Device);
```

the file is assigned to the DOS standard input file (normally the keyboard) associated with file handle number 0.

TYPICAL OPERATION

There are two activities in this session. The first is to use the *reset* statement with a text file and the second uses *reset* with a file of integers.

RESET A TEXT FILE   In this activity, you continue to develop the TEXTIO program that was most recently modified in Module 53, Rewrite.

1. Load the program TEXTIO into the Editor. Add the *reset* statement as shown in the program listing. Add a readln statement at the program's end to keep the output visible on the screen.

```
program TextIO;
uses Crt;
var        S:string;
    Diskfile : text;
begin
    ClrScr;
    assign(Diskfile,'INFO.TXT');
    rewrite(Diskfile);
    writeln(Diskfile,'This information is placed on the disk.');
    reset(Diskfile);
    readln(Diskfile,S);
    writeln(S);
    readln;
end.
```

This *reset* statement positions the file pointer back at the beginning of the file and prepares the file for input.

2. Save and run the program.

```
This information is placed on the disk.
```

The text is first written to the disk, the file is reset, the information is read back from the disk into the variable S, then the information is written to the screen.

RESET A TYPED (INTEGER) FILE   In this activity, you continue to develop the INTIO program that was most recently modified in Module 53, Rewrite.

1. Load the program INTIO into the Editor. Add the *reset* statement as shown in the following listing.

```
program IntegerInOut;
uses Crt;
var     i,j: integer;
    Diskfile: File of Integer;
```

```
begin
    ClrScr;
    assign(Diskfile,'INFO.DAT');
    rewrite(Diskfile);
    for i:= 1 to 10 do write(Diskfile,i);
    reset(Diskfile);
    for i:= 1 to 10 do
    begin
        read(Diskfile,j);
        writeln(j);
    end;
    readln;
end.
```

2. Save and run the program.

```
1
2
3
4
5
6
7
8
9
10
```

The integers are first written to the disk. Then the file is reset and the information read back from the disk into the variable j. After each read operation, the information is written to the screen.

3. Turn to Module 9, Close, to continue the learning sequence.

Module 53
REWRITE

DESCRIPTION

To create a new disk file, first use the *assign* statement to make the association between the program filename and the DOS filename. Then use the *rewrite* statement to initialize the file for processing.

rewrite (*filevar*)   The disk file assigned to the file variable *filevar* with a prior *assign* statement is prepared for processing, and the file pointer is set to the beginning of the file. If *filevar* refers to the name of an existing disk file, the old file is erased and a new one created.

APPLICATIONS

To create a new file for output:

- Declare *filevar* in a *var* statement.
- Associate *filevar* with a DOS file with the *assign* statement.
- Use the *rewrite* statement to set the file pointer at the first position in the file.

One danger in using *rewrite* is the potential for accidentally erasing a previously existing file. To prevent the loss of an existing file, attempt first to *reset* the file. If the *reset* operation is successful (IoResult=0), then require user-confirmation before erasing the file. If the *reset* operation is unsuccessful (IoResult=2 indicates that the file does not exist), then proceed with the *rewrite* operation without user intervention.

The *rewrite* statement is also used to associate a program name with a DOS device. The available devices are:

CON: The console device providing buffered input. Assigned to the DOS device CON:.

LPT1:   The first parallel printer.

LPT2:   The second parallel printer.

LPT3:   The third parallel printer.

COM1:   Serial communications port 1.

COM2:   Serial communications port 2.

INP: The DOS standard input device (file handle 0).

OUT: The DOS standard output device (file handle 1).

ERR: The DOS standard error device (file handle 2).

TYPICAL OPERATION

There are four activities in this session. In the first activity, you add the rewrite statement to the TEXTIO program. In the second activity, you add the rewrite statement to the INTIO program. In the third activity, you investigate the use of IoResult to avoid destroying a previously existing file with the *rewrite* statement. In the fourth activity, you use the *rewrite* statement to treat the DOS device LPT1: (the printer) as a text file for output.

ADD THE REWRITE STATEMENT TO TEXTIO   In this activity you add the statement to create the file INFO.TXT on the disk.

1. Load the program TEXTIO into the Editor.

2. Add the *rewrite* statement as shown in the following listing.

```
program TextIO;
uses Crt;
var        S:string;
    Diskfile : text;
begin
    ClrScr;
    assign(Diskfile,'INFO.TXT');
    rewrite(Diskfile);
    writeln(Diskfile,'This information is placed on the disk.');
    readln(Diskfile,S);
    writeln(S);
end.
```

3. Save the program.

ADD THE REWRITE STATEMENT TO INTIO   In this activity you add the statement to create the file INFO.DAT on the disk.

1. Load the program INTIO into the Editor.

2. Add the *rewrite* statement as shown in the following listing.

```
program IntegerInOut;
uses Crt;
var        i,j: integer;
    Diskfile: File of Integer;
begin
    ClrScr;
```

```
        assign(Diskfile,'INFO.DAT');
        rewrite (Diskfile);
        for i:= 1 to 10 do write(Diskfile,i);
        for i:= 1 to 10 do
        begin
            read(Diskfile,j);
            writeln(j);
        end;
    readln;
    end.
```

USE IORESULT WITH REWRITE   In this activity you check for the existence of a file, create a new disk file, and write a line of text to the file.

NOTE

This program uses the *reset* statement and the *close* statement. They are used here, prior to their appearance in the recommended learning sequence, to better illustrate the use of the *rewrite* statement in combination with IORESULT. The *reset* statement allows you to prepare a file that already exists for use. The *close* statement informs the system that you are finished changing the file.

1. Clear the Editor workspace and type the following program:

```
program SafetyCheck;
uses Crt;
var Stuff : Text;
    Error : Integer;
    Choice: Char;

begin
    ClrScr;
    Assign (Stuff, 'STUFF.TXT');
    {$I-}              {Turn off I/O checking.}
    reset(Stuff);      {Attempt to open as an existing file.}
    Error:=IoResult;
    {$I+}
    If Error=0 then    {The file exists if Error=0}
    begin
        write('STUFF.TXT exists. Erase it (Y/N): ');
        readln(Choice);
        if UpCase(Choice)='Y' then
        begin
            Close(Stuff);
            Rewrite(Stuff);
            Writeln(Stuff,'The old stuff was erased.');
        end;
    end
    else begin
        rewrite(Stuff);
        writeln(Stuff,'Stuff didn''t exist, so here it is.');
```

```
        end;
        Close(Stuff);
        writeln('Press Enter to return to the Integrated Environment');
        readln;
    end.
```

2. Save the program as SAFETY.PAS.

3. Run the program.

No error messages appear on the screen.

4. Load STUFF.TXT into the Editor.

```
  ≡  File  Edit  Search  Run  Compile  Debug  Options  Window  Help   █
 ───────────────────────────── SAFETY.PAS ─────────────────────1───────┐
┌─[■]══════════════════════════ STUFF.TXT ══════════════════════2=[↑]═┐
│Stuff didn't exist, so here it is.
│
│
│
│
│
│
│
```

5. Close the STUFF.TXT Editor window.

6. Run the program.

```
    STUFF.TXT exists. Erase it (Y/N): _
```

7. Type **N** and press **Enter** to leave STUFF.TXT intact.

8. Load STUFF.TXT into the Editor.

```
  ▓  File  Edit  Search  Run  Compile  Debug  Options  Window  Help
 ───────────────────────────── SAFETY.PAS ─────────────────────1───────┐
┌─[■]══════════════════════════ STUFF.TXT ══════════════════════2=[↑]═┐
│Stuff didn't exist, so here it is.
│
│
│
│
│
│
```

The contents of STUFF.TXT remain unchanged.

9. Close the STUFF.TXT Editor window.

10. Run the program.

```
STUFF.TXT exists. Erase it (Y/N): _
```

11. Type **Y** and press **Enter**.

12. Load STUFF.TXT into an Editor window.

```
 ≡  File  Edit  Search  Run  Compile  Debug  Options  Window  Help
 ───────────────────────────── SAFETY.PAS ───────────────────────1──
 ┌─[■]══════════════════════════ STUFF.TXT ═══════════════════════2=[↑]═┐
 │The old stuff was erased.
```

The *rewrite* statement erases the old version of STUFF.TXT, replacing it with the new version.

USING REWRITE WITH THE PRINTER   Use an explicit *rewrite* operation to assign the printer to a program file and place output on the printer.

1. Open a new Editor window and type the following program.

```
program TextPrint;
var Printer : text;

begin
    assign(Printer,'LPT1:');
    rewrite(Printer);
    writeln(Printer,'This output appears on the printer.');
end.
```

2. Save the program TEXTPNT and run the program.

```
    This output appears on the printer.
```

This provides an alternate way to produce program output on the printer.

3. Turn to Module 52, Reset, to continue the learning sequence.

Module 54
RUN MENU

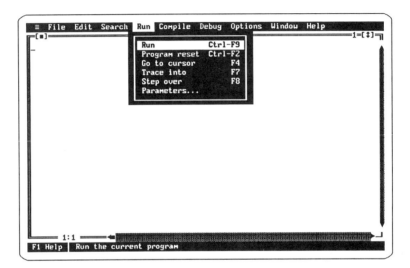

DESCRIPTION

The Run menu allows you to execute and debug programs from within the Turbo Pascal integrated environment. The Run command compiles and executes the program currently loaded in the Editor. The remaining commands control the operation of the integrated debugger.

The Program reset command allows you to restart a program that you are debugging.

The Go to cursor command is like a dynamic breakpoint; you place the cursor on the program line that interests you, then execute the command from the menu or by pressing F4. The program executes until it reaches the line in question, then pauses for your action.

The Trace into and Step over commands select whether the debugger will trace only statements in the main program, or also trace procedures and functions that you call. Trace into traces into the procedures and functions. Although Step over executes procedures and functions, it does not "trace" through them one statement at a time.

The Parameters option displays a dialog box that allows you to specify command-line parameters to be passed to your program, corresponding to the parameters a user would type on the command line when executing the program.

APPLICATIONS

The Program reset command is excellent for use when you want to watch a piece of code execute a second time. Program reset allows you to restart the program without having to recompile the source statements.

The Go to cursor command allows you to skip over tight loops in your code to get immediately to the next point of interest. Sometimes, it is easier to move the cursor, then execute the Go to cursor command than it is to establish permanent breakpoints in the program. The Go to cursor command is also helpful in identifying program code that never executes. If you "know" that a particular piece of program code is responsible for a particular computation or a particular output, place the cursor there and press F4. Many times you will discover that the program never reaches the code in question and that your error is elsewhere.

The Trace into command is used when you are unsure of the interactions between the program you are tracing and the procedures it calls. The Trace into command is probably the most useful from the debugger.

The Step over command is used to step over procedure and function calls, allowing you to skip the execution of a procedure or function that you have previously proven correct.

Normally, the Turbo Pascal debugger automatically switches between the screens when input or output operations occur. However, output operations typically happen more rapidly than you can readily observe in real time. Press Alt-F5 to toggle between the output screen and the Edit/Watch screen at any time.

TYPICAL OPERATION

Continue this activity directly from the typical operation in Module 16, Debug Menu, where you established watch expressions and placed a breakpoint in the source statements.

1. Press **Alt-R** to drop down the Run menu. Type **T** to activate the Trace into command. Press **Alt-W** and type **A** to cascade the windows so that both are visible on the screen.

   Turbo Pascal compiles the program and highlights the word "begin" at the start of the program. Notice that the debugger skipped the *program* statement and the *var* statement.

```
 ≡  File  Edit  Search  Run  Compile  Debug  Options  Window  Help
┌──────────────────────────── ASSIGN.PAS ─────────────────────────1─┐
│program Assign;                                                     │
│uses Crt;                                                           │
│var x, y, z: real;                                                  │
│    i, j, k: integer;                                               │
│    s, t, r: string[255];                                           │
│    b      : boolean;                                               │
│                                                                    │
│begin                                                               │
│─   ClrScr;                                                         │
│    i := 2 + 3;                                                     │
│    j := 27350 - 21845;                                             │
│    k := i * 2 + 1;                                                 │
│    x := 2 / 3;                                                     │
│    y := 3.14159 * 5 * 5;                                           │
│    z := x + y;                                                     │
├─[■]═════════════════════════ Watches ══════════════════2═[↑]═┐    │
│    j: 5505                                                    │    │
│    k: 11                                                      ▓    │
│    z: 79.206416667                                           ▒    │
│    r: ''                                                      ▪    │
└──────────────────────────────────────────────────────────────────┘
  F1 Help  F7 Trace  F8 Step  ↵ Edit  Ins Add  Del Delete  F10 Menu
```

2. Press **F8** to advance one line. The highlight bar rests on the ClrScr statement. The highlighted statement is the statement that is about to be executed.

3. Press **F8** to execute the ClrScr statement and advance one line. Notice that your screen quickly switches to display the cleared screen, then returns to the integrated environment.

4. Press **F8**, executing the statement I := 2 + 3. The highlight rests on the line J := 27350 − 21845. Notice the value of "J" in the Watch window at the bottom of the screen.

5. Press **F8**, executing the statement. Notice that the value of J changes to 5505 from its previously undefined state.

```
 ≡  File  Edit  Search  Run  Compile  Debug  Options  Window  Help
┌──────────────────────────── ASSIGN.PAS ─────────────────────────1─┐
│program Assign;                                                     │
│uses Crt;                                                           │
│var x, y, z: real;                                                  │
│    i, j, k: integer;                                               │
│    s, t, r: string[255];                                           │
│    b      : boolean;                                               │
│                                                                    │
│begin                                                               │
│─   ClrScr;                                                         │
│    i := 2 + 3;                                                     │
│    j := 27350 - 21845;                                             │
│    k := i * 2 + 1;                                                 │
│    x := 2 / 3;                                                     │
│    y := 3.14159 * 5 * 5;                                           │
│    z := x + y;                                                     │
├─[■]═════════════════════════ Watches ══════════════════2═[↑]═┐    │
│    j: 5505                                                    │    │
│    k: 11                                                      ▓    │
│    z: 79.206416667                                           ▒    │
│    r: ''                                                      ▪    │
└──────────────────────────────────────────────────────────────────┘
  F1 Help  F7 Trace  F8 Step  ↵ Edit  Ins Add  Del Delete  F10 Menu
```

6. Press **Ctrl-F9**, activating the Run command. Notice that the highlight bar stops at your breakpoint, the statement r := s + t. Notice also that the values of K and Z now reflect the results of the execution of their respective assignment statements.

7. Press **F8** to execute the statement r := s + t. Notice that the values of s and t are concatenated to form the value of r.

8. Press **Down Arrow** until the cursor is under the writeln statement that displays the value of K. Then press **F4** to advance the execution of the program to the cursor location.

9. Press **Alt-F5** to switch to the output screen. (This is the same as selecting User screen from the Run menu.)

```
The value of I is: 5
The value of J is: 5505
```

Notice that the output screen contains the results of the first two *writeln* statements.

10. Press **Alt-F5** to return to the integrated environment.

11. Press **Ctrl-F9** to continue running the program.

```
The value of I is: 5
The value of J is: 5505
The value of K is: 11
The value of X is:  6.6666666667E-01
The value of Y is:  7.8539750000E+01
The value of Z is:  7.9206416667E+01
The value of R is: The cow jumped over the moon.
The value of B is: TRUE
```

The program stops at the *readln* statement, waiting for you to press Enter.

12. Press **Enter** to return to the integrated environment.

```
 ≡  File  Edit  Search  Run  Compile  Debug  Options  Window  Help
[■]════════════════════════ ASSIGN.PAS ═══════════════════════1=[↑]┐
   i := 2 + 3;
   j := 27350 - 21845;
   k := i × 2 + 1;
   x := 2 / 3;
   y := 3.14159 × 5 × 5;
   z := x + y;
   s := 'The cow jumped';
   t := ' over the moon.';
   r := s + t;
   b := true;
   writeln('The value of I is: ',i);
   writeln('The value of J is: ',j);
   writeln('The value of K is: ',k);
   writeln('The value of X is: ',x);
═ 22:1 ═══════◄▓▓▓▓▓▓▓▓▓▓▓▓▓▓▓▓▓▓▓▓▓▓▓▓▓▓▓▓▓▓▓▓▓▓▓▓▓▓▓▓▓▓▓▓▓▶┘
════════════════════════════ Watches ═════════════════════════2─
   j: 5505
   k: 11
   z: 79.206416667
   r: 'The cow jumped over the moon.'

 F1 Help  F2 Save  F3 Open  Alt-F9 Compile  F9 Make  F10 Menu
```

13. Turn to Module 76, Window Menu, to continue the learning sequence.

Module 55
SEARCH MENU

DESCRIPTION

The Search menu provides the key to locating specific portions of your program in the Editor and for performing text replacements. When you press Alt-S the Search menu appears. The available options include:

FIND   In a long program it is convenient to be able to jump immediately to a specific spot. The Editor Find command allows you to find any sequence of characters. You activate the Find dialog box either by selecting Find from the Search menu, or by pressing Ctrl-Q-F. The following dialog box is displayed.

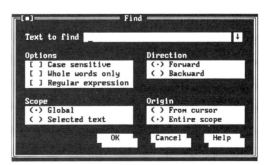

The Text to find field is where you type what you are looking for. Options affecting the way the search is conducted are selected either with the mouse or with the keyboard. With the mouse, point to the desired option and click the left mouse button to change its setting. With the keyboard, use the Tab key to move between option groups, and the Up Arrow and Down Arrow to move between options in a particular group. Change the setting of the desired option by pressing the Spacebar.

REPLACE   Sometimes you want to change a number of occurrences of one text pattern to another. You may want to rename a constant or variable. You may want to change all references to the text string "Hit Return" to "Press Return," a less destructive way of interacting with the keyboard. The Editor provides a Replace command to perform these activities. You may find and replace strings of characters up to 30 characters long. The string to find and the string to replace with do not have to be the same length.

Activate the Replace dialog box either by selecting Replace from the Search menu, or by pressing Ctrl-Q-A on the keyboard.

The Replace dialog box is similar to the Search dialog box with the addition of a field to hold the replacement text.

SEARCH AGAIN   This option repeats the most recent Find operation.

GO TO LINE NUMBER   Jumps to the specified line number in the Editor workspace.

FIND PROCEDURE   Locates a specific procedure.

FIND ERROR   Locates an error based on its hexadecimal memory address.

APPLICATIONS

Find, Replace, and Search again are similar in function to the corresponding functions in any word processor or editor. The Go to line number option is especially useful when locating errors found by the command-line version of the Turbo Pascal compiler. Compiler errors are reported by the command-line compiler in terms of line number. The Go to line number option allows you to quickly locate such errors. The Find procedure option is useful for locating the text of a Pascal procedure. While the name of a procedure frequently appears throughout a program, searching for the procedure definition can be tedious. This option understands the syntax of Pascal and only identifies procedures by name. The Find error option is useful for locating run-time errors, which are reported by the system in terms of a hexadecimal address representing a segmented memory address. Even if you don't understand memory addressing, transcribing the address displayed in the error message into the Find error dialog box allows you to find the offending statement in the program text.

TYPICAL OPERATION

This activity follows directly from the activity begun in Module 21, Edit Menu.

First, change all occurrences of "simple" to "hard." This requires the use of the find-and-replace procedure.

1. Press **Ctrl-Q-A** to begin the find-and-replace procedure.

2. Type **simple** as the Text to find, press **Tab**, then type **Hard** as the New text and press **Enter**.

3. Press **Tab** to move the cursor to the Options block. Press **Down Arrow** until "Prompt on replace" is highlighted. Press **Spacebar** to deselect the option.

4. Press **Tab** until "Change all" is highlighted. Press **Enter** to perform the replacements.

5. Press **F2** to display the Save File As dialog box.

6. Type **HARD** as the program name and press **Enter**.

7. Press **Alt-R** to access the Run menu, and press **Enter** to run the program.

8. Press **Enter** to return to the integrated environment.

9. Turn to Module 23, File Menu, to continue the learning sequence.

Module 56
SEEK

DESCRIPTION

Sequential files are ideal for storage of data that is always processed in a specific order, or for small quantities of data that remain in computer memory for manipulation. However, when information is needed from the middle of a large file, the sequential-access file operations take too long. Therefore, a fast mechanism is required to locate any specific record in a file.

seek(*recnum*)   *Recnum* is a *longint* value greater than or equal to 0 specifying the position in the file to place the file pointer. (A long integer can represent values as large as 2,147,483,647.)

Seek cannot be used on *text* files.

APPLICATIONS

To locate a specific record in a file, you could *reset* the file pointer to the beginning of the file. (The first record in the file is record number zero.) Next you could perform enough *readln* operations to advance the file window to the desired location. This procedure is quite cumbersome. Fortunately, Turbo Pascal provides the *seek* procedure to place the file pointer at any arbitrary point within the file.

CREATING A FILE OF RECORD   Typically, the most useful base type for a random-access file is *record*, but applications exist for files of integer types, real types, and Boolean.

One application for a random-access file is in a computerized order-taking system. When a customer calls the company to place an order, the person taking the order can type the catalog number of the product on the keyboard, and the computer responds with the number of units on hand. The salesperson can then tell the customer whether or not a sufficient quantity of goods is on hand to fill the order. This problem could be solved with a sequential file, but it might require a linear search of thousands of records to find the product.

A number of strategies exist for using random-access files to make this process more efficient. You have already used a binary-search strategy to search an array. If you know the number of records in a random access file, you can also use a binary search to search a file.

A more primitive method is to let the stock number of the product be the record number in the file. While this method has a number of limitations in practice, it makes a good place to begin an exploration of random-access files.

TYPICAL OPERATION

In this session you create a random-access file of inventory records.

First, create a datafile to serve as the database for the inventory system.

The datafile might look like this:

```
STOCK #  DESCRIPTION      QUANTITY PRICE
      1 | Aluminum Canoe |     3 | 472.50 |
      2 | Backpack Stove |    24 |  37.25 |
      3 | Fishing Rod    |    18 |  12.95 |
      4 | Backpack       |    22 |  77.69 |
      5 | Nylon Tent     |     8 | 168.99 |
      6 | Cook Kit       |    12 |  23.79 |
      7 | Dining Fly     |     8 |  39.95 |
      8 | Pliers         |    22 |   3.95 |
      9 | Sleeping Bag   |    14 |  56.00 |
     10 | Foam Pad       |    10 |   9.95 |
```

The use of the word "record" is confusing in Pascal. This program has two kinds of records.

Each line item in the inventory is called a record. Because the strategy of this program uses the stock number as the record number, you do not need to store the stock number as an entry in the record—it is implied from the position of the record within the file.

The data structure used for the file variable is also a record. A record data structure is designed to associate data of different types. In this program, the description is represented as string[16], the quantity as an integer, and the price as a real. A weak programming method is to define three files: a file of string[16], a file of integer, and a file of real. You have already had experience creating user-defined ordinal type variables. The record is a user-defined structured variable.

1. If you are continuing your work session from a previous module, clear the Editor workspace. Otherwise, start Turbo Pascal.

2. Start the Editor and type the following program:

```
program Create;
uses Crt;
type Item = record
               Description:string[16];
               Quantity:integer;
               Price:real
            end;
var Stock:file of Item;
```

```
        Current:item;
        Count:longint;

    begin
        assign(Stock,'STOCK.DAT');
        rewrite(Stock);
        seek(Stock,1);
        for Count:=1 to 10 do
        begin
            ClrScr;
            writeln('Item number ',Count,':');
            write('Enter the DESCRIPTION: ');
            readln(Current.Description);
            write('Enter the QUANTITY: ');
            readln(Current.Quantity);
            write('Enter the PRICE: ');
            readln(Current.Price);
            write(Stock,Current);
        end;
        close(Stock);
    end.
```

A fully developed inventory program would have an open-ended input routine to add stock to the inventory file. However, for this illustration, a *for* loop gets information about ten items and writes it in the file.

You have used the *writeln* statement to write text to a file. When the information is not text, the *write* statement is used. Turbo Pascal enforces strict type checking when writing to a file. Therefore, the only type variable you can write to the file Stock is an Item variable.

The *rewrite* statement positions the file window at position 0. Since a stock number of 0 is unusual, waste a file location and use a seek statement to advance the file window to location 1.

The variable Current is an Item-type variable. There is more than one way to refer to the values in Current. When referring to the individual fields, or parts, of the variable, you use a period to separate the record name from the field name. You write assignment statements as follows:

```
        Current.Description:='Reflector Oven';
        Current.Quantity:=75;
        Current.Price:=69.95;
```

Once each set of data has been defined, it is written to the file with the *write* statement.

You refer to all the fields of a record variable at once by using only the name of the record variable. You do not include the names of the individual fields. The statement

```
    write(Stock,Current)
```

writes all the information in the record to the disk file.

The *write* statement advances the file pointer each time it is used, making it unnecessary to use *seek* to position the file at each successive record.

3. Save the program as CREATE then run the program.

4. Enter the data for the database.

STOCK #	DESCRIPTION	QUANTITY	PRICE
1	Aluminum Canoe	3	472.50
2	Backpack Stove	24	37.25
3	Fishing Rod	18	12.95
4	Backpack	22	77.69
5	Nylon Tent	8	168.99
6	Cook Kit	12	23.79
7	Dining Fly	8	39.95
8	Pliers	22	3.95
9	Sleeping Bag	14	56.00
10	Foam Pad	10	9.95

Now that the file is created, write the Pascal program statements necessary to access it in a random-access manner.

NOTE
Because this file is not a text file, you cannot examine it with the Turbo Pascal Editor.

Even though the file was created sequentially, because it is a file of record instead of a text file it can be accessed in any order.

5. Clear the Editor workspace and type the following program:

```
program Inventory;
uses Crt;
type Item = record
                Description:string[16];
                Quantity:integer;
                Price:real;
            end;

var Stock:file of Item;
    Current:Item;
    Choice:Longint;

begin
    ClrScr;
    assign(Stock,'STOCK.DAT');
    reset(Stock);
    Choice:=1;          {Initialize the reference variable.}
    while Choice in [1..10] do
    begin
```

```
            write('Enter the stock number: ');
            readln(Choice);
            if Choice in [1..10] then
            begin
                seek(Stock,Choice);
                read(Stock,Current);
                with Current do
                    writeln(Description:16,Quantity:5,Price:8:2);
            end;
        end;
    end.
```

The *reset* statement is used to open the file because the file already exists.

The main loop of the program consists of asking the user for a stock number, accessing the file, and displaying the information about the item. Terminate the program with a request for a record out of the range of the file.

The use of the full name for the fields of a record variable is often cumbersome. The Pascal *with* statement allows you to shorten the variable names. Use a *with* statement to specify the name a record variable, then any references to a field name are assumed to refer to the *with* record variable name. When the *with* statement refers to several statements, you may enclose the statements in a *begin/end* group.

6. Save the program as INVENT then run the program.

```
    Enter the stock number: _
```

7. Type **0** and press **Enter**.

```
    Enter the stock number: 0
    Nylon Tent          8    160.99
    Enter the stock number: _
```

8. Type **2** and press **Enter**.

```
    Enter the stock number: 0
    Nylon Tent          8    160.99
    Enter the stock number: 2
    Backpack Stove    24      37.25
```

9. Experiment with additional stock numbers. Verify that the program works as expected.

10. Type **0** and press **Enter** to end the program.

This example was purposely kept primitive to illustrate the fundamental concept of accessing a random-access file. A program written for actual use would need many additional statements to arrange the information in a pleasing fashion on the screen, make the program easy to use, and protect itself against a wide variety of errors.

11. Turn to Module 25, FileSize, to continue the learning sequence.

Module 57
SET

DESCRIPTION

Pascal provides a built-in data structure called the *set* that has much in common with sets in mathematics. In mathematics, a set is a collection of objects or elements. Examples are the set of natural numbers less than six, the set of vowels, and the set of consonants. The general concept of a set is largely unrestricted. You could talk about the set of things in your pocket. This set might include a comb, a quarter, a nickel, a pocketknife, a paperclip, and a piece of gum. In the first three examples, all of the members of the set are of the same type: a set of numbers or a set of letters. The elements in the set of things in your pocket have little in common except for being in your pocket.

To declare a set data type:

```
type settype = set of basetype;
```

To declare a set type within a *var* statement:

```
var varname : set of basetype
```

settype   Is a new set data type containing elements of *basetype*.

basetype   Specifies a simple type. It can be integer, byte, real, char, Boolean, or a user-defined enumerated type.

varname   Specifies the name of a new set variable comprised of elements of *basetype*.

SET DEFINITION   Pascal places a restriction on membership in a set that requires all the members of a set to be drawn from the same base type. This base type must be a scalar or subrange type. For example,

```
Type Digit: Set of 0..9;
```

creates a set of the numeric digits. The declaration

```
Type Vowel = Set of ('A','a','E','e','I','i','O','o','U','u');
```

creates a set containing the vowels, both uppercase and lowercase.

Sets do not have to be based on predefined types. They can also be defined on user-defined base types. For example,

```
Type Color=(Red,Blue,Green,Cyan,Magenta,Yellow);

var Primary, Addcolor, Subcolor: Set of Color;

begin
    Primary:=[Red,Blue,Green,Cyan,Magenta,Yellow];
    Addcolor:=[Red,Blue,Green];
    Subcolor:=[Cyan,Magenta,Yellow];
```

defines a base type of COLOR that contains six primary colors. Two sets are defined for the additive and subtractive primary colors.

SET OPERATIONS   Sets that have the same base are manipulated with the set operators

```
+  Union
-  Difference
*  Intersection
```

Using the specifications above, some available operations are:

```
[Red,Blue] + [Cyan] is [Red,Blue,Cyan]
Addcolor - [Blue] is [Red,Green]
[Red,Blue,Cyan] * Subcolor is [Cyan]
```

SET COMPARISONS   Sets can be compared in Boolean expressions. The available operators are:

```
=  Equals
<> Not equals
IN Membership
>= Is a superset of
<= Is a subset of
```

For example,

```
[Red,Green] = [Green,Red] is True
[Red,Green] <> [Cyan] is True
[Red,Green] = [Red] is False
```

For two sets to be equal, they must have exactly the same elements. The elements in a set are not ordered.

```
(Red in Primary) = True
```

because the element RED is a member of the set Primary.

```
(Subcolor <= Primary) = True
```

because every member of Subcolor is a member of Primary.

```
(Primary = Addcolor) = True
```

because the set Primary contains all the elements in set Addcolor.

```
(Primary  = Primary) = True
(Primary >= Primary) = True
(Primary <= Primary) = True
```

because every set is equal to itself, is a superset of itself, and is a subset of itself. Also remember that the empty set, [ ], is a subset of every set.

SET LIMITATIONS   Turbo Pascal imposes several limitations on sets. These limitations are specific to the Turbo Pascal Compiler, which vary with limitations imposed by other Pascal Compilers.

- The maximum number of elements in a set is 256.
- A set based on an integer subrange has a lower bound of 0 and an upper bound of 256.

APPLICATIONS

The concept of set membership is a powerful and useful concept in developing programs. A single check to see if an element is a member of a set can replace multiple *if* comparisons resulting in code that is easier to write, easier to read, and more likely to be correct.

Remember that you can only compare and operate on sets of the same base type. If you define the following sets:

```
var ASCII : set of char;
    Digit : set of 0..9;
    Le100 : set of 0..100;
    Code  : set of 0..255;
```

the intersection of set Digit and Le100, Digit*Le100, is a valid operation because, although they are defined on different subranges, the base type of both subranges is integer.

The intersection of set Digit and ASCII, Digit*ASCII, is not a valid operation because the sets are defined on different base types.

A test of set membership, 100 *in* Digit, is valid (although false). It is false because 100 is outside the subrange 0 . . 9 defined for Digit, 100 is an integer, and the subrange 0 . . 9 is a subrange of the integers.

A test of set membership, 'A' *in* Digit, is not valid, because 'A' is not a *char*, which is the base type of ASCII.

TYPICAL OPERATION

Set notation provides a powerful way to express a number of ideas in Pascal. In this session you develop a program to count the number of vowels in a sentence typed at the keyboard. The program has three main parts:

- Input each character in a sentence.
- Test each character and increment a counter.
- Output the result.

The key code in this program is the test operation to determine whether a specific letter is a vowel. If the tested letter is stored in the variable CHECK, and the vowel counter is in COUNT, the following code could be used to implement the process:

```
If (Check = 'A') or (Check ='a') then Count:=Count+1
else if (Check = 'E') OR (Check = 'e') then Count:=Count+1
else if (Check = 'I') OR (Check = 'i') then Count:=Count+1
else if (Check = 'O') OR (Check = 'o') then Count:=Count+1
else if (Check = 'U') OR (Check = 'u') then Count:=Count+1;
```

Not only is this wordy, it lacks clarity. Using a set to define the vowels,

```
['A','a','E','e','I','i','O','o','U','l']
```

the entire comparison is reduced to a single *if* construct,

```
if Check in ['A','a','E','e','I','i','O','o','U','u']
    then Count:=Count+1;
```

Using set notation, the entire comparison is elegantly expressed as a single simple statement.

Making use of the *UpCase* function, the statement is expressed even more compactly as

```
if UpCase (Check) in ['A','E','I','O','U']
    then Count:=Count+1;
```

The first program development step is to develop a strategy for the program solution. The use of set operations is limited to ordinal variable types. You can make use of the fact that Turbo Pascal treats a string as an array of characters. A useful strategy is as follows:

- Input a sentence from the keyboard.
- Use a counter variable to keep track of the running total of the number of vowels.
- Use a *for* loop to travel the length of the string, examining each character in the string for potential set membership. Increment the vowel counter if the character is a member of the set.
- Display the number of vowels on the screen.

1. If you are continuing your work session, clear the Editor workspace. Otherwise, start Turbo Pascal.

2. Start the Editor and type the following program:

```
program Vowel;
uses Crt;
var Check : string[80];
    Count, Index:integer;

begin
    ClrScr;
    Count:=0;
    writeln('Enter a sentence.');
    readln(Check);
    for Index := 1 to Length(Check) do
        if UpCase(Check[Index]) in ['A','E','I','O','U']
            then Count:=Count+1;
    write('There are ',Count,' vowels in the sentence.');
    readln;
end.
```

3. Save the program as VOWEL and run the program.

4. Type **Every good boy does fine.** and press **Enter**.

```
Enter a sentence.
Every good boy does fine.
There are 9 vowels in the sentence.
```

5. Verify the correct operation of the program with additional test sentences.

6. Turn to Module 50, Record, to continue the learning sequence.

Module 58
SIMPLE DATA TYPES

DESCRIPTION

Turbo Pascal provides predefined simple data types including integers, real numbers, Boolean, and character data.

INTEGERS Integers are the positive whole numbers, negative whole numbers, and zero. Turbo Pascal provides five data types to represent integers.

Shortint   Whole numbers in the range of –128 . . 127. A *Shortint* occupies one byte of memory.

Integer   Whole numbers in the range –32768 . . 32767. An *Integer* occupies two bytes in memory.

Longint   Whole numbers in the range –2147483648 . . 2147483647. A *Longint* occupies four bytes of memory.

Byte   Whole numbers in the range 0 . . 255. A *Byte* occupies one byte in memory.

Word   Whole numbers in the range 0 . . 65535. A *Word* occupies two bytes of memory.

REALS Real numbers are used for expressing decimal values. Turbo Pascal supports five types of real numbers. If your computer is equipped with a math co-processor, Turbo Pascal uses it to increase the computation speed of all real data types except the basic *real* type.

Real   Decimal numbers that provide both positive and negative decimals in the range of 2.9×10^{-39} through 1.7×10^{38} and maintain 11 significant digits of accuracy. The standard *real* occupies six bytes in memory. It does not benefit from a math co-processor, even when one is available.

Single   Decimal numbers providing both positive and negative values in the range of 1.5×10^{-45} to 3.4×10^{38} and maintaining 7 or 8 digits of accuracy. The *Single* type is the smallest of the real number types, using only four bytes of memory.

Double   Decimal numbers providing both positive and negative values in the range of 5.0×10^{-325} to 1.7×10^{308} and maintaining 15 or 16 digits of accuracy. The *Double* type uses eight bytes of memory.

Extended   Decimal numbers providing both positive and negative values in the range of 1.9×10^{-4951} to 1.1×10^{4932} and maintaining 19 or 20 digits of accuracy. The *Extended* type uses ten bytes of memory.

Comp   Whole numbers in the range of $-2^{63}+1$ to $2^{63}-1$, which is about -9.2×10^{18} to 9.2×10^{18}. A *Comp* occupies eight bytes of memory. Although mathematically an integer, Turbo Pascal treats *Comp* data as a real number.

NON-NUMERIC TYPES

Boolean   A *Boolean* value can be either *True* or *False*. *True* and *False* are defined so that *False* <*True*. *Boolean* data occupies one byte in memory.

Char   One character in the ASCII character set. *Character* data occupies one byte in memory.

APPLICATIONS

INTEGERS   One of the built-in data types of Pascal is the integer. Integers include the whole numbers—positive, negative, and zero. In mathematics the set of integers consists of $\{\ldots, -3, -2, -1, 0, 1, 2, 3, \ldots\}$.

The internal representation of integers in the computer's memory provides both benefits and limitations. Integer arithmetic is very fast. The computer can manipulate whole numbers much faster than it can decimals. Integers are also precise. Unlike real numbers, which approximate values with floating point representation (the computer's answer to logarithms), integer values are stored as exact representations. These benefits come at a price. The set of integers in Pascal does not extend infinitely in both directions.

Range of Integers   Turbo Pascal allows you to optimize the performance of your use of integers in terms of speed, size, and memory requirements. When you must store a large number of small values, use either the *Shortint* or *Byte* types to conserve memory. When performing arithmetic on numbers in the range $-32767 \ldots 32767$, use the standard *Integer* type for high speed calculations. (Integer arithmetic is faster than *Shortint* and *Byte* arithmetic.) When the magnitude of the values extends beyond 32767 but is still within the two billion mark, use the *Longint* type. If your application requires absolute accuracy in dealing with numbers larger than two billion, use the real *Comp* type instead, restricting your application to machines with a co-processor. The Comp type is excellent for writing financial applications where absolute precision is required. Treating all monetary values in terms of cents or mils provides the accuracy required by financial applications, and yet it does not limit you to the small ranges of magnitude available with the standard integer types.

Turbo Pascal provides a predefined constant, *Maxint*, equal to 32767, the largest value that can be represented by the *Integer* type.

Mixing Integers The Integer types are, in general, compatible with each other. The exception to absolute compatibility is when passing values to procedures and functions. In this case, the values should be of the same integer type.

REALS The internal representation of real numbers in the computer's memory also provides both benefits and limitations. Integers are limited in magnitude but provide absolute precision. Real numbers can be considerably larger and smaller, both in range and in magnitude. With real arithmetic 1 + 1 does not necessarily equal 2, it may equal 1.99999999999999999999 instead. This does not pose a problem for scientific and engineering computing, where significant digits and tolerances are part of the field. It does, however, limit the application of real numbers to the solution of financial problems, where all the pennies must add up, even when representing numbers as large as the national debt.

BOOLEANS Boolean data can have the value of either true or false. Turbo Pascal provides two predeclared identifiers, *True* and *False*, to make working with Boolean data easier. *Boolean* data is often used to control the action of the *if* statement in branching, and the *repeat* and *while* looping structures.

CHARS Character data is based on the ASCII character set. The data type *char* is useful when working with single characters.

Turn to Module 42, Numbers, to continue the learning sequence.

Module 59
SOUND and NOSOUND

DESCRIPTION

Turbo Pascal provides the facility to use the built-in speaker on the IBM PC and compatibles through two procedures located in the *Crt* unit.

Sound(I)*frequency*   *Frequency* is an integer representing cycles per second. This procedure turns on the PC's speaker and leaves it on. The sound continues while other instructions execute, after the program terminates, even after a return to DOS from Turbo Pascal.

Nosound   Turns off the PC's speaker.

APPLICATIONS

To make music requires some knowledge of the relationship between musical notes and frequency. In general, given the frequency of any note, the note a half-step above any note is found by multiplying the frequency of the note by the 12th root of 2. The standard tuning note in music is an "A" with a frequency of 440 cycles per second.

TYPICAL OPERATION

In this session you play a chromatic scale on the computer's speaker.

1. If you are continuing your work session, clear the Editor workspace. Otherwise, start Turbo Pascal.

2. Enter the Editor and type the following program:

```
program Music;
uses Crt;
var Pitch:real;
        i:integer;
begin
    Pitch:=220;
    for i:=1 to 12 do
    begin

        {Multiply pitch by the 12th root of 2 for the next note.}
        Pitch:=Pitch*exp(ln(2)/12);
        Sound(Trunc(Pitch));
```

```
        end;
        Nosound;
    end.
```

3. Save the program as MUSIC. (You need it in Module 17, Delay.)

4. Run the program.

The scale plays rapidly.

5. Turn to Module 17, Delay, to continue the learning sequence.

Module 60
STRING

DESCRIPTION

A string constant is a sequence of characters enclosed in single quotes.

```
'This is a string constant.'
```

To enclose a single quote or an apostrophe in a string, use two single quote characters together. This situation arises in words such as *isn't* and *don't*. For example, the expression

```
'If it isn''t broken, don''t fix it!'
```

is the proper expression of the string constant

```
If it isn't broken, don't fix it!
```

A one-character string containing only a single quote or apostrophe is written as a series of four single quotes:

```
''''
```

A string containing no characters at all is written as two single quotes with no space between them:

```
''
```

This is the shortest possible string, a string with a length of 0. It is referred to as the empty string or the null string. The maximum length of a string in Turbo Pascal is 255 characters.

In addition to manipulating strings as a unique data type, it is also possible to refer to the individual characters that comprise the string. You refer to individual characters using array notation. If S is a string, then S[1] is the first character in the string, S[2] is the second character, S[3] is the third, and so on.

CAUTION

When you refer to a string using array notation, Turbo Pascal does not protect you from yourself. In particular, you are allowed to refer to *any* character in the string, whether it has a meaningful value or not. If, for example, the string S has the value 'Hello,' then the value of S[10] is specifically undefined and contains random garbage from the computer's memory.

String data with a length of one is different than *char* data. The two may not be used interchangeably, although it is a simple matter to convert from one type to the other.

Turbo Pascal allows the concatenation of strings with the + sign. Concatenation means to connect or join together. For example, the string expression

```
'Remember ' + 'the ' + 'Alamo!'
```

evaluates as

```
'Remember the Alamo!'
```

APPLICATIONS

There are two ways of storing character information in Pascal. Only single characters may be stored as *char* data. English words are not often treated as single characters, but rather as groups of characters; words, phrases, and sentences are more natural. Groups of characters comprising words, sentences, or phrases are stored in a data type called *string*. Turbo Pascal provides the *string* data type to handle groups of characters. Unlike other data types, a string does not have a fixed length in memory. The length of a string can change during the execution of a program.

The digits 0 through 9 are also characters. When you have a number in your program that is not manipulated mathematically, it is usually better to define it as a string instead of an integer or a real number. Examples include Zip codes, telephone numbers, and Social Security numbers.

TYPICAL OPERATION

In this session, use the *Writeln* command to display strings on the screen illustrating the features of string definition and concatenation.

1. If you are continuing from a previous module, press **Alt-F** and type **N** to clear the Editor workspace; otherwise, type **TURBO** from the DOS prompt to start Turbo Pascal.

2. Press **Alt-E** to enter the Editor and type the following program.

```
program Strings;
uses Crt;
begin
    ClrScr;
    writeln('Remember ' + 'the ' + 'Alamo!');
    writeln('');
    writeln('Don''t cry over spilled milk.');
    readln;
end.
```

3. Press **Alt-F** to drop down the File menu and type **S** for save. Type **STRINGS** as the program name and press **Enter**.

4. Press **Alt-R** and **Enter** to run the program.

```
Remember the Alamo!

Don't cry over spilled milk.


```

The computer performs the concatenation of the three strings making up the first line of the output and displays them on the screen. The blank line between the two output lines is from displaying the empty string. The third line shows the effect of typing two single quote characters in the middle of a literal string.

5. Press **Enter** to return to the integrated Turbo Pascal environment.

6. Turn to Module 40, Naming, to continue the learning sequence.

Module 61
STRING FUNCTIONS

DESCRIPTION

Turbo Pascal provides several functions for use in manipulating text. The functions are designed for use with string data, but simple assignment allows character data to become string data. As a result, these functions are also useful for work with character data.

The following string functions return string values:

Concat(*S1,S2, . . . ,Sn*)   Any number of strings *S1*, *S2*, *S3*, etc. specified when calling this function. The string returned is the concatenation of the strings *S1 . . Sn*.

Copy(*Source,Index,Size*)   *Source* is a string. *Index* and *Size* are integers. The function returns *Size* characters from *Source* starting with character *Index*. If *Size* is too large, the function does nothing.

The following functions return a value of integer:

Length(*Source*)   *Source* is a string. Returns the number of characters in the string.

pos(*Pattern,Source*)   *Source* and *Pattern* are strings. If *Pattern* appears within *Source*, the function returns the position of the first character of the match. If no match is found, the function returns zero.

For example, the statements

```
First:='A rolling stone';
Middle:=' gathers';
Last:=' no moss.';
```

assign string values to First, Middle, and Last.

The statement

```
Sentence:=concat(First,Middle,Last);
```

assigns the value "A rolling stone gathers no moss." to the variable Sentence. The concat function lets you concatenate as many strings as you like, placing them end to end to form one long string. You are responsibe for making sure you have defined the target string (in this case Sentence) long enough to hold the result of the concatenation. If you do not, you may get a "value range error." Normally, when working with Turbo Pascal, the + operator is used for string concatenation—unless compatibility with other Pascal systems is required.

Using the variable definitions above, the statement

```
Phrase:=copy(Sentence,3,7);
```

assigns the value "rolling" to the string variable Phrase. The function begins the copy operation with the third character and copies a total of seven characters.

For example, if

```
Sentence=''A rolling stone gathers no moss.''
```

the statement

```
HowLong:= length(Sentence);
```

assigns the value 32 to the integer variable HowLong. Characters, spaces, and punctuation all count in figuring the length of the string.

If Pattern="the," the statement

```
Start:= pos(Pattern,Sentence)
```

assigns the value 19 to the integer variable Start because the pattern "the" is found starting with the 19th character in the string variable Sentence.

APPLICATIONS

String functions are fundamental to manipulating text. For example, in a program to print mailing labels, you may have a variable called Name, containing a person's last name, followed by a comma, a space, and the first name. You want to print the name on the label as the first name, a space, and then the last name.

Assume the variable Name contains the value "Buhalog, Diane"

```
Name:='Buhalog, Diane';
```

The comma is the key to separating the first name from the last name — not the space. The *pos* function allows you to determine the position of the comma in the string.

```
CommaPosition:=pos(',',Name);
```

In the example, 8 is assigned to CommaPosition. The next step is to extract the first and last names. You can extract the last name with the *copy* function:

```
LastName:=copy(Name,1,CommaPosition-1);
```

This statement begins the copy operation with the first character position in Name, and continues for CommaPosition–1, or seven characters. The value 'Buhalog' is assigned to LastName. You can extract the first name with another call to the *copy* function.

```
FirstName:=copy(Name,CommaPosition+2,Length(Name)-CommaPosition+2)
```

With this statement, you use the *length* function to compute the number of characters to copy.

The *concat* function (or the + operator) is used to put the name back together again for printing.

```
FullName:=concat(FirstName,' ',LastName);
```

The value of FullName can be printed on the label.

TYPICAL OPERATION

In this session you write a complete program to reverse the order of a person's name in the format of lastname, comma, firstname.

1. Start Turbo Pascal, or clear the Editor workspace and continue with your work session.

2. Start the Editor and type the following program:

```
program StrFunc;
uses Crt;
var Name, Lastname, Firstname, Fullname : String[80];
    CommaPosition : integer;

begin
    ClrScr;
    write('Enter a name in the form Lastname, Firstname: ');
    readln(Name);
    CommaPosition:=pos(',',Name);
    LastName:=copy(Name,1,CommaPosition-1);
    FirstName:=copy(Name,CommaPosition+2,Length(Name)-CommaPosition+2);
    Fullname:=concat(FirstName,' ',Lastname);
    writeln('The name is:',FullName);
    readln;
end.
```

3. Save the program as STRFUNC then run the program.

```
Enter a name in the form Lastname, Firstname:
```

4. Type **Van de Bogart, Tom** and press **Enter**.

```
Enter a name in the form Lastname, Firstname: Van de Bogart, Tom
The name is: Tom Van de Bogart
```

Notice that keying on the space in Van de Bogart would produce flawed output.

5. Press **Enter** to return to the Turbo Pascal system.

6. Continue the learning sequence with Module 62, String Procedures.

Module 62
STRING PROCEDURES

DESCRIPTION

String procedures provide additional ways of manipulating string information. String procedures are different from string functions in that the result of the procedure is returned as one of the parameters of the procedure. Unlike a string function, the name of a string procedure is never used as a term of a string expression. The procedures provided allow insertion into strings, deletion from strings, and conversion between string data and numeric data types. The format of the string procedures is as follows:

```
Insert(source, destination, index)
```

source	A string specifying the string to insert.
destination	The string where the insertion takes place.
index	An integer representing the character position in *destination* where the insertion begins.

```
Delete(destination, index, size)
```

destination	The string where the deletion takes place.
index	An integer representing the character position in *destination* where the deletion begins.
size	An integer specifying the number of characters to delete from the string.

```
Val(StringValue, NumericVariable, ErrorCode)
```

StringValue	A string literal, or a string variable, or a string expression. It may contain neither leading nor trailing spaces.
NumericVariable	A real variable or an integer variable. The value of *StringValue* is converted to a number, and the result is placed in *Numeric Variable*.

ErrorCode   An integer variable. If there are no errors in the conversion process, the value of *ErrorCode* is 0. If there is an error, *ErrorCode* contains the position of the error within *StringValue*. If *ErrorCode* is not zero, the value of *NumericVariable* is undefined.

```
Str(NumericValue,StringVariable);
```

NumericValue   A numeric literal, numeric variable, or numeric expression. It can be either real or integer.

StringVariable   A string variable.

You can use the same field width specifiers on *NumericValue* that you use for specifying the format of numeric output in the *write* statement.

The *insert* procedure allows you to insert a substring into a target string. The string *source* is inserted in string *destination* starting at position *index*. For example,

```
S:=' green';
D:='The moon is made of cheese.';
Insert(S,D,20);
write(D);
```

produces as output

```
The moon is made of green cheese.
```

Look carefully at the definition of string S. Notice the definition includes a space character before the "g" in "green." This is the space that is placed between "of" and "green." The space between "green" and "cheese" is the same space that previously preceded "cheese." The *insert* procedure treats a space exactly like any other character. The *delete* procedure removes a substring from another string. The removed string may be located anywhere within the target string. The delete operation begins at position *index* of the string *destination*. *Size* is the number of characters removed from *destination*. The resulting string is *size* characters less than it was originally. For example, the program segment

```
D:='The pink elephant ate cheese for lunch.';
Delete(D,22,11);
write(D);
```

produces the output

```
The pink elephant ate lunch.
```

After all, everyone knows that pink elephants don't eat cheese.

CAUTION

If you specify an impossible delete operation, particularly if *index* + *size* is greater than the length of the target string variable, the *delete* procedure does nothing at all.

APPLICATIONS

Many programmers accept all input from the keyboard as *char* or *string* variables, then convert the strings to numbers for assignment to numeric variables with the *Val* procedure. By accepting all input as characters and strings, there is no possibility that a user can provide invalid input and generate a type-mismatch I/O error.

For example,

```
program Valdemo;

var S:string[20];
    N:real;
    E:integer;
begin
    S:='123.45';
    Val(S,N,E);
    Write(N:7:2);
end.
```

When run, the program produces the number 123.45 as output.

The Turbo Pascal procedure *Str* is the inverse of *Val. Str* converts a numeric value into a string value.

```
program Strdemo;

var S:string[20];
    N:integer;
begin
    N:=1492;
    Str(N,S);
    write(S);
end.
```

When run, the program produces the string "1492" as output. If you change the *Str* procedure call to read:

```
Str(N:7,S);
```

when run, the program produces the string "1492" as output, providing three leading spaces in the string.

TYPICAL OPERATION

Use the *insert* and *delete* procedures to manipulate the example strings.

1. Start Turbo Pascal, or clear the Editor workspace and continue your work session.

2. Type the following program:

```
program StrProc;
uses Crt;
var S,D:string[80];

begin
    ClrScr;
    S:=' green';
    D:='The moon is made of cheese.';
    Insert(S,D,20);

    writeln(D);
    D:='The pink elephant ate cheese for lunch.';
    Delete(D,22,11);
    writeln(D);
    readln;
end.
```

3. Save the program as STRPROC then run the program.

```
The moon is made of green cheese.
The pink elephant ate lunch.
```

The operations behave as expected.

4. Press **Enter** to return to the integrated environment.

5. Turn to Module 32, If, to continue the learning sequence.

Module 63
SYSTEM MENU

DESCRIPTION

The System menu is located at the far left of the integrated environment's menu bar. It appears as three short horizontal lines. You activate the System menu by clicking the icon with the mouse, pressing Alt-Spacebar, or by pressing F10 and then pressing Enter.

There are three items on the System menu: About, Refresh display, and Clear desktop. The About selection displays the version of Turbo Pascal and the copyright notice. The Refresh display command repaints the contents of the screen. The Clear desktop command closes all the windows that are open on the screen.

APPLICATIONS

When moving from one computer system to another, use the About option on the System menu to verify the revision level of the compiler. Software developers often maintain older versions of compilers for performing maintenance on established software. In such cases it is useful to be able to verify from within the system which level of the compiler you are currently working with.

It is possible that a Turbo Pascal program may go astray and corrupt the display. When running Turbo Pascal under a multitasking DOS extender (such as Desqview or Windows) other programs may corrupt the Turbo Pascal display. In such cases, the Refresh display command may help to restore your system.

The Clear desktop command closes all the windows that are open on the desktop at once. This is often easier than closing the windows one at a time.

TYPICAL OPERATION

In this session you use the System menu commands.

1. Start Turbo Pascal.

2. Press **Alt-Spacebar** or click on the System menu icon with the mouse.

3. Type **A** to choose the About command. The dialog box appears as follows.

4. Press **Enter** to close the dialog box.

5. Press **F1** to display the Turbo Pascal help system.

6. Press **Alt-Spacebar** to display the System menu, then type **C** to select the Clear desktop command.

7. Notice that both the help system and the edit window disappear from the integrated environment desktop.

8. Turn to Module 21, Edit Menu, to continue the learning sequence.

Module 64
TEXT

DESCRIPTION

All input and output operations in Turbo Pascal are performed with files. Many programs use only the predefined files *input* and *output*; however, most applications making use of disks for data storage must define additional files. All operations are performed with the file variable, defined in a *var* statement. Turbo Pascal allows you to create files of any type, except a file of files, but only predefines one file type, *text*. To define a filetype of *text* use the statement

```
type filetype = text;
```

where *filetype* follows the Pascal rules for naming.

To declare a text file variable use the statement

```
var filevar : text;
```

where *filevar* follows the Pascal rules for naming. It does not have to follow the DOS rules for filenames.

TEXT FILE BUFFERS   By default, text files are defined with a file buffer size of 128 bytes. This means that Turbo Pascal works with the information 128 bytes at a time. This buffer size is adequate for most applications; however, disk-intensive programs, such as a database program, may benefit from a larger file buffer. You specify the size of the buffer with the *SetTextBuf* procedure. The format for the procedure is

```
SetTextBuf (filename,buffer,size)
```

filename	is the name of the text file. You must not use the *SetTextBuf* procedure on an open file.
buffer	is the name of the buffer. It makes sense to declare the buffer as an *array* of *char*.
size	is a word specifying the size of the buffer. This parameter is optional. If omitted, Turbo Pascal uses the *sizeof(buffer)* to determine the buffer size.

The following program fragment demonstrates the creation of a 1K (1024 byte) buffer:

```
var filename : text;    buffer   : array[1..1024] of char;
begin
    Assign (filename,'DISKFILE.TXT');
     SetTextBuf(filename,buffer);
    Reset(filename);
```

You can change the size of the text buffer by changing the size of the buffer array.

APPLICATIONS

Turbo Pascal provides the predefined filetype *text* for working with text files. Text files are different from other types of files in that they are not simply a collection of values of a particular type. Although a text file is composed of characters, it is organized into lines terminated by a carriage-return/line-feed sequence, and the End-of-File is marked by an end-of-file marker, which is Ctrl-Z. The lines of a text file are not necessarily the same length. In practice, they are seldom the same length. Text files can only be processed sequentially. In addition, input and output cannot be performed simultaneously to a text file.

TYPICAL OPERATION

In this session you define a text file that will be used for program output.

1. Open the Editor window and type the following program fragment.

```
program TextIO;
uses Crt;
var        S:string;
    Diskfile : text;
begin
    ClrScr;
    writeln(Diskfile,'This information is placed on the disk.');
    readln(Diskfile,S);
    writeln(S);
end.
```

2. Save the fragment as TEXTOUT.

NOTE

An *assign* statement, *reset* statement, and a *rewrite* statement are also required to run this program.

3. Turn to Module 24, File Of, to continue the learning sequence.

Module 65
TEXTBACKGROUND

DESCRIPTION

Each text character consists of a small box with both a text color and a background color. The background color is set with the *textbackground* procedure. The form of the procedure call is

```
textbackground(value);
```

value   is an integer expression in the range 0 .. 7.

The background colors are more limited than the text colors. Only the "dark" colors can be used as background colors. The following constants are defined by the *Crt* unit and are available for setting colors:

Code	Color
0 :	Black
1 :	Blue
2 :	Green
3 :	Cyan (sky-blue)
4 :	Red
5 :	Magenta
6 :	Brown
7 :	LightGray

The background color is set with procedure *textbackground*. The expressions

```
textbackground(5);
```

and

```
textbackground(Magenta);
```

both select magenta as the text background.

MONOCHROME DISPLAY NOTE

LightGray (color 7) as a background color shows up as white on the IBM Monochrome Display only when it is used with a text color of black. This creates reverse image characters. Black (color 0,8,16,24) as a foreground color shows up as black only when used with a background color of 0 (which makes the characters invisible) or 7 (which creates reverse image characters). Other combinations of foreground and background colors produce white-on-black results.

APPLICATIONS

Modification of the text background area gives increased control over the layout of screen displays. One effective technique is to use different color background areas for different areas of the screen or different types of displays. For example, you could use a blue background for displaying unrestricted information, and a red background for information the user should recognize as privileged. As with text foreground colors, it is easy to overdo the use of color. With too many colors on the screen, all the user sees is color, so that it obscures rather than highlights the information.

Many combinations of foreground and background colors are unreadable. Other combinations are ugly. When using color in a program, it is an excellent programming practice to allow the user the capability to change your choice of colors.

When changing color background, keep in mind that you do not change the background color of characters that are already on the screen. You only change the background color of characters that you write with the new background color. If you want to change the color of the entire screen to the new background color, use the *ClrScr* command to clear the screen. *ClrScr* sets the color of the entire screen to the current background color.

TYPICAL OPERATION

In this session you examine all possible combinations of text foreground and background colors.

1. If you are continuing your work session, clear the Editor workspace. Otherwise, start Turbo Pascal.

2. Start the Editor and type the following program:

```
program Combinations;
uses Crt;
var FColor, BColor : integer;

begin
    ClrScr;
    for BColor:= 0 to 7 do
    begin
        textbackground(BColor);
        ClrScr;
        For FColor:=0 to 15 do
        begin
            textcolor(FColor);
            writeln('This is color ',FColor,' on color ',BColor);
        end;
        write('Press Enter to continue.');
        readln;
    end;

end.
```

3. Save and run the program.

4. Press a key to see each set of screen colors.

5. Turn to Module 29, Gotoxy, to continue the learning sequence.

Module 66
TEXTCOLOR

DESCRIPTION

The *TextColor* procedure is part of the *Crt* unit. When you are in one of the text modes, either 40 or 80 columns, characters can be displayed on the screen in 16 different colors. The colors are referred to by number (0 . . 15), but the *Crt* unit provides 16 predefined integer constants to make remembering color numbers easier and programs more readable. The color (or attribute on the monochrome display) of the characters in text is selected by the *TextColor* procedure.

```
textcolor(value);
```

value   is an integer expression in the range 0 . . 31.

The IBM Monochrome Display can only produce green text, but it does provide two levels of brightness and an underline feature that are activated by the assignment of colors.

The colors available for text and their numbers are included in the following table.

Code	Color	Monochrome
0 :	Black	Black
1 :	Blue	Underlined white
2 :	Green	White
3 :	Cyan (sky-blue)	White
4 :	Red	White
5 :	Magenta	White
6 :	Brown	White
7 :	LightGray	White
8 :	DarkGray	Black
9 :	LightBlue	High intensity underlined
10 :	LightGreen	High intensity
11 :	LightCyan	High intensity
12 :	LightRed	High intensity

Code	Color	Monochrome
13 :	LightMagenta	High intensity
14 :	Yellow	High intensity
15 :	White	High intensity

The numbers 16 . . 31 are the blinking versions of the colors 0 . . 15.

If your color monitor is not fully compatible with an IBM color monitor, it is possible that the light colors look exactly like their dark counterparts.

The Integer parameter of textcolor can be a number, variable, or one of the predefined constants. For example,

```
Textcolor(2);
```

produces green text and is identical to the statement

```
TextColor(Green);
```

Remember that you do not have to assign values to the color names. The constants are predefined by Turbo Pascal. If you want the characters to blink, add 16 to the color number. This technique works on both the color displays and the monochrome display. Blinking green characters can be produced with these statements:

```
Textcolor(2+16);
Textcolor(18);
Textcolor(Green+16);
```

or, you can make use of another predefined Turbo Pascal constant, Blink, and write the procedure call as:

```
TextColor(Green+Blink);
```

which results in a highly readable program. This final technique is the one recommended to make your programs readable both to you and others.

APPLICATIONS

The effective use of color can add to the readability of your screen displays. Color is effective for highlighting important information on the screen. In financial programs, negative values are often displayed as red text.

There are three cautions about the use of color text. First, it is easy to get carried away and use too many colors on the screen at one time. Resist this temptation. Screen displays with more than four colors are seldom effective. Blinking text should be used only for rare occasions—typically for pointing out cautions or warnings. Second, not all color combinations are readable on all monitors. Almost everything is readable on an Enhanced Color Display; most color text is readable on a standard RGB color monitor, but many color combinations are unusable on a composite video monitor, either color or black and white. It is good programming practice to allow the program user to modify the choice of colors or to disable the use of color altogether. Third, the monochrome display shows blue as an underline. This can either work against you, or you can use this to your advantage when writing a word processor: many word processors use blue to designate underlined text. When the program is used on a monochrome monitor, the text appears on screen underlined.

TYPICAL OPERATION

In this session you display colored text on the screen in each of the available textmodes. If you have a composite monitor, the black and white textmodes disable the generation of color text. If you have an RGB color monitor, there is no difference between the black and white and the color modes.

1. If you are continuing your work session from the previous module, clear the Editor workspace. Otherwise, start Turbo Pascal.

2. Start the Editor and type the following program:

```
program Colortext;
uses Crt;
var Mode,Color:integer;
begin
    for Mode:=0 to 15 do
    begin
        TextMode(Mode);
        For Color:=0 to 15 do
        begin
            TextColor(Color);
            write('This is mode ', Mode);
            writeln(' and color ', Color);
        end;
        {Pause before showing the next display}
        writeln('Press Enter to continue');
        readln;
    end;
    {Reset the display to 80 column color text
      (or whatever you need) before ending}
    TextMode(C80);
end.
```

3. Save and run the program.

4. Press **Enter** to see each screen combination.

Your results look different depending on your computer setup. If you are using an IBM Monochrome display, all screens look the same (although only 40 columns are available in the 40-column modes). If you are using an RGB color monitor (the cable has a 9-pin or 15-pin connecter where it plugs into the back of the computer), you see color on all the displays. If you have a composite color monitor (the cable plugs into a round connector on the back of the computer), all modes work as specified. If you have a composite monochrome monitor, the color displays appear in different shades or textures.

5. Turn to Module 65, Textbackground, to continue the learning sequence.

Module 67
TEXTMODE

DESCRIPTION

The *Textmode* procedure is included as part of the *Crt* unit. Turbo Pascal supports five text modes. Each mode of operation has different capabilities. You can switch between modes with these statements:

Textmode(BW40);   40 columns of black and white text. BW40 is a predefined Turbo Pascal constant with the value 0.

Textmode(C40);   40 columns of color text. C40 is a predefined Turbo Pascal constant with the value 1.

Textmode(BW80);   80 columns of black and white text. BW80 is a predefined Turbo Pascal constant with the value 1.

Textmode(C80);   80 columns of color text. C80 is a predefined Turbo Pascal constant with the value 3.

Textmode(Mono);   80 columns of text on a monochrome monitor.

After using graphics, you can return to the most recently used text mode with the statement:

```
Textmode(Last);    The last active text mode.
```

Using the procedure *Textmode* without any parameters clears the screen, but it does not change the number of columns or the availability of color.

The black and white text modes affect only monitors connected to the composite video connector (round RCA jack) on a color graphics adapter (CGA). They do not disable color on an RGB color monitor connected to the color graphics adapter. They have no effect on EGA or VGA text.

APPLICATIONS

When 80-column color text is produced on a monochrome composite video monitor, the results are often unreadable. The black and white text modes allow you to disable the production of color at the composite video output of the color graphics card.

Unfortunately, while it is possible to determine whether a machine is equipped with a monochrome display adapter, a color graphics adapter, or an enhanced color graphics adapter, there is no effective way to determine whether a RGB monitor or a composite monitor is plugged into a color graphics adapter. Two solutions that are commonly used are to ask the user which type of monitor is in use, or to check for a command-line parameter to suppress the generation of color.

TYPICAL OPERATION

In this session you place text on the screen in each of the four available text modes.

1. If you are continuing your work session from a previous module, clear the Editor workspace. Otherwise, start Turbo Pascal.

2. Start the Editor and type the following program:

```
program TextModeDemo;
uses Crt;
var Mode : integer;
begin
    for Mode:=0 to 3 do
    begin
        Textmode(Mode);
        writeln('This is textmode ',Mode);
        readln;
    end;
end.
```

3. Save and run the program.

```
This is textmode 0
```

4. Press **Enter** repeatedly to see each text mode.

If you have a monochrome display card in your machine, you see no difference on the screen among the four options. A color graphics adapter, enhanced color graphics adapter, or video graphics array adapter produce a large character set in the 40-column mode.

5. Turn to Module 28, Function, to continue the learning sequence.

Module 68
TURBO VISION

DESCRIPTION

Turbo Vision is an applications framework included with Turbo Pascal. Turbo Vision packages many of the objects that comprise the Turbo Pascal integrated environment in a way that allow your programs to easily inherit the professional user interface of the Turbo Pascal environment.

It is useful to differentiate Turbo Vision from libraries of functions and procedures. On the surface, Turbo Vision appears similar to the many libraries of procedures and functions that are available commercially and from user groups to provide windows, menus, mouse support, file viewers, and similar functionality. Procedure and function libraries are typically provided as source code modules, allowing you to modify them to suit your needs. Turbo Vision is a collection of objects — you don't modify the source code of the basic objects, you extend them through the process of object inheritance. As a result, the fully debugged code that forms the foundation of the object is never modified. You are never faced with having to rewrite someone else's program that you may not fully understand.

The foundation of Turbo Vision is the application object, TApplication. You never change TApplication — you modify it by extending existing objects and by defining new objects.

All Turbo Vision applications, regardless of complexity, have a simple main program begin-end group, similar to the following:

```
begin
    MyApplication.Init;
    MyApplication.Run;
    MyApplication.Done;
end.
```

All Turbo Vision applications share the look and feel of the Turbo Pascal integrated environment. The top line of the screen is a Menu bar. The bottom line is a status line. The remainder of the screen is a desktop that is initially a half-tone dot pattern. Each of these elements, the menu bar, the status line, and the desktop are objects. Although their behavior can be modified by extension, by default they behave as their counterparts in the Turbo Pascal integrated environment. In other words, when you use the mouse to click on a word on the menu bar, a menu drops down and a highlight bar provides an indication of the currently selected menu item.

Turbo Vision applications are inherently event-driven. This means that there is a central event-dispatcher that takes care of getting all input from the user.

APPLICATIONS

Borland International has invested thousands of hours in the development of a high quality user interface for Turbo Pascal. As you begin an applications development effort, an important first question is whether you have the time or resources to create a higher-quality, more fully debugged text-mode user interface than the one provided by the Turbo Pascal integrated environment. If the answer to that question is "no," then Turbo Vision is the foundation of a quality interface that you simply "inherit" with your purchase of Turbo Pascal. Borland requires no royalty payments for the use of the Turbo Vision objects in your programs.

TYPICAL OPERATION

In the first typical operation you displayed the words "This is a simple as it gets!" on the computer screen. In this activity, you display the same message, Turbo Vision style.

1. Open a new Editor window.

2. Type the structure of the program.

```
program SimpleVision;
uses Objects, Drivers, Views, Menus, Dialogs, App;
type PSimpleApp = ^TSimpleApp;
     TSimpleApp = object(TApplication)
     end;

var Simple : TSimpleApp;


begin
    Simple.Init;
    Simple.Run;
    Simple.Done;
end.
```

Turbo Vision applications typically make use of a drop-down menu, a status line, one or more dialog boxes, and a central event handler.

3. Declare methods for the TSimpleApp objects as shown.

```
program SimpleVision;
uses Objects, Drivers, Views, Menus, Dialogs, App;

type PSimpleApp = ^TSimpleApp;
     TSimpleApp = object(TApplication)
       procedure InitMenuBar; virtual;
```

```
      procedure InitStatusLine; virtual;
      procedure MessageBox;
      procedure HandleEvent(var Event: TEvent); virtual;
    end;
var Simple : TSimpleApp;
```

4. Now provide the code to specify the menu bar. The menu will contain two entries, one to display the dialog box and the other to exit the program.

```
      procedure MessageBox;
      procedure HandleEvent(var Event: TEvent); virtual;
    end;

procedure TSimpleApp.InitMenuBar;
var R: TRect;
begin
  GetExtent(R);
  R.B.Y := R.A.Y + 1;
  MenuBar := New(PMenuBar, Init(R, NewMenu(
    NewSubMenu('~M~enu',hcNoContext, NewMenu(
    NewItem('~S~imple','',0, BoxCmd, hcNoContext,
    NewLine(
    NewItem('E~x~it','Alt-X', KbAltX, cmQuit, hcNoContext, nil)))), nil))));
end;

var Simple : TSimpleApp;
```

5. The identifier "BoxCmd" requires a definition. Event constants are best specified as constants in a *const* declaration.

```
program SimpleVision;
uses Objects, Drivers, Views, Menus, Dialogs, App;

const BoxCmd = 100;

type PSimpleApp = ^TSimpleApp;
     TSimpleApp = object(TApplication)
```

6. Add the program statements to initialize and define the status line. The status line will specify that F10 displays the menu and that pressing Alt-X exits the program.

```
      procedure MessageBox;
      procedure HandleEvent(var Event: TEvent); virtual;
    end;

procedure TSimpleApp.InitStatusLine;
var R: TRect;
begin
    GetExtent(R);
    R.A.Y := R.B.Y-1;
    StatusLine := New(PStatusLine, Init(R,
      NewStatusDef(0, $FFFF,
        NewStatusKey('', kbF10, cmMenu,
```

```
        NewStatusKey('~Alt-X~ Exit', kbAltX, cmQuit, nil)), mil)));
    end;

procedure TSimpleApp.InitMenuBar;
var R: TRect;
begin
    GetExtent(R);
```

7. Create a dialog box to display the message. The dialog box requires an "OK" button to acknowledge the message.

```
        procedure MessageBox;
        procedure HandleEvent(var Event: TEvent); virtual;
      end;

procedure TSimpleApp.MessageBox;
var R: TRect;
    D: PDialog;
    C: Word;
begin
    R.Assign(20, 5, 60, 14);
    D :=New(PDialog, Init(R, 'Simple Box'));

    R.Assign(6, 2, 35, 3);
    D^.Insert(New(PStaticText,
        Init(R, 'This is as simple as it gets!')));

    R.Assign(16, 5, 24, 7);
    D^.Insert(New(PButton, Init(R, 'Ok', cmCancel, bfNormal)));

    C := Desktop^.ExecView(D);
end;

procedure TSimpleApp.InitStatusLine;
var R: TRect;
begin
    GetExtent(R);
```

8. Write the event handler.

```
        procedure MessageBox;
        procedure HandleEvent(var Event: TEvent); virtual;
      end;

procedure TSimpleApp.HandleEvent(var Event: TEvent);
begin
    TApplication.HandleEvent(Event);
    if Event.What = evCommand then
    begin
        case Event.Command of
            BoxCmd: MessageBox;
        else
            Exit;
        end;
```

```
        ClearEvent(Event);
    end;
end;
```

```
procedure TSimpleApp.MessageBox;
var R: TRect;
    D: PDialog;
    C: Word;
```

9. Check the complete program against the following listing.

```
program SimpleVision;
uses Objects, Drivers, Views, Menus, Dialogs, App;

const BoxCmd = 100;

type PSimpleApp = ^TSimpleApp;
     TSimpleApp = object(TApplication)
       procedure InitMenuBar; virtual;
       procedure InitStatusLine; virtual;
       procedure MessageBox;
       procedure HandleEvent(var Event: TEvent); virtual;
     end;

procedure TSimpleApp.HandleEvent(var Event: TEvent);
begin
    TApplication.HandleEvent(Event);
    if Event.What = evCommand then
    begin
        case Event.Command of
            BoxCmd: MessageBox;
        else
            Exit;
        end;
        ClearEvent(Event);
    end;
end;

procedure TSimpleApp.MessageBox;
var R: TRect;
    D: PDialog;
    C: Word;

begin
    R.Assign(20, 5, 60, 14);
    D := New(PDialog, Init(R, 'Simple Box'));
    R.Assign(6, 2, 35, 3);
    D^.Insert(New(PStaticText,
        Init(R, 'This is as simple as it gets!')));
    R.Assign(16, 5, 24, 7);
    D^.Insert(New(PButton, Init(R, 'Ok', cmCancel, bfNormal)));
    C := Desktop^.ExecView(D);
end;
```

```
procedure TSimpleApp.InitStatusLine;
var R: TRect;
begin
    GetExtent(R);
    R.A.Y := R.B.Y-1;
    StatusLine := New(PStatusLine, Init(R,
      NewStatusDef(0,$FFFF,
        NewStatusKey('',kbF10,cmMenu,
        NewStatusKey('~Alt-X~ Exit', kbAltX, cmQuit, nil)),nil)));
end;

procedure TSimpleApp.InitMenuBar;
var R: TRect;
begin
  GetExtent(R);
  R.B.Y := R.A.Y + 1;
  MenuBar :=New(PMenuBar, Init(R, NewMenu(
    NewSubMenu('~M~enu',hcNoContext, NewMenu(
    NewItem('~S~imple','',0, BoxCmd, hcNoContext,
    NewLine(
    NewItem('E~x~it','Alt-X', KbAltX, cmQuit, hcNoContext, nil)))), nil))));
end;

var Simple : TSimpleApp;

begin
    Simple.Init;
    Simple.Run;
    Simple.Done;
end.
```

10. Run the program. Press **Alt-M** to drop down the menu.

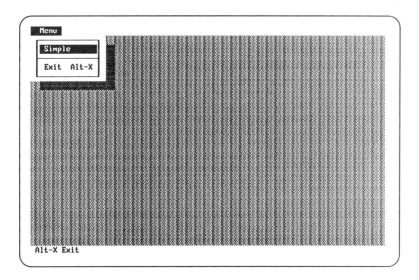

11. Type **S** to open the dialog box.

12. Press **Enter** to close the dialog box.

Experiment with the menu. Open the dialog box. Move it around the desktop. Try both the keyboard and mouse controls. Notice that the program environment is similar to the workings of the Turbo Pascal integrated environment.

There are certainly more statements in this program than in the first simple program of the learning sequence, However, the increase in functionality provided by such a modest increase in the number of program statements is completely out of proportion to the small increase in program statements. Additional information about the Turbo Vision objects is found in the *Turbo Vision Guide* included with Turbo Pascal 6.0.

13. This completes the learning sequence.

Module 69
TYPE

DESCRIPTION

Pascal provides a number of data types including *integer, byte, char, string,* and *real* for your use. If these data types do not meet your needs, you can create additional data types using the *type* statement. The *type* statement is generally placed as the first statement following the *program* statement.

```
type type-name = type-description;
```

or

```
type type-name = type-description;
     type-name = type-description;
     type-name = type-description;
          |              |
     type-name = type-description;
```

type-name   is the name you assign to the new data type. It must follow the Turbo Pascal rules for names.

type-description   is the definition of the type.

APPLICATIONS

Not all data is easily represented by integer, real, string, and character types. If you write a program to manage school records, one item you can keep track of is student classification: Freshman, Sophomore, Junior, and Senior. If you wish, you can assign an alphabetic or numeric code to each class, but then you have to remember the code system. Pascal provides an easier way by allowing you to create your own types. The statement,

```
type Level = (Freshman, Sophomore, Junior, Senior);
```

creates a new data type called LEVEL. It is possible to declare a LEVEL type variable, just as you can create an integer or character type variable. The statement,

```
var Class: Level;
```

declares a variable named CLASS of type LEVEL. You can use this variable in assignment statements:

```
Class:=Sophomore;
Class:=Junior;
```

Notice the values SOPHOMORE and JUNIOR are not enclosed in quotation marks. CLASS is not a string variable. Attempting an assignment such as CLASS:='SENIOR' creates a Compiler type-mismatch error message.

User-defined types are ordinal, meaning that they can be placed in order. The order depends on the order in the type definition. In the example above, FRESHMAN <SOPHOMORE <JUNIOR <SENIOR (where < is less than). Because of the ordering of user-defined types, you can use these variables as an index in a *for* loop. For example,

```
for Class:=Freshman to Senior do Printclass;
{Assume PRINTCLASS is a previously defined procedure.}
```

prints a class list of each class as the variable CLASS takes on the values FRESHMAN, SOPHOMORE, JUNIOR, and SENIOR. Note that the order in which the values appear in the *type* statement is the definition of order. The computer does not understand that schools are arranged this way.

You can use a user-defined type variable in a *case* statement. For example,

```
case class of
     Freshman    : writeln('This student is a freshman.');
     Sophomore   : writeln('This student is a sophomore.');
     Junior      : writeln('This student is a junior.');
     Senior      : writeln('This student is a senior.');
end;
```

Here is another example: A hotel elevator might have buttons labeled B (basement), L (lobby), M (mezzanine), 1, 2, 3, 4, 5, 6, 7 and R (rooftop swimming pool). A computer program to control the hotel elevator system needs to process floor choices when guests press the elevator buttons.

One way to handle this situation is to assign a number to each button in the computer program. For example, B is 1, L is 2, M is 3, 1 is 4, 2 is 5, 3 is 6, and so on. If this method does not confuse the programmer who writes the program the first time, it will certainly confuse the programmer who has to change the program to handle a change in the system, such as an additional elevator. Remembering that 2 is 5 and that 7 is 10 is asking too much.

A better way to handle this situation is with a user-defined data type. A statement such as

```
type Floor : (Basement,Lobby,Mezzanine,First,Second,Third,Fourth,
              Fifth,Sixth,Seventh,Roof);
```

creates a useful data type for the solution of this particular problem.

Of course, the computer needs special hardware to process the signals to and from the elevator. Once done, you can assign a value to a FLOOR type variable named CHOICE. The variable declaration looks like this:

```
var Choice : Floor;
```

Once CHOICE is assigned a value, a *case* statement is used to select the proper floor.

```
case Choice of
    Basement        : StopatB;
    Lobby           : StopatL;
    Mezzanine       : StopatM;
    First           : Stopat1;
    Second          : Stopat2;
    Third           : Stopat3;
    Fourth          : Stopat4;
    Fifth           : Stopat5;
    Sixth           : Stopat6;
    Seventh         : Stopat7;
    Roof            : StopatR;
    end;
  end.
```

In this illustration, assume that all the STOPAT procedures are already defined.

SUBRANGES   It is also possible to declare a data type which is a subrange of another type. For example:

```
type Natural = 1..Maxint;
```

defines NATURAL as the positive integers. NATURAL is a subrange of integer. Subranges are not limited to integers. You can declare a subrange of any ordinal data type. A subrange can be declared on the character set; for example,

```
type Firstsix = 'A'..'F'
```

declares FIRSTSIX as a subrange of *char*. You are not limited to subranges of predeclared data types. If you declare

```
type Class = (Freshman, Sophomore, Junior, Senior);
```

you could also declare UPPERCLASSMAN as:

```
type Class = (Freshman, Sophomore, Junior, Senior);
     Upperclassman = Sophomore..Senior;
```

There are three reasons for using a subrange or an enumerated type. The first is to take advantage of Pascal's strict type checking to check for out-of-range values. Allowing the computer to perform these checks helps prevent errors. A second reason is to save space. Enumerated types and subranges with fewer than 255 possible values occupy only a single byte of memory. The third reason is to improve the readability and maintainability of your program. Specifying the data type as precisely as possibly allows you to follow the structure of your program more easily when you come back to it after a period of time.

The intrinsic functions *ord*, *succ*, and *pred* work with enumerated types and subranges in the same manner as they work with integers.

TYPICAL OPERATION

In this session you define a new type, BigString, which is defined as a string with a maximum length of 255 characters.

1. If you are continuing your work session, clear the Editor workspace. Otherwise, start Turbo Pascal.

2. Start the Editor and type the following program:

```
Program TypeDef;
uses Crt;
type BigString = String[255];
var Phrase1, Phrase2, Sentence : BigString;

begin
    ClrScr;
    Phrase1:= 'The sooner you get behind';
    Phrase2:= 'the more time you have to catch up.';
    Sentence:=Phrase1 + ',' + Phrase2;
    writeln(Sentence);
    readln;
end.
```

3. Save the program as TYPEDEF then run the program.

```
The sooner you get behind, the more time you have to catch up.
```

All operations are performed using your newly defined data type BigString. You can do anything to a BigString that you can do with an ordinary string.

4. Turn to Module 64, Text, to continue the learning sequence.

Module 70
UNIT

DESCRIPTION

Unit *UnitName*

UnitName   is a Pascal identifier used to provide a name for the unit.

In addition to the predefined units provided with Turbo Pascal, the software allows you to create your own units. The *Unit* statement is the first statement in the unit. Use the *Unit* statement instead of the *Program* statement to differentiate between a program and a unit.

The Turbo Pascal Compiler compiles units into a proprietary object format, and places them on the disk with the DOS file extension of TPU.

APPLICATIONS

Units provide a powerful mechanism to split programs into logical, reusable segments. You might add a unit to perform window operations, a unit for a mouse interface, or a unit to provide screen-oriented input routines for standard data formats.

The use of units allows you to more easily develop your programs in pieces, isolating the code under development from code that you know is error-free. In addition to physically isolating segments of your code, the fact that units are compiled individually can substantially lower the compile time for large programs because you do not have to recompile those portions of the program each time you compile the program.

The *Make* and *Build* commands on the Run menu become significant when you include your own units in programs that you develop. When you select *Make*, the system compares the DOS directory date and time on each unit source file (file extension PAS) with the corresponding TPU file. If the unit has been modified since it was last compiled, it is automatically recompiled. When you select *Build*, Turbo Pascal recompiles every unit that the program depends on. If you are conscientious about maintaining the correct time and date in your computer system, the *Make* command can save considerable compile time. If, however, you are not as consistent as you might like in setting the date and time, you may find it advantageous to use the *Build* command. In any event, when a program using units fails to behave as you think it should, performing a *Build* assures you that the program you are testing actually reflects the most recent version of each of the separate pieces.

Turn to Module 34, Interface, to continue the learning sequence.

Module 71
USES

DESCRIPTION

Instead of building Turbo Pascal as a single giant system, Borland implemented it as a central core, with optional (but included at no additional cost) units. You may selectively include these units in your programs, and you may write additional units yourself to extend Turbo Pascal.

The *Uses* statement allows Turbo Pascal programs to make use of procedures that are contained in these separately compiled units. When writing a program, place the *Uses* statement immediately following the *Program* statement. List the required units, separated by commas, and conclude the statement with a semicolon. When writing units that refer to other units, the *Uses* statement may be placed either after the *Interface* statement or after the *Implementation* statement.

APPLICATIONS

The units included with Turbo Pascal include the following:

Crt   Contains routines that help manipulate text on the screen.

Graph   Contains routines for creating graphics on the screen.

Printer   Provides a simple printer interface for printing from within your programs.

DOS   Contains routines for accessing PC-DOS/MS-DOS interrupt procedures and built-in functions, plus procedures for manipulating files and directories on the disk.

Graph3   Contains routines for maintaining compatibility with programs that were first written with Turbo Pascal version 3.0. It is inadvisable to use Graph3 in writing new programs.

These units are physically located in the disk file TURBO.TPL that forms a part of the Turbo Pascal package.

You can also write and compile additional units yourself. This procedure is described more fully beginning in the *Unit* module.

Turbo Pascal units are also available from computer bulletin boards, from the Turbo Pascal forum on Compuserve, on USENET, and commercially from companies such as Blasise Computing and TurboPower Software.

Regardless of the source of your units, whether included in the Turbo Pascal library, purchased from a third party, or written personally, you must include the name of the unit in a *Uses* statement for any program that depends on information defined in a unit.

TYPICAL OPERATION

The use of the *Uses* statement is demonstrated in the *ClrScr* module.

Turn to Module 10, ClrScr, to continue the learning sequence.

Module 72
VAR

DESCRIPTION

The *var* statement reserves space for data in the computer's memory and assigns a name to the space. The *var* statement does not place any value in the memory at the location. At the start of the program, the value of all variables is undefined until you assign each variable a value with the assignment operator.

Variable declaration:

```
var name {,name} : type
   {name {,name} : type};
```

name   is the name of the variable.

type   is the type of the variable or list of variables.

Variable assignment:

```
name := expression
```

name   is the name of the variable.

expression   is a Pascal expression with the same type as *name*. It can be a literal, a variable, or an expression constructed from literals, variables, and operators.

: =   is the Pascal assignment symbol. It causes Pascal to evaluate the expression on the right side of the sign and place the result in the variable location on the left side of the sign. The symbol = is a symbol for equality, and it is not interchangeable with the symbol : =.

VARIABLE DECLARATION   Pascal requires all variables to be declared, which is accomplished with the *var* statement. The *var* statement requires you to list each variable you use in the program and to specify the variable's type. Program variables are declared following the *program* statement and before any procedure definitions, function definitions, and the *begin* statement for the program block.

To declare a single variable use the statement

```
var name : type;
```

where *name* is the name of the variable and *type* is the type of the variable.

You create the name according to Turbo Pascal's rules for naming. The type can be a scalar type including *integer, byte, real, char*, and *Boolean*; a *string*; a structured type including *array, record*, or *set*; or a user-defined type, that is defined in a *type* statement.

Scalar types are declared by using the word *integer, shortint, longint, byte, real, char*, or *Boolean* as the variable type. When you declare a string variable you must state the maximum length of the string by enclosing a number between 0 and 255 in square brackets immediately following the word String. For example, String[10] refers to a string that can have a maximum of ten characters. String[255] specifies the longest possible string. Declaration of Arrays, Records, and Sets are discussed in the modules by those names. Declaration of user-defined types is defined in the Type module.

To declare several variables of the same type, use the statement in the form

```
var name1, name2, name3 : type;
```

You may declare as many variables as you like in a single *var* statement.

```
var name : type1;
    name1, name2, name3 : type2;
    name4, name5 : type3;
```

For example, a typical variable declaration looks like the following:

```
var Count, Index      : Integer;
    Choice            : Char;
    Hours, Payrate    : Real;
    Name, Address     : String[30];
    City              : String[15];
    State             : String[2];
    ZipCode           : String[9];
    Current           : Boolean;
```

The spacing is purely decorative. Spacing is used to make the specification more readable. To the computer, it could just as well be written like this:

```
var Count,Index:Integer;Choice:Char;Hours,Payrate:Real;Name,Address
:String[30];City:String[15];State:String[2];ZipCode:String[9];Current
:Boolean;
```

Spacing is irrelevant to the Turbo Pascal Compiler. Spacing is important, however, for making Pascal programs understandable to both yourself and others.

This variable declaration, in either form, specifies Count and Index as *integer* variables. Choice is declared as a *char* variable. It would be used for keeping track of a single character, for example, pressing a menu choice letter such as "E" for Edit from the Turbo Pascal Main menu. Hours and Payrate are specified as *real*. This allows them to keep track of fractional hours, and payrates such as 18.75 dollars per hour. Name and Address are both declared as strings with a maximum length of 30. City is declared as a string with a maximum length of 15. State is a string with a maximum length of 2. ZipCode is declared as a string with a maximum length of 9. Zip codes are never added or multiplied, so there is no reason to demand the computational abilities of real numbers. Many Zip codes are larger than 32767, the largest integer, and Canadian codes contain both letters and digits. Current is declared as a *Boolean* variable. It could be assigned the value *True* if a person were a current employee, or *False* if a person were a past employee.

VARIABLE ASSIGNMENT   Now that you know how to name a variable, look at the method of placing data in the variable's location. This task is accomplished with the assignment statement. The symbol := is used as the assignment operator in Pascal. It is composed of two characters—a colon and an equal sign. Assignment statements could look like the following:

```
Pay:=135.23;
Tax:=89.21;
```

The first statement takes the number 135.23 and places it in location PAY. The second statement takes the number 89.21 and places it in location TAX.

The value of one variable can be placed in the location of another variable. For example,

```
Pay:=135.23;
Tax:=Pay;
```

places the number 135.23 in location PAY, then takes the contents of location PAY (which is 135.23) and places it in location TAX. When the above two statements are executed, the variables PAY and TAX contain the value 135.23.

APPLICATIONS

One of the real advantages of computer programs is the ability of the programmer to designate certain variables in the program and to have the computer manipulate them to produce specified output. The computer programs you have written so far have produced messages on the screen. The programs have the single purpose of printing a single message. They are not designed to have any flexibility. They cannot print different words or different numbers. They cannot switch output devices and place output on the printer or in a disk file without rewriting the program. To perform tasks more complex than printing a simple message on a single output device, you need additional tools. Variables are one of these powerful tools.

A variable is a location in the computer memory used to store information. This location has much in common with a mailbox. The computer program can place information in the location and change that information. The computer needs to know two things about these locations (mailboxes) to create and use them. First, the computer must have a name for the location, and second, the computer must know what kind of information the location must contain. Just as mailboxes must be different sizes to accommodate letters and packages, variable locations must be different sizes to accommodate different types of data.

Do not confuse the symbols for assignment (:=) and equality (=). The statement

```
Count = Count + 1
```

is a statement of mathematical equality that is never true. The statement

```
Count := Count + 1;
```

is a valid and extremely useful assignment statement that means:

- Take the number stored in location COUNT.
- Add 1 to the number.
- Place the result in COUNT.

Assignment and equality are two completely different concepts.

TYPICAL OPERATION

In this session you declare variables, assign them values, and display the values on the screen.

1. If you are continuing from the previous module, press **Alt-F** and type **N** to clear the Editor workspace; otherwise, type **TURBO** from the DOS prompt to start Turbo Pascal.

2. Press **Alt-E** to start the Editor and type the following program.

NOTE
Typing the *writeln* statements is easiest if you use the Editor Block commands. After typing the first *writeln* statement, use the F7 and F8 keys to mark "writeln('The value of" as a block. Then use the Block copy command, Ctrl-K-C, to copy the block for each succeeding *writeln* statement.

```
program Assign;
uses Crt;

var X, Y, Z: real;
    i, j, k: integer;
    S, T, R: string[255];
```

```
    B       : Boolean;

begin
    ClrScr;
    i:=2+3;
    j:=27350 - 21845;
    k:=I * 2 + 1;
    X:=2/3;
    Y:=3.14159 * 5 * 5;
    Z:=X + Y;
    S:='The cow jumped';
    T:=' over the moon.';
    R:=S+T;
    B:=True;
    writeln('The value of I is: ',i);
    writeln('The value of J is: ',j);
    writeln('The value of K is: ',k);
    writeln('The value of X is: ',x);
    writeln('The value of Y is: ',y);
    writeln('The value of Z is: ',z);
    writeln('The value of R is: ',r);
    writeln('The value of B is: ',b);
    readln;
end.
```

3. Press **Alt-F** for the drop-down File menu, then type **S** to save the program. Type **ASSIGN** as the program name and press **Enter**.

4. Press **Alt-R** and press **Enter** to run the program.

```
    The value of I is: 5
    The value of J is: 5505
    The value of K is: 11
    The value of X is:    6.6666666667E-01
    The value of Y is:    7.8539750000E+01
    The value of Z is:    7.9306416666E+01
    The value of R is: The cow jumped over the moon.
    The value of B is: TRUE
```

The computer appears to have provided the correct answers. In the *Write and Writeln* module you learn column formatting specifications to control column alignment and width of your output.

5. Press **Enter** to return to the Turbo Pascal environment.

6. Turn to Module 16, Debug Menu, to continue the learning sequence.

Module 73
VIRTUAL

DESCRIPTION

You change the resolution of an object reference from compile-time resolution to run-time resolution through the addition of the keyword *virtual* following the declaration of the object method. A method that is declared *virtual* at any point in an object heirarchy must be declared as *virtual* in all instances of the method throughout the heirarchy.

Additionally, any object that contains a *virtual* method must have a *constructor* method. See Module 15, Constructor, for additional information on *constructor* methods.

APPLICATIONS

In the ScrnObj unit, both Point and Ball have methods named ChangeLocation that are designed to move them on the screen. The static method ChangeLocation, as defined in Ball, overrides the static method ChangeLocation as defined in Point. When moving either object, you must use the specific method for that type object. With a larger assortment of objects, keeping track of the variations would be as inconvenient as requiring separate versions of the *write* statement to deal with each different data type. With a virtual method, the compiler figures out which definition of ChangeLocation to use when the program is run.

One of the advantages of object-oriented programming is the extensibility of objects. When you create these object definitions in a unit, it is possible to distribute a programming toolkit consisting of a source code listing of the *interface* section and a compiled .TPU file, retaining the source code of the *implementation* section as private information. The use of *virtual* methods allows the user of the unit to extend the object definition and have access to all of the required programming interfaces without having access to the source code of the object and method definitions.

Sometimes, for speed and memory efficiency, you may decide that a particular method will never need extension, and you may elect to use the default of static methods. However, the amount of overhead imposed by virtual methods is small, and it is difficult to anticipate in advance every possible application in which an object might be used.

Module 73

TYPICAL OPERATION

In this session you modify the ScrnObj unit to make the ChangeLocation methods virtual. You add a method, MoveTo, to move a generalized object on the screen.

1. Load the unit SCRNOBJ.PAS (most recently used in Module 44, Object) into the Turbo Pascal Editor.

2. Add the keyword *virtual* following the ChangeLocation methods declaration for Point and Ball in the interface portion of the unit as shown in the following listing.

```
Unit ScrnObj;
interface
type Point = object
   X, Y : word;
   procedure Initialize(XPos,YPos : word);
   procedure ChangeLocation(XDisplacement,YDisplacement : integer); virtual;
   function XLocation : word;
   function YLocation : word;
end;

Ball = object(Point)
   Radius : word;
   procedure Initialize(XPos,YPos,Size: word);
   procedure ChangeLocation(XDisplacement,YDisplacement : integer); virtual;
end;
```

3. Add the MoveTo method heading to the definition of Point in the interface section of the unit as shown.

```
interface
type Point = object
   X, Y : word;
   procedure Initialize(XPos,YPos : word);
   procedure ChangeLocation(XDisplacement,YDisplacement : integer); virtual;
   function XLocation : word;
   function YLocation : word;
   procedure MoveTo(XPos,YPos : word); virtual;
end;
```

4. Add the definition of the MoveTo method to the implementation section of the unit as shown.

```
function Point.YLocation;
begin
    YLocation:=Y;
end;

procedure Point.MoveTo;
var StartX, StartY, DeltaX, DeltaY : integer;
begin
    StartX:=XLocation;
    StartY:=YLocation;
```

322

```
    DeltaX:=XPos - StartX;
    DeltaY:=YPos - StartY;
    ChangeLocation(DeltaX, DeltaY);
end;

procedure Ball.Initialize;
begin

    Point.Initialize(XPos,YPos);
```

Notice that the reference to ChangeLocation in procedure MoveTo does not specify whether to use Point.ChangeLocation or Ball.ChangeLocation. The virtual nature of Change Location allows Turbo Pascal to figure it out for itself when the program executes.

Before compiling the unit, you must add a *constructor* for each object. You do this in Module 14, Constructor.

5. Save the unit.

6. Turn to Module 14, Constructor, to continue the learning sequence.

Module 74
WHILE

DESCRIPTION

The *while* loop is similar to the *repeat* loop. The *repeat* loop always executes at least once; the *while* loop may never execute.

Simple *while* loop:

```
while condition do statement;
```

Compound *while* loop:

```
while condition do
begin
    statement;
    statement;

    statement;
end;
```

condition   is a Boolean expression. If *condition* is never false, the loop executes forever.

statement   is a Turbo Pascal statement. Notice that a semicolon is not required after the last *statement* in the compound form of the *while* loop.

APPLICATIONS

The "test" portion of a *repeat* loop is located at the bottom of the loop. As a result, the code in the loop is always executed at least once. Sometimes you may not want a loop executed at all. The *while* loop performs the same function as the *repeat* loop, except that the "test" is at the top of the loop.

Many times when reading a disk file, you do not know exactly how many records or entries the file contains. Pascal provides an end-of-file function, *Eof*, which is set every time an input operation is processed. When the last record or line of a diskette file is read, *Eof* is set to *true*. In general, it is impossible to guarantee that the file you read actually contains data. A file could contain only an end-of-file marker. In this case, the first *read* operation would attempt to read past the end-of-file and generate an I/O error. It is best to test for end-of-file immediately after opening the file with the *reset* statement.

TYPICAL OPERATION

READ A TEXT FILE In this session you write a program to read a text file from a diskette as the source of input for the program. Since all Turbo Pascal Editor files are text files, use the file RESET.PAS from the *Reset* module as the data for this session.

The program must first use the *assign* statement to associate the disk file RESET.PAS with the program file Infile. The *reset* statement is used to "open" the diskette file and prepare it for reading. A *while* statement is then used to read the disk and write to the screen until the end of the file is reached.

1. If you are continuing your work session, clear the Editor workspace. Otherwise, start Turbo Pascal.

2. Enter the Editor and type the following program:

```
program List;
uses Crt;
var infile:text;
    line:string[80];
begin
    ClrScr;
    assign (Infile, 'List.pas');
    reset(Infile);
    while not Eof(Infile) do
    begin
        readln(Infile,Line);
        writeln(Line);
    end;
    readln;
end.
```

The file specification "Infile" as the first parameter in the *readln* statement serves the same function as the file specification in a *writeln* statement. It tells the computer that the operation is performed on the file, not on the default I/O device.

3. Save the program with the name LIST then run the program.

```
program List;
uses Crt;
var infile:text;
    line:string[80];
begin
    ClrScr;
    assign (Infile, 'List.pas');
    reset(Infile);
    while not Eof(Infile) do
    begin
        readln(Infile,Line);
        writeln(Line);
    end;
```

```
        readln;
    end.
```

A *while* statement is the preferred structure to use to read to the end of a file. A *repeat* statement always attempts at least one read. If the file has no data, the *repeat* generates an error when it attempts to read beyond the end-of-file.

USING A WHILE LOOP WITH STANDARD I/O   It is possible to use a *while* loop to read from the DOS standard input file and write to the DOS standard output file.

1. Clear the Editor workspace and type the following program:

```
program Transfer;
Var Ch:char;
begin
    while not Eof(Input) do
    begin
        read(Ch);
        write(Ch);
    end;
end.
```

2. Save the program.

Because all filenames are specified through the operating system, you do not need to *assign* or *reset* any files in the program.

For maximum flexibility, the program works with the files on a character-oriented basis. This sounds inefficient, but remember that the operating system buffers the input and output operations. Therefore, the system does not perform a physical read operation or a physical write operation every time you read or write a character.

The program uses the *Eof* function to check the standard Turbo Pascal file *Input*.

3. Press **Alt-C** to drop down the Compile menu.

4. Type **D** to change the Destination to Disk.

5. Type **C** to compile the program to a .EXE file on disk.

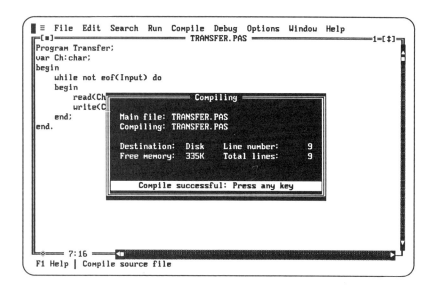

```
 ▌ ≡  File  Edit  Search  Run  Compile  Debug  Options  Window  Help
 ┌[■]══════════════════════ TRANSFER.PAS ══════════════════════1═[↕]═┐
 Program Transfer;
 var Ch:char;
 begin
     while not eof(Input) do
     begin
         read(Ch┌═══════════════ Compiling ═══════════════┐
         write(C│                                         │
     end;      │  Main file:  TRANSFER.PAS               │
 end.          │  Compiling:  TRANSFER.PAS               │
               │                                         │
               │  Destination:  Disk    Line number:   9 │
               │  Free memory:  335K    Total lines:   9 │
               │                                         │
               │    Compile successful: Press any key    │
               └═════════════════════════════════════════┘


 └═*═══ 7:16 ═══◄▌▒▒▒▒▒▒▒▒▒▒▒▒▒▒▒▒▒▒▒▒▒▒▒▒▒▒▒▒▒▒▒▒▒▒▒▒▒▒▒▒▒▌►┘
 F1 Help │ Compile source file
```

6. Press **Alt-F** to drop down the File menu.

7. Type **Q** to quit Turbo Pascal and return to the DOS prompt.

DOS I/O redirection uses the symbol to specify the input file and to specify the output file.

8. Type each of the following commands and observe the effect of I/O redirection.

What you type: **What it does:**

TRANSFER <LIST.PAS>CON: Assigns the file RESET.PAS as the input file and the DOS console as the output device. The file contents are displayed on the screen. Note that the specification of CON: as the output file is actually redundant, as CON: is the default value.

TRANSFER <LIST.PAS >RESET..TXT   Assigns the file RESET.PAS as the input file and RESET.TXT as the output file.

TRANSFER <LIST.PAS>LPT1:   Assigns the file RESET.PAS as the input file and LPT1:, the printer, as the output device. Produces a listing on the printer.

You can also use TRANSFER as a DOS filter with full support for DOS pipes.

DIR|TRANSFER >DIR.TXT

The output of the DIR command is sent to the input of the TRANSFER filter, and its output is placed in the disk file DIR.TXT.

An interesting modification of the TRANSFER program is the creation of a data encryption DOS filter. Instead of simply reading the file from the input device and writing it unmodified to the output device, encode the file before writing it. One simple encoding technique is to add 128 to the ASCII value of the character before writing it. One advantage of this method is that the same program used for encoding also decodes.

1. Clear the Editor workspace and start the Editor.

2. Use the Editor Block-Read procedure to import the file TRANSFER.PAS. (Press **Ctrl-K-**and type **R** to begin the read process.)

3. Rename the program Code, and add the encoding assignment statement as shown.

```
program Code;
var Ch:char;
begin
    while not Eof(Input) do
    begin
        read(Ch);
        ch:=chr(ord(ch)+128);
        write(Ch);
    end;
end.
```

4. Press **Alt-F** and type **W** to save the program as CODE.

5. Press **Alt-C** and type **D** to change the compiler destination to disk. Type **C** to compile the program to an .EXE file. Then exit Turbo Pascal.

6. Type the following commands and notice the operation of the program.

What you type:

What it does:

CODE <LIST.PAS

Places an encoded version of the program on the screen.

CODE <LIST.PAS >LIST.CRP

Places an encoded version of the program in the file LIST.CRP.

CODE <LIST.CRP

Decodes the file LIST.CRP and places the results on the screen.

DIR|CODE   Places a coded directory on the screen.

DIR|CODE|CODE   Sends the output of the DIR command to
                                                CODE for encoding, which sends its
                                                output to CODE for decoding, which
                                                sends its output to the screen. This is
                                                definitely the long way around to place
                                                the directory on the screen, but it does
                                                demonstrate some of what can be done
                                                with pipes and I/O redirection.

INFINITE LOOPS   Beginning programmers often forget to assure that a loop will
actually end, which creates an infinite loop.

1. Clear the Editor workspace and type the following program:

```
program Forever;

begin
    while 1=1 do
        writeln('This program will run forever if not stopped.');
end.
```

2. Run the program.

```
This program will run forever if not stopped.
This program will run forever if not stopped.
This program will run forever if not stopped.
```

The Break key is the upper right key on most keyboards. (The word "Break" is printed on
the front of the key instead of the top.)

3. Press **Ctrl-Break** to end the program.

4. Start the Editor. Modify the program as follows:

```
program Forever;
var TheEndOfTime : boolean;

begin
    TheEndOfTime:=False;
    repeat
        writeln('This program runs till the end of time.')
    until TheEndOfTime;
end.
```

5. Run the program.

```
      |           |           |
      |           |           |
  This program runs till the end of time.
  This program runs till the end of time.
  This program runs till the end of time.
```

6. Press **Ctrl-Break** to end the program.

Writing programs you must stop by pressing Ctrl-Break is exceptionally poor programming style. The examples here are straightforward enough for you to see immediately that they cannot end by themselves. Beware, however, of subtle programming bugs that can cause a loop to never end.

When you write a program loop, make certain that statements inside the scope of the loop change the loop condition so that the loop eventually terminates. Keeping loops short through the use of procedures and careful indentation of program steps makes it easier to verify correct structure.

7. Turn to Module 67, Textmode, to continue the learning sequence.

Module 75
WINDOW

DESCRIPTION

The *window* procedure is part of the *Crt* unit. It is possible to redefine the active text screen area as a portion of the full screen with the *window* procedure. Once you specify an active window, all text commands relate to that window — the remainder of the screen is protected until you redefine the active window to include those parts.

```
window(x1,y1,x2,y2)
```

(x1,y1)   specifies the x and y coordinates of the upper left corner of the window.

(x2,y2)   specifies the x and y coordinates of the lower right corner of the window.

The upper left corner of the screen is (1,1), and the lower right corner of the screen is (80,25) or (40,25), depending on the current width of the screen as defined by *textmode*.

The action of the *gotoxy* procedure is modified to make all coordinates refer to the window, not the screen. *Gotoxy(1,1)* places the cursor in the upper left corner of the current window, not the physical screen. *ClrScr* clears only the current window, not the entire screen.

APPLICATIONS

Using multiple windows in software is a popular, contemporary design strategy employed by professional applications software. Although many individuals equate windows with graphical user interfaces, the Turbo Pascal integrated environment is an excellent example of an effective use of text windows.

Use the *window* command to create multiple text windows on the screen to serve multiple program functions. Creating these windows with the *window* command makes it easier to manipulate multiple text windows.

If you define your own text windows without using the *window* command, you must also write your own routines for clearing the screen and your own *gotoxy* procedure for working inside your windows. When you use Turbo Pascal's *window* command to construct windows, you modify the text output commands to affect only the desired screen window. As a result, the Compiler takes care of many of the tedious details of window management.

TYPICAL OPERATION

To illustrate the use of text windows, modify the Fill program to create a window on the screen at the end of the program.

1. If you are continuing your work session, clear the Editor workspace. Otherwise, start Turbo Pascal.

2. Start the Editor and use the Block Read operation to import the file FILL.PAS from the Gotoxy module.

3. Modify the program as shown.

```pascal
program Windows;
uses Crt;

procedure Fill;
var symbol:char;
    x,y,foreground,background:integer;

begin
    Textmode(C80);
    randomize;
    repeat
        x:=1+Random(80);
        y:=1+Random(24);
        foreground:=Random(16);
        background:=Random(8);
        symbol:=chr(Random(127)+128);
        Textcolor(foreground);
        Textbackground(background);
        Gotoxy(x,y);
        write(symbol);
    until keypressed;
end;

procedure OpenWindow;
begin
    window(15,5,65,10);
    Textcolor(white);
    Textbackground(blue);
    ClrScr;
    Gotoxy(10,2);
    write('On a clear day, I can see forever.');
    readln;
    {Reset the screen to a full screen of white on black.}
    window(1,1,80,25);
    Textcolor(white);
    Textbackground(black);
end;
```

```
begin
    Fill;
    OpenWindow;
    readln;
end.
```

Resetting the window to correspond to the full physical screen at the end of the program is good programming technique.

4. Save the program as WINDOWS and run the program.

5. Press **Enter** to open the window.

On a clear day, I can see forever.

A blue window with a white message is displayed.

6. Press **Enter** to end the program.

7. Press **Enter** to return to the Turbo Pascal environment.

8. Turn to Module 5, Array, to continue the learning sequence.

Module 76
WINDOW MENU

DESCRIPTION

The Window menu provides the methods for changing the appearance of the Turbo Pascal desktop. When you activate the Window menu, by pressing Alt-W or by clicking on Window in the menu bar with the mouse, the Window menu appears.

Use the Size/Move command, which has a shortcut keystroke of Ctrl-F5, to change the size of windows on the screen.

The Zoom command, which has a shortcut keystroke of F5, expands the current window to fill the screen. Selecting Zoom again shrinks the window to its previous size.

The Tile command arranges all the windows on the screen in such a way that no window overlaps another window.

The Cascade command arranges all the windows on the screen in an overlapped, cascaded manner.

The Next command, which has a shortcut keystroke of F6, makes the "next" window active. Repeatedly activating the Next command cycles through all of the windows on the desktop, making each, in turn, active. The ordering of the windows is constant and depends on the order that the windows were created or opened.

The Previous command, which has a shortcut keystroke of Shift-F6, cycles through the windows on the desktop exactly as the Next command, with the exception of reversing the order of the cycling.

The Close command, which has a shortcut keystroke of Alt-F3, closes the current window and removes it from the integrated environment desktop. If you have not saved the most recent changes to the window (in the case of an edit window) you are prompted with a dialog box that allows you to do so.

The Watch command is used to activate the Watch window where the values of variables and expressions can be monitored during source-level debugging.

The Register command opens a CPU Register window that allows you to monitor the contents of the CPU registers in the computer and the status of the CPU flags.

The Output command opens a window on the output screen created by the execution of the Turbo Pascal program.

The Call stack command, which has a shortcut keystroke of Ctrl-F3, opens a window showing the procedures that a program called to reach a particular point in its execution.

The User screen command, which has a shortcut keystroke of Alt-F5, switches to a full-screen view of the output screen. Pressing F5 again toggles you back into the integrated environment.

The List command, which has a shortcut keystroke of Alt-0, presents a dialog box listing all the active windows on the desktop. You may select a new active window by highlighting the desired window either with the Up Arrow and Down Arrow keys or the mouse, then jumping to the window by pressing Enter, clicking the OK button with the mouse, or double clicking the name of the window with the mouse.

APPLICATIONS

There are two ways to size and move windows on the desktop. The keyboard method is to select the Size/Move command from the Window menu and then use the arrow keys to move the window and the shifted arrow keys to resize the window. If you have a mouse, it is usually easier to size the window by placing the mouse cursor at the extreme lower right corner, pressing and holding the left mouse button, dragging the corner into the desired position, and releasing the mouse button. Moving the window with the mouse is equally easy. Place the mouse cursor on the title bar of the window, press and hold the left mouse button, and drag the window into the desired position. Release the mouse button when the window reaches the desired position.

The Next and Previous commands (F6 and Shift-F6) can frequently be used together to switch between adjacent windows. This can be especially useful when using the integrated environment's clipboard to copy and paste program code between windows.

The Watch window automatically becomes active when you activate Watches in the Debug menu. However, you may find it useful to put the Watch window aside during your editing activities to allow you the use of the full-screen view of your program code.

The CPU Register window is invaluable for low-level debugging activities, especially when working with the INTR and MSDOS procedures and with INLINE assembly code in your program. This window is designed for very low-level debugging activities for monitoring advanced program code. You won't need this window as you learn Turbo Pascal, but as you push the limits of the language, its constant visual monitoring of the CPU status is invaluable.

The Output window is useful for limited monitoring of a program's output, especially in the early testing stages. However, when working with a program having a full-screen user interface, especially one where random portions of the screen are updated, the User screen option is far more useful.

Frequently in debugging you find a program executing a portion of the code at an unexpected time. The Call stack window helps you answer the question, "How did my program get here?" It is especially useful when combined with the "Go to cursor" command (F4) on the Run menu. When exploring a troublesome piece of code, place the cursor at the start of the code and press F4 to run the program to that position. Then activate the Call stack window to determine how the program arrived at that point. The results are often enlightening and frequently not as expected. With that, you have the basis for further exploration of program logic faults.

The User screen command is more useful than the Output command when working with full-screen user interfaces and with graphics. Although the Output window can monitor line-oriented, scrolling output, only the User screen can show the full range of activity on an 80x25 full screen text application or with a graphics application.

The List command allows you to keep track of the windows on the integrated environment's desktop. During a busy programming session, it is not unlikely that you will have a fair number of windows open at the same time — possibly more than you can easily keep track of in your head. The List command displays a complete list of the open windows and allows you to jump between windows in a random order. When many windows are open at once, this can be quicker than the Next window and Previous window selection techniques.

TYPICAL OPERATION

In this session you practice using the commands on the Windows menu.

1. Begin the activity by loading the program ASSIGN.PAS into the first Editor window.

```
 ≡  File  Edit  Search  Run  Compile  Debug  Options  Window  Help
┌─[■]─────────────────────── ASSIGN.PAS ───────────────────────1═[↕]┐
│program Assign;                                                    ▲│
│uses Crt;                                                          ▓│
│var x, y, z: real;                                                 ░│
│    i, j, k: integer;                                              ░│
│    s, t, r: string[255];                                          ░│
│    b     : boolean;                                               ░│
│                                                                   ░│
│begin                                                              ░│
│    ClrScr;                                                        ░│
│    i := 2 + 3;                                                    ░│
│    j := 27350 - 21845;                                            ░│
│    k := i * 2 + 1;                                                ░│
│    x := 2 / 3;                                                    ░│
│    y := 3.14159 * 5 * 5;                                          ░│
│    z := x + y;                                                    ░│
│    s := 'The cow jumped';                                         ░│
│    t := ' over the moon.';                                        ░│
│    r := s + t;                                                    ░│
│    b := true;                                                     ░│
│    writeln('The value of I is: ',i);                              ░│
│    writeln('The value of J is: ',j);                              ▼│
├──── 1:1 ─────◄                                                    ─┘
│ F1 Help  F2 Save  F3 Open  Alt-F9 Compile  F9 Make  F10 Menu        │
```

2. Add Watches including i, j, and r. (Press **Ctrl-F7** to activate the Add Watch dialog box.) Notice that the Watch window becomes the active window.

```
 ≡  File  Edit  Search  Run  Compile  Debug  Options  Window  Help
┌─────────────────────────── ASSIGN.PAS ───────────────────────1───┐
│program Assign;                                                     │
│uses Crt;                                                           │
│var x, y, z: real;                                                  │
│    i, j, k: integer;                                               │
│    s, t, r: string[255];                                           │
│    b     : boolean;                                                │
│                                                                    │
│begin                                                               │
│    ClrScr;                                                         │
│    i := 2 + 3;_                                                    │
│    j := 27350 - 21845;                                             │
│    k := i * 2 + 1;                                                 │
│    x := 2 / 3;                                                     │
│    y := 3.14159 * 5 * 5;                                           │
│    z := x + y;                                                     │
┌─[■]─────────────────────────── Watches ───────────────────────2═[↑]┐
│    i: Unknown identifier                                          ▓│
│    j: Unknown identifier                                          ░│
│    r: Unknown identifier                                          ░│
│                                                                   ░│
│                                                                   ▪│
│                                                                   ▪│
├─────◄                                                             ─┘
│ F1 Help  F7 Trace  F8 Step  ◄┘ Edit  Ins Add  Del Delete  F10 Menu │
```

3. Press **Alt-W** and type **N** (Next window) to make ASSIGN.PAS the active window. Notice that the program text fills the screen.

4. Press **Alt-W** and type **T** to tile the windows on the screen.

```
≡  File  Edit  Search  Run  Compile  Debug  Options  Window  Help
┌─[■]────────────────────────── ASSIGN.PAS ─────────────────────────1=[↑]┐
│program Assign;                                                          ▲│
│uses Crt;                                                                ▓│
│var x, y, z: real;                                                       ▓│
│    i, j, k: integer;                                                    ▓│
│    s, t, r: string[255];                                                ▓│
│    b      : boolean;                                                    ▓│
│                                                                         ▓│
│begin                                                                    ▓│
│    ClrScr;                                                              ▓│
│    i := 2 + 3;                                                          ▓│
│    j := 27350 - 21845;                                                  ▓│
│    k := i * 2 + 1;                                                      ▓│
│    x := 2 / 3;                                                          ▓│
│    y := 3.14159 * 5 * 5;                                                ▼│
│─ 1:1 ══════◄                                                          ►─┘
┌───────────────────────────── Watches ─────────────────────────2─────────┐
│  i: Unknown identifier                                                   │
│  j: Unknown identifier                                                   │
│  r: Unknown identifier                                                   │
│                                                                          │
│                                                                          │
└──────────────────────────────────────────────────────────────────────  │
 F1 Help  F2 Save  F3 Open  Alt-F9 Compile  F9 Make  F10 Menu
```

5. Press **Alt-W** and type **R** to activate the CPU Registers window.

6. Press **Alt-W** and type **L** to display the Window List dialog box.

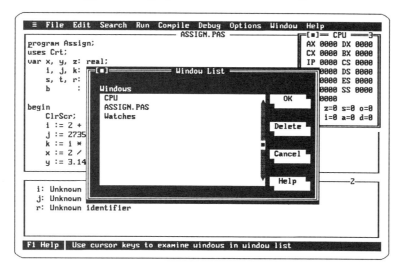

7. Press **Enter** to clear the Window list. Press **F7** to begin tracing the program.

8. Press **F8** until the line "b := true;" is highlighted. Notice that as you press F8 the values in the Watches window are updated.

```
 ≡  File  Edit  Search  Run  Compile  Debug  Options  Window  Help
┌─[■]───────────────────── ASSIGN.PAS ════════════════════════1═[↑]╖
║   ClrScr;                                                        █
║   i := 2 + 3;                                                    █
║   j := 27350 - 21845;                                            █
║   k := i * 2 + 1;                                                █
║   x := 2 / 3;                                                    █
║   y := 3.14159 * 5 * 5;                                          █
║   z := x + y;                                                    █
║   s := 'The cow jumped';                                         █
║   t := ' over the moon.';                                        █
║   r := s + t;                                                    █
║   b := true;                                                     █
│─  writeln('The value of I is: ',i);                              █
║   writeln('The value of J is: ',j);                              █
║   writeln('The value of K is: ',k);                             ─┘
└── 19:1 ═══◄───████████████████████████████████████████████████──┘
├───────────────────────────── Watches ──────────────────────2────┤
│  i: 5                                                            │
│  j: 5505                                                         │
│  r: 'The cow jumped over the moon.'                              │
│                                                                  │
│                                                                  │
└──────────────────────────────────────────────────────────────────
 F1 Help  F7 Trace  F8 Step  F9 Make  F10 Menu
```

9. Continue pressing **F8** until the line "readln;" is highlighted. Then press **Alt-F5** to switch to the User screen.

```
The value of I is: 5
The value of J is: 5505
The value of K is: 11
The value of X is:  6.6666666667E-01
The value of Y is:  7.8539750000E+01
The value of Z is:  7.9206416667E+01
The value of R is: The cow jumped over the moon.
The value of B is: TRUE
```

10. Press any key to return to the integrated environment.

11. Press **Alt-Spacebar** to activate the System menu, then type **C** to clear the desktop.

12. Turn to Module 13, Const, to continue the learning sequence.

Module 77
WITH

DESCRIPTION

Use *with* to simplify references to record data structures in your programs. The reference to a field within a record consists of the name of the record, followed by a period, and the name of the individual field. This notation can become cumbersome when you must repeatedly reference many fields in the same record. The *with* statement allows you to state the name of the record once and then assume that name for the scope of the statement.

For example, consider the record

```
var Customer      : record of
            Name  : string[30];
          Street  : string[30];
            City  : string[12];
           State  : string[2];
             Zip  : string[10];
       end;
```

To display the customer information, you might use statements similar to the following:

```
writeln(Customer.Name);
writeln(Customer.Street);
write(Customer.City,' ',Customer.State,'  ',Customer.Zip);
```

The repetition of "Customer" in each statement is avoided through the use of the *with* statement as shown in the following equivalent statements.

```
with Customer do
begin
    writeln(Name);
    writeln(Street);
    write(City,', ',State,'  ',Zip);
end;
```

The resulting statements are both easier to type and easier to read. When using the *with* statement, it is not an error to be redundant, as shown in the following statements.

```
    with Customer do
    begin
        writeln(Customer.Name);
        writeln(Street);
        write(City,' ',State,'  ',Zip);
    end;
```

Notice that the use of "Customer" in the reference "Customer.Name" is redundant.

APPLICATIONS

When your program requires multiple references to individual fields of the same record, use the *with* statement to lessen the amount of required typing and increase the readability of the resulting program. Where references to individual fields are scattered, the additional overhead of the *with* statement is counterproductive.

TYPICAL OPERATION

In this session you assign values to the fields in a record using standard record.field notation, then display the values on the screen using the notation of the *with* statement.

1. Start Turbo Pascal, or clear the Editor workspace, and type the following program.

```
program Withdemo;
uses Crt;
var Customer : record
            Name : string[30];
          Street : string[30];
            City : string[12];
           State : string[2];
             Zip : string[10];
      end;

begin
    ClrScr;
    Customer.Name:='Al Smith';
    Customer.Street:='1234 Orange Drive';
    Customer.City:='Smallville';
    Customer.State:='TX';
    Customer.Zip:='76218-1923';
    with Customer do
    begin
        writeln(Name);
        writeln(Street);
        writeln(City,', ',State,' ',Zip);
    end;
    readln;
end.
```

2. Save the program as WITHDEMO, then run the program.

```
Al Smith
1234 Orange Drive
Smallville, TX  76218-1923
```

3. Press **Enter** to return to the integrated environment.

4. Turn to Module 41, New, to continue the learning sequence.

Module 78
WRITE and WRITELN

DESCRIPTION

The *write* statement is an output statement to place the value of one or more expressions on an output device or in an output file.

The *writeln* statement is an output statement to place the value of zero or more expressions on an output device or in an output file, then issue a carriage return. The format of the statements is

```
write ({filename,} expression {,expression});
writeln ({filename,} {,expression});
```

filename   If you do not include a value for *filename*, the output of the *write* or *writeln* statement is sent to the default DOS output device. This is usually the screen, but it can be any output device or file if you have used the DOS I/O redirection facilities to change DOS's default output device. If you specify a value for *filename*, it can be either a DOS device or a disk file.

expression   can be any valid Turbo Pascal expression.

THREE OUTPUT METHODS   There are two methods available to produce output with Turbo Pascal. The first method is through PC/MS-DOS. The second method is through the *Crt* unit. The DOS method is generic and produces programs that run on a variety of MS-DOS machines including some that are only somewhat IBM PC-compatible. When you use the *Crt* unit as the basis for your output, you sacrifice the ability to run your program on sort-of-IBM-compatible computers for greatly enhanced speed, and you lose some powerful screen control procedures available on fully IBM-compatible machines. The standard file *Output* is predeclared by Turbo Pascal and is available for use with the *writeln* statement.

DOS *Output*   This is the default output file. This is assigned to the DOS default output device. Under most circumstances, this device is the screen. However, DOS output can be redirected; Turbo Pascal supports the redirection of standard output.

CRT *Output*   When you include the statement *uses Crt* in your program, the meaning of the *Output* device changes. Instead of funneling all of your output through DOS, Turbo Pascal writes the information to the BIOS (Basic Input Output System) or, for even faster performance, directly to the video memory. If you want to use the *Crt* unit and still allow the redirection of DOS output, you must add the statements

```
Assign(Output,'');
 Rewrite(output);
```

to your program.

TurboVision *Output*   The TurboVision unit provides an output field object that handles all aspects of screen handling for you.

CONTROLLING COLUMN WIDTH   You add a column width specification to any output field by following the name of the variable, or the expression, with a colon and a number. If the field width is greater than the width of the output, the output is right justified in the field. Turbo Pascal has different rules for the format of each defined type of data. If you do not specify the column width for a variable, literal, or expression, it is displayed according to the following rules:

Integer	The output occupies one space for each digit, plus one space for a leading minus sign if the number is negative.
Real	The output occupies ten spaces for a *real* or 16 spaces for a math co-processor type. The exponent occupies two places for the basic *real* type and four places for all co-processor types.
Char	The output occupies a single space.
String	The output occupies one space for each position of the string in use. The actual length of the string is the determining factor. The length declared in the *var* or *type* statement only sets a maximum length.
Boolean	If the value is True, the output occupies four spaces, the length of the word True. If the value is False, the output occupies five spaces, the length of the word False.

If the field width is less than the width of the output, the width specification is ignored and default formatting is used.

DECIMAL FORMATTING FOR REAL DATA   Unless you include a format specification in your *write* or *writeln* statement, real values are printed in exponential notation. Exponential, or scientific, notation is useful for applications involving very large and very small numbers, where there are many leading or ending zeroes. Although scientists and engineers often work with exponential notation, decimal notation is more familiar to most people. Decimal notation is preferable for most applications.

DECIMAL REPRESENTATION An additional specification is available to provide decimal representation for real data. You specify the number of digits to the right of the decimal place by following the field-width specification with a second colon and a number.

The first position of the total field is reserved for the sign. When planning real output, consider the total field width. Account for one sign position, digits to the left of the decimal place, the decimal point, and digits to the right of the decimal point. Turbo Pascal ignores requests for more than 20 places to the right of the decimal point.

If you do not provide for sufficient positions to the left of the decimal point, the program ignores your format specification and uses exponential notation. This prevents proper alignment of decimal numbers.

APPLICATIONS

When performing output, use the *write* statement when you want to continue output on the same line of the display (or the same record in the file). Use the *writeln* statement when you want to advance to the next line or record.

You can use the *writeln* statement by itself or with only an output filename to force the output to the next line or record without performing any output.

The statements

```
write('A rolling stone');
write(' gathers no moss.');
writeln;
```

produce the same output as the single statement

```
writeln('A rolling stone gathers no moss.');
```

To advance the printer three lines without producing output, you can write

```
uses Printer;

begin
    {Other statements}
    writeln(Lst);
    writeln(Lst);
    writeln(Lst);
```

You can use a variable value as the filename if you want. In this way, the same set of *write* or *writeln* statements can be used to produce output on the screen, printer, and a disk file. Making multiple use of statements saves work when writing programs. For example, notice the following set of statements:

```
Device:='Lst';
write(Device,'Never do today');
writeln(Device,' what can just as well be put off until tomorrow.');
```

Changing the value of Device to 'Output' places the output on the DOS output device, which is normally the screen. Specifying a user-defined filename allows you to place program output in a disk file. This is an excellent technique when you want to incorporate program output as input to another program, possibly your spreadsheet, database, or word processor.

Pascal's standard output format for real data is not always easy to read. While scientific notation is appropriate for expressing the extremely large and small numbers that often appear in engineering calculations, people who are not engineers generally prefer the more familiar decimal notation for real data.

The variable column width for integer data makes it impossible to use default integer formatting when producing columns of integers in the program output. Specifying a column width allows all integer data to line up right justified in a uniform-width field.

When specifying output, it is necessary to distinguish between the name and the value of a variable. For example, if Count is declared as an integer variable and assigned the value 17, the statement *write(Count);* produces "17" as output. The statement *write('Count');* produces "Count" as output. Anything enclosed in single quotation marks is displayed literally on the screen. Entries not enclosed in quotes are interpreted as variables, and the value is displayed.

TYPICAL OPERATION

In this session you use options in the *writeln* statement to control the output device and display format of program output. If you have a printer available, make sure that it is properly connected, has paper, and is turned on.

1. Start Turbo Pascal, or use the File/New option to clear the Editor workspace in your continuing session.

The program in this typical operation builds on the program developed in the Variables module. Using the Editor block-read procedure lets you import the statements from the file ASSIGN.PAS to save typing effort.

2. Press **Ctrl-K** and type **R** for Read-Block.

3. Type **ASSIGN.PAS** and press **Enter**.

4. Press **Alt-D** (Debug) and type **BC** (Breakpoints/Clear all) and press **Enter** to guarantee that the breakpoints previously set in the program do not interfere with this program.

5. Change the name of the program from "Assign" to "WriteFormats" in the *program* statement.

ADJUST COLUMN WIDTHS   As a first example, examine the effect of a field width of 40 on each *writeln* statement. Use the Editor Replace feature to make the modification easier. The field width specification is placed between the variable name and the right parenthesis in each *writeln* statement. You can take advantage of the fact that the only occurrences of the right parenthesis character are at the ends of the statements you want to change. Therefore, you can perform a global search and replace, replacing all right parentheses with :40).

6. Press **Ctrl-Q** and type **A**.

7. Type **)** in the Text to find field and press **Tab**. Type **:40)** in the New text field. Deselect the Prompt on replace option. Press **Alt-A** to select replace all.

```
 ≡ File Edit Search Run Compile Debug Options Window Help
[■]                              NONAME00.PAS                    1=[↕]
  ClrScr;
  i:=2+3;
  j:=27350 - 21845;
  k:=I * 2 + 1;
  X:=2/3;
  Y:=3.14159 * 5 * 5;
  Z:=X + Y;
  S:='The cow jumped';
  T:=' over the moon.';
  R:=S+T;
  B:=True;
  writeln('The value of I is: ',i:40);
  writeln('The value of J is: ',j:40);
  writeln('The value of K is: ',k:40);
  writeln('The value of X is: ',x:40);
  writeln('The value of Y is: ',y:40);
  writeln('The value of Z is: ',z:40);
  writeln('The value of R is: ',r:40);
  writeln('The value of B is: ',b:40);
  readln;
end.
  28:40
F1 Help  F2 Save  F3 Open  Alt-F9 Compile  F9 Make  F10 Menu
```

8. Press **Alt-F** to drop down the File menu, then type **A** to save the program. Type **WRITE** as the filename and press **Enter**.

9. Press **Alt-R** and type **R** to run the program. Observe the output format.

```
The value of I is:                                          5
The value of J is:                                       5505
The value of K is:                                         11
The value of X is:                            6.6666666667E-01
The value of Y is:                            7.8539750000E+01
The value of Z is:                            7.9206416667E+01
The value of R is:                  The cow jumped over the moon.
The value of B is:                                       TRUE
```

All output is right justified in a 40-character field. Each field is padded on the left with spaces to fill the available column width. All the real data is printed in scientific notation.

10. Press **Enter** to return to the integrated environment.

USE DECIMAL FORMATTING   Next, use the decimal formatting feature to produce the real output in the more familiar decimal notation. You specify the number of places to the right of the decimal point by following the field-width specifier by a colon and the number of positions.

11. Enter the Editor and modify the *writeln* statements by adding decimal specifiers providing three places for X, four places for Y, and five places for Z, as shown.

```
≡  File  Edit  Search  Run  Compile  Debug  Options  Window  Help
[■]═══════════════════ NONAME00.PAS ════════════════1=[↕]
    ClrScr;
    i:=2+3;
    J:=27350 - 21845;
    k:=I * 2 + 1;
    X:=2/3;
    Y:=3.14159 * 5 * 5;
    Z:=X + Y;
    S:='The cow jumped';
    T:=' over the moon.';
    R:=S+T;
    B:=True;
    writeln('The value of I is: ',i:40);
    writeln('The value of J is: ',j:40);
    writeln('The value of K is: ',k:40);
    writeln('The value of X is: ',x:40:3);
    writeln('The value of Y is: ',y:40:4);
    writeln('The value of Z is: ',z:40:5);
    writeln('The value of R is: ',r:40);
    writeln('The value of B is: ',b:40);
    readln;
end.
═ 26:41 ═══◄▐───────────────────────────────
F1 Help  F2 Save  F3 Open  Alt-F9 Compile  F9 Make  F10 Menu
```

12. Save and run the program.

```
The value of I is:                                      5
The value of J is:                                   5505
The value of K is:                                     11
The value of X is:                                  0.667
The value of Y is:                                78.5397
The value of Z is:                               79.20642
The value of R is:              The cow jumped over the moon.
The value of B is:                                   TRUE
```

The values of X, Y, and Z are printed with three, four, and five places to the right of the decimal point respectively.

13. Press **Enter** to return to the integrated environment.

USING UNDERSIZE COLUMN WIDTH   Examine the output when the field width is not sufficiently wide by replacing the field width of 40 with a field width of two.

14. Press **Alt-S** and type **R** to activate the Replace operation.

NOTE

The previous values for find, replace, and options are retained by the Editor. Pressing Enter accepts the value, typing any other key erases the value and overtypes the new value.

15. Type **:40** as the Text to find, press **Tab**, type **:2** and press **Alt-A**.

16. Save and run the program.

```
The value of I is:   5
The value of J is: 5505
The value of K is: 11
The value of X is: 0.667
The value of Y is: 78.5397
The value of Z is: 79.20642
The value of R is: The cow jumped over the moon.
The value of B is: TRUE
```

The first line of output places the number 5 right justified in a field two spaces wide. The second line of output ignores the field width because the number 5505 does not fit in the space provided. The third line, an integer, fits nicely in its two-space column. All remaining output items are too long to fit into a two-space output column.

17. Turn to Module 45, Options, to continue the learning sequence.

Appendix A
ASCII CHARACTER CODES

ASCII value	Character	Control character	ASCII value	Character
000	(null)	NUL	032	(space)
001	☺	SOH	033	!
002	☻	STX	034	"
003	♥	ETX	035	#
004	♦	EOT	036	$
005	♣	ENQ	037	%
006	♠	ACK	038	&
007	(beep)	BEL	039	'
008	◘	BS	040	(
009	(tab)	HT	041	)
010	(line feed)	LF	042	*
011	(home)	VT	043	+
012	(form feed)	FF	044	,
013	(carriage return)	CR	045	−
014	♫	SO	046	.
015	☼	SI	047	/
016	►	DLE	048	0
017	◄	DC1	049	1
018	↕	DC2	050	2
019	‼	DC3	051	3
020	¶	DC4	052	4
021	§	NAK	053	5
022	▬	SYN	054	6
023	↨	ETB	055	7
024	↑	CAN	056	8
025	↓	EM	057	9
026	→	SUB	058	:
027	←	ESC	059	;
028	(cursor right)	FS	060	<
029	(cursor left)	GS	061	=
030	(cursor up)	RS	062	>
031	(cursor down)	US	063	?

ASCII value	Character	ASCII value	Character
064	@	096	'
065	A	097	a
066	B	098	b
067	C	099	c
068	D	100	d
069	E	101	e
070	F	102	f
071	G	103	g
072	H	104	h
073	I	105	i
074	J	106	j
075	K	107	k
076	L	108	l
077	M	109	m
078	N	110	n
079	O	111	o
080	P	112	p
081	Q	113	q
082	R	114	r
083	S	115	s
084	T	116	t
085	U	117	u
086	V	118	v
087	W	119	w
088	X	120	x
089	Y	121	y
090	Z	122	z
091	[	123	{
092	\	124	¦
093	]	125	}
094	^	126	~
095	—	127	△

ASCII value	Character	ASCII value	Character
128	Ç	160	á
129	ü	161	í
130	é	162	ó
131	â	163	ú
132	ä	164	ñ
133	à	165	Ñ
134	å	166	ạ
135	ç	167	ọ
136	ê	168	¿
137	ë	169	⌐
138	è	170	¬
139	ï	171	½
140	î	172	¼
141	ì	173	¡
142	Ä	174	«
143	Å	175	»
144	É	176	░
145	æ	177	▒
146	Æ	178	▓
147	ô	179	│
148	ö	180	┤
149	ò	181	╡
150	û	182	╢
151	ù	183	╖
152	ÿ	184	╕
153	Ö	185	╣
154	Ü	186	║
155	¢	187	╗
156	£	188	╝
157	¥	189	╜
158	Pt	190	╛
159	ƒ	191	┐

ASCII value	Character	ASCII value	Character
192	└	224	α
193	┴	225	β
194	┬	226	Γ
195	├	227	π
196	─	228	Σ
197	┼	229	σ
198	╞	230	μ
199	╟	231	τ
200	╚	232	Φ
201	╔	233	θ
202	╩	234	Ω
203	╦	235	δ
204	╠	236	∞
205	═	237	$\emptyset$
206	╬	238	ϵ
207	╧	239	$\cap$
208	╨	240	$\equiv$
209	╤	241	$\pm$
210	╥	242	$\geq$
211	╙	243	$\leq$
212	╘	244	$\lceil$
213	╒	245	$\rfloor$
214	╓	246	$\div$
215	╫	247	$\approx$
216	╪	248	$\circ$
217	┘	249	$\bullet$
218	┌	250	$\cdot$
219	█	251	$\sqrt{}$
220	▄	252	n
221	▌	253	2
222	▐	254	■
223	▀	255	(blank 'F')

Appendix B
RESERVED WORDS and
PREDECLARED INDENTIFIERS

RESERVED WORDS

The following words are reserved in Turbo Pascal. They may not be redefined by the program.

absolute	external	nil	shl
and	file	not	shr
array	forward	overlay	string
begin	for	of	then
case	function	or	type
const	goto	packed	to
div	inline	procedure	until
do	if	program	var
downto	in	record	while
else	label	repeat	with
end	mod	set	xor

PREDECLARED IDENTIFIERS

Turbo Pascal provides a number of predeclared identifiers. When you redefine these identifiers, you lose the original feature. They are best left with their original meaning.

Addr	EOF	LightMagenta	Red
Append	EOLN	LightRed	Release
ArcTan	Erase	Ln	Rename
Assign	Execute	Lo	Reset
Aux	Exit	LongFilePos	Rewrite
AuxInPtr	Exp	LongFileSeek	RmDir
AuxOutPtr	False	LongSeek	Round
Black	FilePos	LowVideo	Seek
BlockRead	FileSize	Lst	Seg
BlockWrite	FillChar	LstOutPtr	SeekEof
Blue	Flush	Magenta	SeekEoln
Boolean	Frac	Mark	Sin
Brown	GetDir	MaxInt	SizeOf
BufLen	GetMem	Mem	Sqr
Byte	GotoXY	MemW	Sqrt
Chain	GraphBackground	MemAvail	Str
Char	GraphColorMode	MkDir	SSet
ChDir	GraphMode	Move	Succ
Chr	GraphWindow	MsDos	Swap
Close	Green	New	Text
ClrEOL	Halt	NormVideo	TextBackground
ClrScr	HeapPtr	Odd	TextColor
Con	Hi	Ofs	TextMode
ConInPtr	HiRes	Ord	Trm
ConOutPtr	HiResColor	Output	True
Concat	IOresult	OvrPath	Trunc
ConstPtr	Input	Palette	UpCase
Copy	InsLine	Pi	Usr
Cos	Insert	Plot	UsrInPtr
CrtExit	Int	Port	UsrOutPtr
CrtInit	Integer	PortW	Val
CSeg	Intr	Pos	WhereX
Cyan	Kbd	Pred	WhereY
DarkGray	KeyPressed	Ptr	White
DelLine	Length	Random	Write
Delay	LightBlue	Randomize	WriteLn
Delete	LightCyan	Read	Yellow
Draw	LightGray	ReadLn	
Dseg	LightGreen	Real	

Appendix C
SYNTAX

The following is not the formal definition of Turbo Pascal. It represents a brief summary of the major control structures of the language, but does not suppose to be exhaustive.

: : =	Means "is defined as."
|	Means "or."
{ }	Enclose items which may be repeated zero or more times.
[ ]	Enclose items which are optional.

Each element of the language is printed in normal type. Each reserved word is printed in boldface.

```
assignment statement ::=
    variable-name:=expression

case-statement ::=
    case expression of
        constant-list: statement {;
        constant-list: statement}
    end

statement::=

    statement |
    begin
        statement {;
        statment}
    end

for-statement ::=
    for ordinal-variable := start-value [down]to end-value do statement

function ::=
    procedure procedure-name
        [([var] variable-name {variable-name}:type-name
        {;[var] variable-name {variable-name}:type-name})]:type-name;
    {constant-declaration}
    {variable-declaration}
    statement{;
    statement}
end:
```

```
if statement : :=
    if Boolean-expression then
        statement
    else
        statement

procedure ::=
    procedure procedure-name
        [([var]variable-name {variable-name} : type-name
        {;[var]variable-name {variable-name} : type-name})]
    {constant-declaration}
    {variable-declaration}
    {procedure or function}
    begin
        statement {;
        statement}
    end;

program ::=
    [program program-name]
    {constant-declaration}
    {variable-declaration}
    {function-declaration and/or procedure-declaration}
    begin
        statement {;
        statement}
    end.

read-statement ::=
    read([filename,]variable-name{,variable-name})

readln-statement ::=
    readln([filename,]variable-name{,variable-name})
repeat-statment ::=
    repeat statement until Boolean-expression

while-statement ::=
    while Boolean-expression do statement

write-statement ::=
    write([filename,]variable-name{,variable-name})

writeln-statment ::=
    writeln([filename,]variable-name{,variable-name})
```

Appendix D
EXERCISES

1. *About This Book*
   a. For what kind of person is this book designed?
   b. Why was Pascal designed?
   c. If you are learning Turbo Pascal, what sequence should you follow to go through this book?
   d. What is the significance of the numbered steps in the Typical Operations sections of each module?

2. *Sample Session*
   a. When should you use the compile-to-disk feature of Turbo Pascal?
   b. What happens if you neglect to specify a Work file before selecting the Editor from the Main menu?
   c. What do you type to start Turbo Pascal from the DOS prompt?
   d. Under what conditions should you include error messages?
   e. What statement identifies the name of a Turbo Pascal program?
   f. What statement places output on the screen?
   g. What punctuation separates Turbo Pascal statements?
   h. What punctuation ends a Turbo Pascal program?
   i. What statement clears the text screen?

3. *Absolute*
   a. What Turbo Pascal statement does the Absolute declaration modify?
   b. What memory protection is provided to prevent modifying important system resources with the *absolute* declaration?
   c. In specifying an absolute address, the first portion of the address is the _____ an the second portion is the _____.
   d. Beginning a number with a dollar sign ($) indicates that it is what kind of number?

4. *Arithmetic*
   a. What is the difference between the operators / and *div* in performing division?
   b. What is the result of the operation 7 *mod* 3?
   c. What is the result of the operation 7 *div* 3?
   d. Evaluate 2 + 3 * 4.
   e. What data type is compatible with byte data?
   f. How are integers stored in the computer?

5. *Array*
   a. Can the lower bound of an array be specified as a decimal?
   b. What characters are used to enclose the bounds of an array in the array definition?
   c. What characters are used to enclose the subscript of an array in an array reference?
   d. Can array subscripts be characters?
   e. What delimiter is used to separate the subscripts in a multiple-dimensional array?
   f. What looping control-structure is frequently used to examine each element in an array for processing?

6. *Assign*
   a. As what type must *filevar* be defined prior to the *assign* statement?
   b. If the *DOS-filename* is not specified as a literal, what data type must it be?
   c. What purpose does the *assign* statement serve?

7. *Case*
   a. What type variable is appropriate for the case selector?
   b. What does the notation 'B'..'D' indicate when used in a *case* statement?
   c. If the selector variable must be a real number, what statement should be used instead of the *case* statement?

8. *Character Functions*
   a. What effect does the *UpCase* function have on special symbols, such as #, &, @, and *?
   b. What name is given to the character code system for your computer?
   c. What function allows you to send special codes to the printer?

9. *Close*
   a. What happens when you close an output file?
   b. What danger is there in leaving files open longer than necessary?
   c. How can you minimize the number of open files in a program?

10. *ClrScr*
    a. Where is the cursor placed after issuing the *ClrScr* command?
    b. The *ClrScr* statement clears only the _____ screen.

11. *Comments and Compiler Directives*
    a. The _____ compiler directive controls the number of simultaneous open files.
    b. The _____ compiler directive has two meanings, depending on whether it is followed by a + or –, or a filename.
    c. To disable run-time checks of array indices, use the _____ compiler directive at the _____ of the program.
    d. A compiler directive is written by following the { symbol with a ____, the directive, and closing with a }.

12. *Compile Menu*
    a. What is the difference between a Make and a Build?
    b. What kind of file is created when you specify "Disk" as the destination?
    c. How is the link operation performed in Turbo Pascal?

13. *Const*
    a. Constants are similar to _____.
    b. Constants have _____ value in a program.
    c. True and False are predefined _____ constants.

14. *Constructor*
    a. A _____ object always requires a constructor.
    b. What type of method must a constructor be?
    c. May an object have more than one constructor method?

15. *CRT Unit*
    a. What is the advantage of using AssignCrt?
    b. What is the disadvantage of using AssignCrt?
    c. What do InsLine and DelLine do?
    d. What statement is necessary to take advantage of the features of the Crt unit?

16. *Debug Menu*
    a. How do you check the value of an expression while debugging?
    b. How do you modify the value of a variable or constant while debugging?
    c. What is the difference between Standalone debugging and Integrated debugging?
    d. What is a watch?
    e. What is a breakpoint?
    f. How do you establish a breakpoint?
    g. How do you jump to a breakpoint?

17. *Delay*
    a. The delay statement is calibrated in _____.
    b. Turbo Pascal gets its timing information from the _____ _____.
    c. The delay statement _____ the execution of a program for the specified length of time.

18. *Destructor*
    a. What is the relationship between dispose and an object destructor?
    b. What types of objects require destructors?
    c. Must you take specific steps to determine the size of a dynamically allocated object in memory when you create an object destructor?

19. *Directory Functions*
    a. You should not erase an _____ file.

    b. The _____ procedure creates a new subdirectory.

    c. In the *GetDir* procedure, drive 0 is which disk drive?

    d. Directory operations are best performed with _____ files.

20. *Dispose and Mark/Release*

    a. To release the memory occupied by a single data structure, use the _____ statement.

    b. To release all memory beyond a specified point, use _____ and _____.

    c. Dispose, Mark and Release should _____ all be used in the same program.

    d. The _____ statement leaves a hole in the dynamic memory space where other data can be stored.

21. *Edit Menu*

    a. What key combination moves the cursor to the top of the file?

    b. What key combination moves the cursor to the bottom of the file?

    c. How do you toggle between Insert and Overwrite?

    d. How do you mark the beginning of a block?

    e. How do you mark the end of a block?

    f. How do you move a block?

    g. How do you copy a block?

    h. In a find-and-replace operation, how do you specify replacement of all occurrences of the string?

    i. In a find-and-replace operation, what combination of options specify replacement of the next 7 occurrences, as whole words only, without paying attention to case?

22. *File*

    a. The *file* statement creates an _____ file.

    b. Untyped files have a record length of _____ bytes.

    c. An untyped file is compatible with _____ files.

23. *File Menu*

    a. When you load or save files, what is the default file extension?

    b. What is the function of the New command on the File menu?

    c. What is the difference between "Save" and "Save as"?

    d. How can you execute programs, such as DOS commands, without needing to exit Turbo Pascal?

24. *File of*

    a. The reserved word *file of* creates a _____ file.

    b. The most useful typed file is a file of _____.

    c. A text file can be considered as a file of _____.

25. *FileSize*
    a. The first record in every file is record _____.
    b. The record beyond the last entry in the file is computed as _____.

26. *For*
    a. The index of a *for* loop must be what data type?
    b. Can a *for* loop use an increment other than 1?
    c. What is the value of the index variable when a *for* loop terminates?
    d. What word is used to decrement instead of increment the index variable in a *for* loop?
    e. If the starting value of a *for-to* loop is greater than the final value, how many times does the loop execute?
    f. For what kinds of loops is the *for* structure ideally suited?

27. *Forward*
    a. When do you use the *forward* statement?
    b. What does it mean for procedures to be mutually recursive?

28. *Function*
    a. A variable defined inside a function is _____ to the function.
    b. If a variable in a function has the same name as a variable in the main program, how does the function resolve the name conflict?
    c. What makes a function recursive?
    d. Why are recursive functions used?
    e. What type values can a function return?

29. *Gotoxy*
    a. The cursor is placed in the upper left corner of the screen by the statement *gotoxy*(_____,_____).
    b. The first parameter is the (horizontal/vertical) specification.
    c. The second parameter is the (horizontal/vertical) specification.
    d. The cursor is placed in the lower left corner of the screen by the statement *gotoxy*(_____,_____).
    e. The *gotoxy* procedure determines coordinates relative to (the physical screen/the active window).

30. *Graphics Unit*
    a. Color graphics produced by the IBM CGA adapter provides _____ dots horizontally and _____ dots vertically.
    b. Monochrome graphics provides _____ dots horizontally and _____ dots vertically.
    c. How do you determine the graphics hardware installed in the computer?
    d. In point (_____,_____) is the upper left corner of the graphics screen.
    e. The _____ procedure places a single point on the screen.

    f. The files ending in _____ must be available to use the extended graphics features of Turbo Pascal.

    g. The graphics screen is cleared with a call to procedure _____.

31. *Help Menu*

    a. How does the Copy example command on the Edit menu relate to the Turbo Pascal help system?

    b. Describe two methods for accessing help information about a particular command.

32. *If*

    a. The *if* statement controls performance based on a _____ expression.

    b. It is always incorrect to place a _____ immediately before the word *else*.

    c. A compound if statement is formed by enclosing a series of statements between the reserved words _____ and _____.

    d. The relations and have _____ precedence then *and* and *or*.

33. *Implementation*

    a. What is the difference between the Interface portion of a unit and the Implementation portion?

    b. Where do you place unit initialization code?

    c. When is the initialization code for a unit executed?

    d. What is the difference between the procedure headings in the Interface portion of the unit and the corresponding headings in the Implementation portion?

34. *Interface*

    a. What portions of a unit belong in the Interface section?

    b. What is the scope of variables defined in the Interface portion of a unit?

    c. How do you make a data type available to the calling program?

35. *Intr*

    a. The *Intr* procedure allows you to access _____ interrupts.

    b. Where do you find information about the software interrupt system?

    c. How to you send information to the interrupt system?

    d. How do you examine the results of the interrupt system?

36. *IoResult*

    a. To use *IoResult*, you must use the _____ compiler directive.

    b. What does IoResult code 04 mean?

    c. What error results if you try to erase the printer?

    d. What happens to the program if an I/O error occurs under system control?

37. *Keypressed*
    a. *Keypressed* is a _____ function.
    b. *Keypressed* is commonly used in combination with _____.

38. *Move*
    a. What protection does Turbo Pascal provide when you use the Move statement?
    b. What sort of compatibility must be provided between the source and destination data structures?

39. *MsDOS*
    a. Where do you find additional information about DOS services?
    b. Where do you put the number of the DOS service you request?
    c. How does the DOS service communicate its results back to the program?

40. *Naming*
    a. What is the alternate way to writing the symbol {?
    b. What would happen if you named a function *Cos*?
    c. What would happen if you named a variable *type*?
    d. May names begin with a number?
    e. What is the maximum length of an identifier?
    f. Is the underscore (_) significant in names?

41. *New*
    a. What is another name for the area in the computer's memory used for dynamic memory?
    b. You access a dynamic variable through use of a _____.
    c. The _____ statement allocates space for another dynamic variable.
    d. You identify a pointer by what symbol?
    e. To create a linked list, at least one entry in the record must be a _____.
    f. Creating a linked list is easiest with _____ pointers.
    g. A pointer that points nowhere should have the value _____.

42. *Numbers*
    a. What are the two kinds of numbers in Turbo Pascal?
    b. A number containing the letter E is a _____ number.
    c. Binary arithmetic uses only the digits _____ and _____.
    d. Hexadecimal arithmetic uses the symbol _____ to represent the number 10 (decimal).
    e. In hexadecimal arithmetic, F+1 is what number?
    f. Integers are represented as _____ bytes in memory.

43. *Numeric Functions*
    a. The natural logarithm of a number is returned by the ____ function.
    b. _____ returns a random real number.
    c. Convert a real number to an integer with either _____ or _____.

44. *Object*
    a. An object is an extension of what Pascal data type?
    b. What is a method?
    c. When should you use the *self* parameter?
    d. What is encapsulation?
    e. What special steps are required to define an object in a unit?

45. *Options Menu*
    a. When would you want to use the disk for the link buffer?
    b. How do you specify where on the disk Turbo Pascal files are located?
    c. How many lines of text can Turbo Pascal display on a VGA screen?
    d. How do you accommodate the display needs of a laptop computer's LCD display?

46. *Printer Unit*
    a. What statement must be placed in your program to use the Printer unit?
    b. What two methods are available for placing output on the printer?
    c. What limitations are there on printing with the Printer unit?

47. *Procedure*
    a. What are the restrictions on variable type for procedure parameters?
    b. When do you use the word *var* in a procedure heading?
    c. What compiler directive allows you to relax the strict type checking of parameters?
    d. When should you use value parameters?
    e. What is a formal parameter?
    f. What is an actual parameter?
    g. What is a local variable?

48. *Read and Readln*
    a. If the first parameter in a *read* or *readln* statement is the name of a file, what happens?
    b. What is the difference between *read* and *readln*?
    c. What device do you use for input when you do not want characters to automatically echo to the screen?
    d. How do you enable input redirection?
    e. What can you examine to determine if you are at the end of an input line?

49. *Readkey*
    a. What is the ASCII code for the Escape key?
    b. How can you tell that an extended ASCII code is pending?
    c. What is the code for Alt-A?

50. *Record*
    a. How is a *record* different than an *array*?
    b. What symbol is used to separate the record name from the field name?
    c. What advantage can an array of records have over a two-dimensional array?
    d. How can you avoid having to specify both a record name and a field name in referencing information in a record?

51. *Repeat*
    a. What type expression terminates a *repeat* loop?
    b. What is the minimum number of times a *repeat* loop is performed?
    c. Why is a *repeat* loop preferable to a *for* loop in performing searches?
    d. Why is a *repeat* loop excellent for input error trapping routines?

52. *Reset*
    a. What happens if you *reset* a file that does not exist?
    b. What happens when you use *reset* of a file that has been previously opened with either *reset* or *rewrite*, but not closed?
    c. What happens if you *reset* a predefined Turbo Pascal file?

53. *Rewrite*
    a. What statement must you use to associate the program file with the DOS file before using the *rewrite* statement?
    b. What happens when you use *rewrite* to open an existing file?
    c. What is the value of IoResult if the *rewrite* operation is successful?

54. *Run Menu*
    a. When should you use the Program Reset command?
    b. How can you toggle between the program screen and the output screen?
    c. When should you use the To Cursor command?

55. *Search Menu*
    a. Describe two methods for activating a search operation.
    b. Of what use is the Find error command on the Search menu?

56. *Seek*
    a. What kind of files can *seek* not be used on?
    b. What is the maximum number of records that can be accessed with *seek*?
    c. What is the value of the first record in every file?

57. *Set*
    a. All members of a set must come from the same _____ type.
    b. The base type of a set must be a _____ or _____ type.
    c. Set membership is examined with the _____ operator.
    d. Set union is performed with the ___ operator.

e. The symbol = means _____.

f. The maximum number of elements in a Turbo Pascal set is _____.

58. *Simple Data Types*

a. The range of byte values is _____ to _____.

b. The possible values of a Boolean variable are _____ and _____.

c. What type is best for storing single character data?

d. What type is necessary when storing decimal numbers?

59. *Sound and NoSound*

a. After starting a note with *Sound*, how long does the note continue playing?

b. How do you compute the notes of the chromatic scale?

c. What is the function of *NoSound*?

d. What does the parameter of the *Sound* procedure represent?

60. *String*

a. What is a string?

b. What makes a string different than all other data types?

c. How do you represent a single quote in a string?

d. What is concatenation?

e. What is the concatenation operator?

61. *String Functions*

a. Why use the *concat* function instead of the concatenation operator?

b. How do you write the *copy* function to return the leftmost characters of a string?

c. How do you write the *copy* function to return the rightmost characters of a string?

d. How do you find out the length of a string?

62. *String Procedures*

a. Write the statement to insert the word "bad" into the sentence, "Who's afraid of the big bear?"

b. What limitation is there on the string parameter to the *val* procedure?

c. What is the purpose of the *Str* procedure?

63. *System Menu*

a. What two methods are available for activating the System menu?

b. When would you want to select the Refresh display option?

c. What is the value of the Clear desktop option?

64. *Text*

a. What is the buffer size of a text file?

b. How do you change the buffer size of a text file?

c. What determines the end-of-line in a text file?

d. What is the code for end-of-file?

65. *Textbackground*
    a. What color corresponds to the number 5?
    b. When you change the text background color, what happens to the background color of text already on the screen?
    c. How do you change the background color of the entire screen?

66. *Textcolor*
    a. What colors of text produce underline on the IBM Monochrome display?
    b. How do you cause text to blink on the screen?
    c. What is the value of the constant *Red*?

67. *Textmode*
    a. What effect does *Textmode(bw80)* have on an RGB monitor?
    b. What effect does *Textmode(bw80)* have on a composite monitor?
    c. What happens when you try to display color text on a black and white composite monitor?
    d. How do you access the 40-column text mode on the IBM PC?

68. *Turbo Vision*
    a. What is a TApplication?
    b. What is the difference between Turbo Vision and a procedure or function library?
    c. How do you modify the behavior of a Turbo Vision object?

69. *Type*
    a. Where is the type statement usually placed in a program?
    b. Why is it useful to define your own data types?
    c. Define a type called Months consisting of the months January through December.
    d. Define Summer as a subrange of Months including June through August.

70. *Unit*
    a. What type of file is created when you compile a unit?
    b. What is the relationship of Make and Build to developing programs containing units?
    c. How do you differentiate a unit from a program?

71. *Uses*
    a. What is the purpose of the *uses* statement?
    b. Where should the *uses* statement be placed in the program?
    c. How do you specify the use of multiple units in a single program?

72. *Var*
    a. What is the function of the *var* statement?
    b. Pascal requires _____ variables be declared.

c. The symbol := means _____ .

d. The symbol = means _____ .

73. *Virtual*

    a. What does the use of the Virtual specifier change about the way method references are resolved?

    b. How does the use of virtual methods allow object extensibility?

    c. When should static methods be used instead of virtual methods?

74. *While*

    a. What is the minimum number of times that every *while* loop executes?

    b. What type condition is used to terminate a *while* loop?

    c. When is a *while* loop the best loop to use?

    d. What function does *Eof* serve?

75. *Window*

    a. What statements are modified as the result of the *window* procedure?

    b. What is the default setting for the *window* procedure on an 80-column screen?

    c. What happens when you issue a *ClrScr* command with the window set to less than the full physical screen?

76. *Window Menu*

    a. What is the function of the Register option on the Window menu?

    b. What does it mean to "tile" windows?

    c. How do you view the output screen of a program?

77. *With*

    a. What is the purpose of the *with* statement?

    b. What happens if you use the "record.field" notation inside the scope of a *with* statement, creating a redundancy?

    c. When should you not use the *with* statement?

78. *Write and Writeln*

    a. What is the difference between the *write* and *writeln* statements?

    b. What happens if the first parameter of a *write* or *writeln* statement is a file name?

    c. What happens if you use *writeln* without a parameter list?

    d. How do you specify the width of the output column?

    e. How do you specify the number of decimal places for real output?

    f. If you do not specify an output format, what default format is used for real value output?

    g. If you do not specify an output format, how many columns are used for integer output?

    h. What happens to information enclosed in single quote marks in a *write* or *writeln* statement?

Index